ERRORS OF PSYCHOTHERAPY

BY SEBASTIAN DE GRAZIA

Errors of Psychotherapy

The Political Community

Errors of

Psychotherapy

by Sebastian de Grazia

DOUBLEDAY & COMPANY, INC.
GARDEN CITY, NEW YORK, 1952

Acknowledgments

For their help and encouragement I thank E. M. Kirkpatrick, Renzo Sereno, Pendleton Herring, Gustave von Grunebaum, Harold D. Lasswell, Walter A. Weisskopf, W. Lloyd Warner, Walter Johnson, J. G. Hall, Robert Redfield, Arnold Bergstraesser, Donald Young, Earl S. Johnson, Lionel Blitsten, Charles and Dorothy Hartshorne, Grace Swigart Malakoff, and Elizabeth G. Sullivan.

The research, I wish gratefully to acknowledge, was aided by awards from the American Philosophical Society and the Social Science Research Council.

Thanks are due also to the following authors, publishers, and publications for permission to reprint the material listed below:

Abingdon-Cokesbury Press for excerpt from *The Story of Methodism,* by Halford E. Luccock, Paul Hutchinson, and Robert W. Goodloe, copyright, 1949, by Pierce & Smith.

Appleton-Century-Crofts, Inc., for excerpts from *Crashing Thunder,* by Paul Radin, copyright, 1926, D. Appleton & Company.

Grune & Stratton, Inc., for extracts from *Medical Hypnosis,* by Lewis Robert Wolberg.

Harvard University Press, for extract from *Contemporary Psychopathology,* edited by Silvan Solomon Tomkins; and extracts from "Transference Problems in Schizophrenics," by Frieda Fromm-Reichmann.

Houghton Mifflin Company for extracts from *Counseling and Psychotherapy*, by Carl Rogers, and from *Case Book of Non-Directive Counseling*, by William U. Snyder.

International Universities Press, Inc., for extract from *Practical Aspects of Psychoanalysis*, by Lawrence S. Kubie.

Alfred A. Knopf, Inc., for extracts from *Island of Bali*, by Miguel Covarrubias; and *God Is My Adventure*, by Rom Landau.

McGraw-Hill Book Company, Inc., for extracts from *Mirror for Man*, by Clyde Kluckhohn.

W. W. Norton & Company, Inc., for extracts from *The Case Book of a Medical Psychologist*, by Charles Berg; with special permission from the British publisher, George Allen & Unwin, Ltd.

Psychiatry, for extracts from "The Psychiatry of Enduring Peace and Social Progress," by G. B. Chisholm; "Magical Fright," by John Gillin; and "Conceptions of Modern Psychiatry," by Harry Stack Sullivan.

The Ronald Press Company for excerpts from *Psychoanalytic Therapy*, by Franz Alexander and Thomas Morton French, copyright, 1946, The Ronald Press Company.

Charles Scribner's Sons for three lines from *Last Days of Alice*, by Allen Tate.

Charles C Thomas, Publisher, for extracts from *The Sexual Criminal*, by J. Paul de River, with special permission from the author.

S de G

Florence, Italy

Contents

Introduction

Small gods walk up and down the land. To them, people pray. They pray for relief from disordered passions, but so long as they beseech small gods their peace will be small. They are like children crying for parents they do not know are dead.

The problems of the wayward and the sinful are political and religious, and nothing more. Granted there are times when the political scientist, the student of earthly authority and its relation to the divine, need not occupy himself with the troubles of those who stray from the good path. Those are the times when his duty is to discover the best path for all to walk. He leaves the first problem to others, but only on conditions, saying to them, "It is not so grave, this problem, that I should break away now from my concern for the commonweal." But then there are different times, when the path has been so overrun and trampled that it can no longer serve as a trail for those who seek right conduct, when even those to whom the problem was left—the separate social scientists: the psychologists, the economists, the anthropologists, above all the sociologists—cannot find the path, cannot help as guides, and, strange to behold, cannot remember that the problem originally was entrusted to them by a conditional delegation of religious and political authority.

It then becomes the duty of the political scientist to recall to his friends the limited nature of their charge. He further must examine whether the way of life demanded of his fellow citizens is too strait that so many of them left the path; whether, too, his trustees, now that they have lost sight of the way, still can act as spiritual advisers. He decides then the necessity has come for him to abandon his most elevated work and to take on his most elemental task—restoring wholeness to the body politic.

Too often today the sickness of the body politic is regarded as a local infection that does not materially affect the health of the whole organism. This picture needs turning about. It is the politic body entire that is racked with pain while only an extremity or two, a finger or two, remains in a precarious, insular well-being. Were all the miseries that are labeled "social problems" added up—crime and mental disorder, divorce and desertion, illegitimacy, delinquency, alcoholism, drug addiction, and suicide—they would run into millions and millions. The United States, one should recall, has less than forty million families. A rare family it is whose household is not invaded by one of these apocalyptic riders.

By far the greatest number of these evils fall into a category called mental illness. Its name is Legion, for there are many of them. The pile of victims towers millions higher than any other heap, and reaches over twice as high as all the others put together.[1] What is more, the category is fanning out, like the boundaries of some spreading empire, to capture ever more of the variety of ills that infest the modern world and to contain them in the one dark designation—mental disorder. Today the man who reads, who keeps up with the world, recognizes in the criminal and the deserter and the alcoholic and the suicide the same underlying cause—mental illness. Madness covers the land like a flood.

The Political Community,[2] the forerunner of this book, tried to describe and learn something from modern man's empty lot, and to teach people hard things. It tried to show them that disorder in the political community penetrates every corner of the individual's life, his leisure and loves, his work and play. In the confusion that besets political science today that fact has escaped. Political scientists have preferred the easier and irresponsible position: political science deals with an encapsulated thing called government. But the prominence of mental disorder in the modern community keeps pushing itself before the attention of the theorists of society. It is no longer a problem of curing a few sick. It is no longer a problem of preventing the sick from making the healthy sick. It is a problem of the commonwealth. The whole political community has about it the air of a hospital.

So remarkable is the phenomenon that in an effort to recover the problem a few of the best political scientists have contrived a new name for political science, calling it "social psychiatry." To do this is to forget that political science from the time of Plato has stood as the science of the health of the body politic. A change in vocabulary is unnecessary. Laws are made to preserve the health, the wholeness, the purpose of the political community. When morals and laws are good, the great community is one and whole. When the community is cracked with dissidence, then its morals and laws are bad, and the theologian and political scientist bear a heavy share of the blame.

Whoever concerns himself with trivialities runs the risk of a trifling reputation. Because political scientists have forgotten that their science must rest on the nature of man and that the specialized and unmoral social sciences must be given shape by the comprehensive and moral discipline which is political science, they are becoming identified as little more than fools positive. For this reason their defection has not yet destroyed all hope. Hope remains. There is, there must be, a way out. The present book examines this hope.

Wherein salvation? The ordinary man stakes all on democracy and education. In time this growingly perfect form of government will solve all problems with the assistance of the education and science that flourish under it.[3] The man who reads, however, who keeps up with the world, puts more of his hope in modern social science (within a framework of democracy, of course). And the social scientist himself, in spite of the fact that he knows the history of this hope, that it rings of Auguste Comte and positivism, that it has its modern representatives and extremists, he too, after asserting that he has no illusions about the length of time required, confesses to this hope. What other has he? The leadership of business? Not after the Great Depression. The labor unions? They are too much after their own good. World government, perhaps? Not when people love their countries so well. Religion? Ha! Physical science? When Einstein was asked to choose any person he wished with whom to discuss a momentous problem of civilization, whom did he name? The physicist, Enrico Fermi? The mathematician, Bertrand Russell? No, he turned to the psychologist, Sigmund Freud.[4]

> Dear Professor Freud:
>   The proposal of the League of Nations and its International Institute of Intellectual Co-operation at Paris that I should invite a person, to be chosen by myself, to a frank exchange of views on any problem that I might select affords me a very welcome opportunity of conferring with you upon a question which, as things are now, seems the most insistent of all the problems civilization has to face. This is the problem: Is there any way of delivering mankind from the menace of war? . . . As for me, the normal objective of my thought affords no insight into the dark places of human will and feeling. . . . There are certain psychological obstacles whose existence a layman in the mental sciences may dimly surmise, but whose interrelations and vagaries he is incompetent to fathom; you, I am convinced, will be able to suggest educative methods, lying more or less outside the scope of politics, which will eliminate these obstacles. . . .
>   Yours very sincerely,
>   A. EINSTEIN

There it is. "If we do not place our faith in social science," asks a modern sociologist, "to what shall we look for social salvation?" And another one echoes, "Where else, in any realistic sense, can that [substantial hope] be found?"[5]

The eighteenth century was revolutionary, the nineteenth evolutionary. The twentieth century has jumped back over and recaptured some of the zeal of the enlightened eighteenth. The extension of scientific methods to the personal and social realm during this new century opened up horizons comparable in scope with those of natural science. The future, it has been suggested, will look back to this age as the "first century of the Science of man."[6] While no one, not even the natural scientists themselves, seeks salvation in the demonic power of physical science, to the social sciences all turn with despair written in their eyes. Here is the hope of mankind.

What? What if the opposite were true? What then?

One problem at a time. Since mental disorder looms so large among the afflictions of the community and since in one form or another it affects the work of all social sciences, it well can serve as the test case. Psychotherapy, the science of curing the mind, will be asked here to show its strength, to demonstrate what it does and can do to reduce or eliminate this disease. Psychotherapy the science, with its roots in the biological sciences of medicine and psychiatry and in the social science of psychology, will be asked to show cause for hope. Its life, new and old, will be scrutinized; its principles inspected. The claims it makes will be added and evaluated. The stuff it works with—the mentally disturbed—will be examined. How did they get the way they are? What happens to them before, during, and after treatment? And this treatment, can it be said to cure people and what is a cure and which method cures best? These are some of the questions to be asked.

And when this is all over, something new may have emerged. Some will say that it is old, and praise it for that. Others will cry that psychotherapy has been set back twenty-five hundred years. It does not matter so long as there is in it a new something to help answer the questions.

So now, decide. Sit back and watch unfold before your eyes a play—the modern drive for salvation. Is it epic, farce, or tragedy?

ERRORS OF PSYCHOTHERAPY

CHAPTER ONE

The Cure of One Soul

Let us take a famous case, the case of Dora. Its real
title is "Fragment of an Analysis of a Case of Hysteria,"[1] and it can be found among the collected papers of
Sigmund Freud, the one who discovered the mental cure most
renowned today—psychoanalysis.

When Freud first saw Dora she was, as he says, a girl of
intelligent and engaging looks, in the first bloom of youth.
Yet she was the cause of much worry to her parents. Low in
spirits, disgruntled with herself and her family, on bad terms
with her mother, shunning the company of her friends, she
had gone so far as to write a note bidding her parents good-by.
Life was something she could endure no longer. Her history
was replete with hysterical symptoms—difficulty in breathing,
nervous coughing, hemicranial headaches (possibly migraine),
depression, and loss of voice. In short, *petite hystérie*. One day
after an altercation with her father she had an attack of loss
of consciousness, whereupon the poor man determined to take
her to Freud for help.

After a treatment of just three months Dora left Freud's
care. Fifteen months later she reported to him that her spirits
had risen, her attacks gradually had become less frequent, and
all in all a great improvement had set in. For reasons to be
gone into later, Dora never got the full benefit of psychoanalytic therapy but there can be no doubt that Freud was right
in saying that his short treatment gave her relief.

A remarkable performance, yet one duplicated time upon

time. (This was not an extraordinary case; its fame is due to its priority and its lucidity.) No physical pressure was put on Dora, no injections given, no surgery. If she was cured it was by the healing effect of her dialogue with Freud.

How is it possible for one person to talk to another and cure him? What happens in those situations where the healer and the sick merely look and talk and sometimes touch, where striking cures take place—a paralyzed arm restored to use, a deathly fear of boarding vehicles allayed, a distressing tremor or twitch or muscular spasm, all relieved—without the use of instruments, prescriptions, drugs, or duress? The question is important, the answers to it contradictory. Yet communicative situations of this sort, usually termed psychotherapy, constitute one of the oldest, most trustworthy methods of mind-cure, going back for thousands of years, existing wherever historic man is to be found.

The modern scene offers many schools of psychotherapy that make use of communicative cure.[2] In addition to the psychoanalysts there are the Adlerians, the followers of Jung and of Stekel, the Rankians, the psychobiologists, the hypnotists; there are the many varieties of psychiatry, of counseling, of social service practice; and there are the pastoral and confessional works of ministers and priests. This by no means exhausts the list but it demonstrates the difficulties that lie in wait for anyone trying to discover just what it is in therapeutic conversation that promotes mental health. So many forms with so many differences exist that the problem of a starting point is not easy.

The simplest procedure seems to be this. By taking the successful or relatively successful schools of psychotherapy and by contrasting them with the unsuccessful, one can focus attention on those parts of the communication that are dissimilar and that presumably account for the results, good, bad, or indifferent, of the various therapies. The successful, then, are to be matched with the unsuccessful, and out of the comparison will arise the clues.

CHAPTER TWO

The Panorama of Therapies

The word "psychotherapy" may be new but the idea is old. Modern terminology sometimes hides honorable predecessors. Before the psychiatrist, the psychoanalyst, and the commercial counselor there were those who believed that *divinissimum divinorum est cooperari Deo in salutem animarum,* that it was the most divine of divine things to assist God in caring for the health of souls. Had you explained the word "psychotherapy" to the healers of earlier centuries they would have replied, "Oh yes, you mean the care and cure of souls," for the term itself has its antecedents in two Greek words, *psyche* meaning "the soul" and *therapeia* meaning "cure." Soul-cure is the word.

Look into the most primitive communities that anthropologists have found. There will be a psychotherapist. He fulfills his office in the primitive world under the name of shaman or medicine man. He may be working with his patient for hours or even days on end. His techniques are many, rich, and intricate. Painted on the sand beside him may be a picture, incomprehensible to foreign eyes, but symmetrical and bewilderingly beautiful.

Study the medical papyri of ancient Egypt. The psychotherapist's work is there on the scrolls. His formulas and methods grip the imagination. He seems never to use his pharmacological or surgical skill without making sure that his patient is first prepared psychologically.

Across the Mediterranean in the Greco-Roman world flour-
ished the Asclepian health centers. In these sanitariums the
psychotherapist again appears. The battery of techniques at
his command is fascinating. He and his patient share the impressive architecture, the sun, the air, the quiet, and the pe-
culiarly Greek view—mountain meets the plain and both meet
the sea. In the half a hundred short case histories that the
archaeologists have brought to light he shows a flair for that
most difficult of patients, the skeptical one. Also, in some way
this psychotherapist makes use of the healing power in two
allies, the dream and the drama. Would that more were known
of him.

And that age ushered in by Christianity and dominated by
the Church of Rome, it, too, had its healer of souls. He
originated a system of mental hygiene that was unique. He
spoke a language now mysterious but full of the symbolism of
health. In a church setting he wove together a private therapy
of words and a public one of ceremony. From what can be
learned of him, he was remarkably efficient.

But of the varieties of mental healing throughout history,
the fullest accounts and the most acceptable evidence of success
should be offered by the psychotherapies of the present day.
They are the ones that for the most part are devoted to modern
scientific requirements of accuracy, objectivity, and the numerical expression of results. One finds, indeed, that in this
area a group of studies of a statistical nature exists.[1] Within
this group differences should appear which, expressed in figures, might separate successful from unsuccessful psychotherapies.

That there is a variation in the figures of these studies is
clear to even the most casual observer. Out of 70 cases, for
example, 91 per cent were improved; out of 4000 cases, 69
per cent were cured; out of 952 cases, 60 per cent were improved; out of 37 cases, 100 per cent were recovered; out of
the cases of the Berlin Institute for Psychoanalysis, 38 per cent
were cured and 19 per cent improved; and out of the Chicago

Institute for Psychoanalysis, 22 per cent were cured and 51 per cent improved. There is only one thing wrong—no respectable statistician would consider these figures useful to the purpose at hand.

They are presented in tabular form, it is true; they are expressed in percentages and averages, true; they are treated in a variety of fairly complex statistical ways, also true. But the whole exercise is simply another instance (so common to an age that bows before quanta) wherein the statistical techniques applied outrun the data.

Some therapists and some schools of therapy claim that of the persons they treated as many as ninety or one hundred per cent were cured. Such claims could be divided by two or four or six, depending on the divider's friendliness to the particular form of mind-cure under examination. Other therapists or schools, more humble, mark the lower margin by assigning themselves a grade of thirty per cent or so. A curing rate of one third seems to be the point where it is felt that the firm should go out of business. It falls below marginal utility. No psychotherapy, it seems, claims to save less than this proportion of souls.

What are the units employed in these studies? First of all there is the "case." What is the definition of a case? Whom do the psychiatrist and psychologist and mental hospital accept and whom do they turn away? Obviously the definition of a case hinges on the definition of the mentally ill. Who, then, is ill? The answer is not to be found in these studies.

The type of treatment designated must be considered also. Here, too, is a lack of precision. Some studies speak of a psychoanalytic therapy but others preface the phrase with the word "orthodox," leaving the reader with the necessity of determining which is the more orthodox psychoanalytic treatment when the practitioners themselves disagree. One quantitative study speaks of using "a short intensive treatment based primarily on Adlerian psychotherapy and somewhat on Freudian psychoanalysis"; another of a treatment that aimed at "purging the subconscious," at suggestion and the "development of insight"; another of a "non-directive counseling technique"; of a group therapy method using answers to anonymous questions; of a psychoanalytic technique described as "conversing with the patient in the language of the unconscious and interpreting the unconscious to the patient at every single opportunity." To group any of these studies into one class that could be compared with another would be most difficult.

The fragmentation of one school of therapy after another into smaller schools brings the further problem of getting together enough cases to add up to a statistical inquiry. A number of these quantitative studies are the reports of single psychotherapists on the sum total of their own patients alone, a number necessarily small from a statistical view.

Last in the order of ambiguities to be found in these figures is that in the most important item of the number of "cures." What constitutes a cure varies greatly from one therapist to the next. Usually no definition is given that could be considered adequate for statistical purposes. And it does not increase accuracy to make distinctions, as many of these studies do, between "cured" and "much improved," "improved," "recovered," or "slightly improved." It is as though a quantitative study of coal tonnage were being made that used the terms "long," "short," "gross," and "net" tons without definitions. This matter of the meaning of the term "cure" will be gone into later in greater detail. It presents the strongest block to any scientific or statistical study of cures.

There would be small gain from reproducing or combining the figures from these studies into a grand table. Seeing such a table, one might suppose it to be valuable, but on learning of the vagueness of the units, one is no longer impressed. Furthermore, inaccuracy and unreliability in the data can be compensated by no amount of elaboration and care in subsequent statistical operations. Under present procedures, in which neither "case" nor "treatment" nor "cure" is reliably defined, that is, defined so that different observers could agree in their classifications, a statistician would not be shocked to discover someday that the number of cases cured was greater than the number of cases treated, just as in an African colony it was found once that more children died under the age of one year than were born. To present and treat heterogeneous units as though they were homogeneous is statistical rhetoric.

For those persons who cannot rid themselves of a respect for quantitative data, let it be reported that even those who uncritically accept therapeutic figures can make little out of them. A recent survey made by a psychiatrist concluded that "the therapeutic statistics of psychiatry appear to justify only the conclusion that the essential factors in cures are still unknown." This study did have some reservations to make about the statistics.[2] The expression of qualifications, however, which is also a part of every acceptable statistical study, does not decrease their magnitude, nor limit their damage to the study.

The statistical confusion in which psychotherapists often work is revealed in another psychiatrist's candid statement:

> From the practical scientific point of view I am not satisfied with my work as, unfortunately, I cannot say how many of my patients would have improved without my help. I am as dissatisfied as I am when I read that with insulin one can have results varying from 26 per cent to 88 per cent. On the other hand, one reads papers that show normal remission rates with occupational therapy or with prolonged narcosis up to 54.6 per cent whilst Langfeldt states that 67 per cent of atypical schizophrenics improve without treatment.[3]

Pruned of its technical details, this admission bears a certain similarity to a fourteenth-century story of Petrarch, the famous Italian poet, humanist, and critic of the medical profession. A famous physician once told him that "if 100 or 1000 individuals of the same age and the same constitution and mode of life at one and the same time were attacked by the same disease, and half availed themselves of the physicians while the others acted without medical advice following their natural instincts and discretion, there could be no doubt whatsoever that the second half would happily recover." Petrarch was being malicious; his modern counterpart is not.

Obviously a change of approach to the problem is necessary. Up to this time it could be hoped that reliable statistical differences might be found among the various therapies and that these differences might highlight the significant factors in cures. Now such an expectation must be abandoned. Later, the failure of this approach will be recalled. At present, since no more comprehensive or trustworthy figures than these are available, modern psychotherapists ought to be given the benefit of the doubt. Grant, if you will, that they produce cures, that so far they have been too busy helping people to worry about tabulations, that they are confident enough of the value of their work that they do not question that the persons who leave their doors are much better off. Then the unsupported word of the president of the Division of Clinical and Abnormal Psychology of the American Psychological Association can be accepted. "At the best, psychotherapy probably gives significant help to only forty to sixty per cent of the clients who are subjected to its procedures."[4]

But generosity to modern psychotherapists should be matched by generosity to other workers in the vineyard—the minister, the priest, yes, even the so-called quack, and most certainly the primitive, ancient, and medieval healers of the psyche—for the evidence of their therapeutic success is no less reliable. This would have been hard to believe had not the present estimates been demonstrated to be something less than trustworthy. In addition these other therapies have some evidence in their own right. There is a crude, practical test in the very fact of their past and present existence.

Consider the following case, the case of Alicia. When brought to the psychotherapist, Alicia was a woman of rather dull intelligence, just past middle age, married, poor but respected by the community. She complained of not feeling well. Depressed in mind, neglectful of her household duties and work, avoiding contact with friends, she feared that her sickness would eventuate in death. Her symptoms included diarrhea, loss of appetite, pains in the stomach, back, and legs, and occasional fever. She alternated between moods of deep lethargy and moods of fearsomeness and tension, marked by tremor of the hands and rapid and jerky movements. In short, anxiety attacks with depression. After a physician had treated her fever without success, the one who had taken an interest in the case and later described it in detail brought her to the psychotherapist for treatment.

Several therapeutic sessions later Alicia left the psychotherapist's care. She was observed for four weeks after the close of therapy. A new personality seemed to have emergd. The complaints, the nagging of husband and family, the avoidance of friends, and the anxious and depressive symptoms all had disappeared. Both the psychotherapist and the patient judged the therapy to be successful.

Without knowing the time and place and methods of the curing process, one could substitute the name of Freud or any other modern psychotherapist in the place of this healer who, as it happens, was a Guatemalan *parchero* or shaman and whose patient was a Pokomán Indian.[5]

Occasionally one finds that someone has taken the trouble conscientiously to count up the successes or failures of primitive healers, and this, too, is evidence. In the case given above, the reporting anthropologist, in extending his work, gathered the names of thirty-six former patients of six different shamans. Tracking the patients, he managed to get definite confirmation for sixteen of the thirty-six. The rest were deceased or had moved from the vicinity. "In no case did a Ladino who had been named as the recipient of 'cure' from one of the shamans deny the fact."

Sometimes evidence comes from still another quarter—the many cases where the therapy of the primitive has bested that of the white man. To illustrate with another case:

> The [patient's] cold took on the symptoms of influenza, and despite excellent medical care and nursing, he failed to recover. On the contrary, he gradually became weaker and weaker. He lost interest in his surroundings, refused food, and turned his face resolutely to the wall.
>
> His wife, after hearing the verdict of the doctor that he could not live more than another day or two, called in one of the few remaining kahunas [shamans] who were at work in Honolulu at that late date.
>
> The old kahuna listened carefully to the wife's account of what the white doctor had said. He asked a few questions, and then began his treatment. . . .
>
> [After having carried out a "very ancient" therapy involving confession, the shaman promised the patient] that he would be well on the way to recovery. The man's strength did return, he did eat, and he fell fast asleep. When he awakened hours later, he sat up and called for more food. His wife brought thick soup and he was sitting up happily talking with her when the white doctor arrived. He [the doctor] was one long in the Islands and experienced. After a careful examination of his patient he turned to the wife and asked, "You had the other kind of doctor?" She nodded, and he went out shaking his head wonderingly.

Cases such as this and other evidence of the sort mentioned above led a group of social scientists recently to declare that "careful examination of cases gives the distinct impression that the better type of shaman's record compares not unfavorably with that of the modern physician.[6]

So the strange fact will out. All psychotherapies work. Every community has recognized procedures for the handling of mental disorder. These procedures all meet with success. How successful one may be compared with another cannot yet be told. The psychiatrist previously mentioned, whose conclusion about therapeutic statistics was negative, continued his remarks in this vein:

> Nevertheless, one gains the impression that therapy does something and is effective. One gains the impression that certain types of therapy are more effective in particular types of patients than in others. However, the statistics appear to indicate that any therapy is in itself more fundamental than the type employed. There is something basically effective in the process of therapy in general which is independent of the methods employed.[7]

A statistical evaluation of psychotherapy made less than a decade earlier had a similar lesson to draw. "When we examine the available reports of those institutions specializing in intensive psychotherapy applied to the psychoneurotic patient, it is apparent that the different varieties of intensive work have but little difference in their ultimate effectiveness." So be it. Pierre Janet, the Parisian psychiatrist and contemporary of Freud, agrees. "The psychotherapist who understands his patient well and who knows how to use psychological stimulation succeeds with any method that he cares to use."[8]

Joined by this fact, the original problem—what causes a cure?—becomes approachable from an altogether different direction. If all psychotherapies succeed in some measure, perhaps it is what they all have in common that will reveal the bases of mental healing, the understanding and "psychological stimulation" that Janet speaks of. Instead of the method of differences, the method of similarities can be tried.[9]

Yet the techniques of Professor Freud and Parchero Manuel have so many differences. Have they *anything* in common?

At first the problem seems insuperable, so diverse are the practices. But the field already has been limited, one should remember, to those psychotherapies that depend largely on the personal interaction of healer and patient. Therefore the data are to be sought in communication, in the communication that occurs in the peculiar interpersonal setting of psychotherapy. Perhaps formulas can be found like those of Isis, the Egyptian healing goddess, formulas that expel suffering, words that quicken health.

CHAPTER THREE

Neurosis as Moral Disorder

The persons who come to the psychotherapist are all fired in the same crucible. They have thought bad things or done bad deeds, and so they suffer, ground and baked in a hot oven, cooked, no less, in their own galled conscience. This the history and ethnography of psychotherapy reveal.

Among the ancients the prevailing theory was that mental disorders are the result of moral violation. Largely for this reason, in the civilization of the Egyptians, the Hindus, the Chinese, Greeks, and Romans, the art of healing the psyche was carried on by experts in the moral sphere, the priests. The Buddhist monks, for example, taught that humanity suffered from two kinds of afflictions—physical and mental. For physical ailments the drugs of the doctor sufficed but for mental afflictions Buddhist remedies were required. Buddha once told a physician, "You go and heal his body first. I will come later to treat his mental suffering."

In the religious temples where most psychotherapy took place the unrepentant wicked were not suffered, not even, so it was said, "if they bring all the wealth of India and Sardis." Those to whom, as the Greek dramatist Menander puts it, "the beautiful, the good, the holy, the evil were all the same" could not be helped until they showed the desire to cleanse their souls of sin. In one of the preserved fragments of Greek writings the case is told of a man who consorted with Epicureanism.

(To the temple priests, it should be noted, Epicureanism was the equivalent of atheism.)

> The man Euphronius, a wretched creature, took pleasure in the silly talk of Epicurus and acquired two evils from this: being impious and intemperate. . . .
>
> Being grievously stricken with a disease . . . he first besought the healing aid of mortals and clung to them.
>
> The illness was stronger than the knowledge of the physicians.
>
> When he was already tottering close to the brink of death, his friends brought him to the temple of Asclepius. And as he fell asleep one of the priests seemed to say to him that there was one road of safety for the man, and only one remedy for the evils upon him, namely, if he burned the books of Epicurus, moistened the ashes of the impious, unholy, and effeminate books with melted wax and, spreading the plaster all over his stomach and chest, bound bandages around them.
>
> What he had heard he communicated to his friends and they were straightway filled with excessive joy because he did not come out, disdained and dishonored. . . .
>
> And having learned a lesson from him, they followed him forthwith in a good and honorable life.[1]

Upon the portal of the temple of Epidaurus was an inscription that typifies the attitude of the ancient healer of the soul: "It is proper for him who enters the temple to be pure; now to be pure is to have holy thoughts."

In biblical lands also it was held that derangement was due to moral transgression. Mental disorder is an exchange for moral turpitude, and an exchange plentifully paid.[2] According to the Old Testament, simple injuries and ills can be attended to by doctors but the more serious diseases have spiritual roots. The sufferers must repent of their sins, they must heed the moral injunctions and commands and statutes, or else be simply "oppressed and crushed away" until driven mad (DEUTERONOMY 28:33–34). *The Wisdom of Sirach* instructs thus:

> My son, in thy sickness be not negligent: but pray unto the Lord, and he will make thee whole.
>
> Leave off from sin, and order thine hands aright, and cleanse thy heart from all wickedness.
>
> ECCLESIASTICUS 38:9–10

While to the person healed through religious intercession, the advice of the New Testament is "Sin no more, lest a worse thing befall thee" (JOHN 5:14).

In the Middle Ages the idea was indisputably clear—a disordered mind is the result of evil done or evil thought. To illustrate, the *Dialogues* of Caesarius, a learned Cistercian monk of the early thirteenth century, contain the story of a concubine who entered a convent. But even there she was tormented by thoughts of being carnally solicited by a lascivious demon. She continued to be thus obsessed until "she was cleanly confessed." The language of medieval times couched the entire problem in this vein: "Such afflictions are only on account of sin, and occur to those who do not live in a state of grace."[3]

Surveying the primitives, one sees a remarkably consistent adherence to this conception. First of all, their psychotherapist, the shaman or medicine man, is a religious figure and, like the ancient and medieval priest, deeply concerned with knowledge of the moral order. Secondly, their explanation is often most explicit—mental disorder is due to the breaking of taboo, to the infraction of tribal morality. Deceit, murder, adultery, theft, or other acts may be thought conducive to illness. Among the Salteaux Indians, a hunting people of Ojibwa derivation, the following case is recorded, together with numerous others of the same character. The native doctor had cured a woman.

> She was an unmarried woman, and when he first saw her she could not move. But he had the people put fresh brush in the wigwam and when night came he started to doctor her. She got no better, although he gave her good medicine. So finally he said, "You must have done something to bring this sickness on yourself. What was it?" The woman said that she and another girl had played

[sexually] with each other. After this the young woman got better because the medicine could do its work.[4]

Wherever on the world's continents the life of the ruder communities is explored, the belief in the relation of mental disturbance to moral transgression is to be found. Though thus consistent, the primitive's therapeutic concepts and methods, like the modern and the ancient, are not simple. Because of some moral violation, evil demons may be thought to possess the body, or diseased objects may be said to have entered the body, or witches and sorcerers may be offered fertile field for sowing evil, or again the person's soul may abandon his body. The type of therapy applied will be seen then to lead directly from the shaman's ideas of etiology and pathology.

It is sometimes thought that primitive mentality puts all disturbances, of mind and body alike, in this one category of moral violation. Such a view is widespread but mistaken. All primitive communities known to the anthropologist have definite knowledge of bodily medicines which they have collected in a practical fashion. They are none of them therapeutic nihilists. They all use surgical measures, some of them extremely difficult operations, and they all have pharmacopoeias, some simple and some elaborate, many of them containing those filthy items which the Germans expressively label *Dreckapotheke* and which modern writers delight in listing while superiorly lifting the nose. The Greek Hippocrates, the patron saint of modern physicians, was wrong in saying that "the Barbarians make no use of medicine."[5] Medicine men may know much less than the surgeon and the internist but they work just as hard with the pragmatic measures they have.

What is confusing to the ordinary observer is the combining they often do of physical and psychic therapeutics. The reason is that they most often think of illness as affecting the man in all his vitality. They therefore apply a polytherapy for body and soul. While on a military expedition Socrates noticed this about the barbarian Thracians. They knew that the body could

not be cured without curing the mind. Socrates, who so loved
Athens that he could be pulled away from it only by army
service, nevertheless had no hesitations about censuring the
physicians of Hellas for their ignorance. Because this fact was
unknown to them, he charged, the cure of many diseases was
also unknown.

Often, too, for such maladies as cuts, colds, broken limbs,
bites, burns or scalds, the medicine man will use a purely
medical treatment and (as in the Salteaux case just above)
only if the patient does not respond to his herbs and drugs
does he institute psychotherapy. If the cause of the illness is
not manifest the medicine man may inquire into the patient's
dreams, symptoms, transgressions, especially of taboos, may
examine him visually and even by touch to ascertain to what
type of disturbance the ailment belongs. In this he acts no
differently from the modern physician who, meeting with no
success in his organic tests or treatment, refers his patient to
the psychiatrist, nor from the Greek doctor who, if his therapy
failed, expected the patient to repair to the religious temple.[6]

A division of labor such as this between medicine and psychotherapy often appears. Looking back today over the sick-
nesses of those who went to the temple or to the shaman, one
sees that the great part of their symptoms—blindness, deafness,
dumbness, anesthesia, paralysis, obsession—falls easily within
the seemingly ever expanding limits of psychogenic disorder.
The history of healing in the primitive as well as in the ancient
worlds discloses a tendency for body- and soul-curing to go
separate ways and in doing so to contrive an informal but
practical way of differentiating somatic from psychic disturbances. In those communities that blossom into civilizations
a further stage is discernible—the two spheres of therapy come
to grips—but this issue can be better joined later.

The peoples of the past, then, thought of mental disorder
as both a religious and a moral disturbance. It was this fact
that led to the major generalization of the present chapter, that
the person who presents himself for treatment suffers from

a moral affliction. Not only history and ethnography but present-day practice and theory support the thesis, too, and support it more directly.

More is known about the person who consults the psychotherapist today. There are more detailed accounts of the reasons he gives for his being there, and these accounts give a uniform answer.

First of all, he suffers. The patient knows there is something wrong with what he does. It is causing him hardship and pain and humiliation. The suffering he goes through the modern psychotherapist calls "anxiety."

The anguish of the patient, so obvious today as a fact of significance, did not immediately (perhaps because of its very obviousness) catch the notice of the modern psychotherapist. When psychoanalysis first struck public attention it did so through its insistence on the prevalence in the psychoneurosis of sexual disturbances. The furor, popular and academic, raised by this emphasis covered over succeeding shifts in position. In later works Freud, while dropping none of the terminology devised for sexual problems, more and more came to set up anxiety as the central problem of the neurosis. In *The Problem of Anxiety* he appeared to defend the position that "all symptom formation would be brought about solely in order to avoid anxiety . . . so that anxiety would be the fundamental phenomenon and central problem of neurosis." Other observers in the field later came to record that the "one essential factor common to all neuroses . . . is anxieties and the defenses built up against them."[7]

Once anxiety came to the fore, however, another question was inevitable. What is the person anxious about? Why does he suffer?

Of a sudden, then, the "feeling of guilt," hitherto handled with casualness, assumed importance. With the development in psychoanalysis of the concept of the superego, a word approximating "conscience" in meaning, the guilt the patient felt began to attract more systematic attention until it came to be regarded as "the crucial element in the dynamics of neuroses."[8]

The increased theoretical importance given guilt and shame was reflected in Freud's discovery of the neurotic's need for punishment. "This need for punishment is the worst enemy of our therapeutic efforts," he complained.

> It seems as though this factor, the unconscious need for punishment, plays a part in every neurotic disease. . . . As to the origin . . . there can be, I think, no doubt. It behaves like a part of the conscience, like the prolongation of conscience into the unconscious; and it must have the same origin as conscience. . . . If only the words were less incongruous, we should be justified, for all practical purposes, in calling it "an unconscious sense of guilt." . . . The problems raised by the unconscious sense of guilt, its relation to morality, education, criminality and delinquency, is at the present moment the favorite field of investigation for psychoanalysts. Here we have emerged into the open from the mental underworld.[9]

The problem of the neurotic, then, is suffering, but of a particular kind, suffering due to guilt. Few psychotherapists have perceived that, if this is so, every neurotic's history will show him to be tormented by a moral conflict, a conflict of right and wrong. There are many reasons why they have not seen this fact, which will be touched on presently. Here, however, a short case which Wilhelm Stekel, one of that sparkling group of Viennese healers of the early twentieth century, gave in his autobiographical fragments may illustrate the type of conflict a neurosis involves.

> He [the patient] was a cashier in a big bank, and had held this position for some time. He could not cross a square. When he tried to do so, he experienced an intense anxiety, his whole body trembled and he had to go to his destination by some roundabout way.
> It wasn't even of help if someone went with him. In

my practice I had before had several cases of agoraphobia. . . . I asked about his family, about home conditions, and finally the following facts came out. His very
good mother suffered from cholecystitis. The physician
recommended her to go to Carlsbad, but the trip would
cost too much, and my patient was in financial distress.

I had a flash of intuition.

"Does much money go through your hands?"

"Thousands, and hundreds of thousands of guldens."

"Have you never thought that if you ran away with
this money you could save your mother's life?"

The patient blushed and stammered. "The thought
has come into my mind. It was immediately rejected. I
am an honest man, and have no inclination towards becoming a criminal."

Now I explained to him that . . . his phobia was a
means of self-defense against his unconscious criminal
impulse.

The cashier asked: "What can I do?"

"Give up your post as cashier."

"How can I do that? How shall I explain that I am
giving up a job which is entrusted to men of great in-
tegrity?"

"I will give you a certificate to the effect that the
responsibility makes you nervous."

"All right," he rejoined.

After a year . . . his sister . . . told me he had been
transferred to another branch of the bank and that his
agoraphobia had disappeared.[10]

All cases have a similarly moral center. The foreman who
could only stutter incomprehensibly in making reports to his
supervisors was holding back a desire to be abusive, which he
considered wrong. The girl who was afraid to go out in public
was curbing a desire to exhibit herself and be promiscuous,
which she considered evil. One can read through the standard
books of cases and, wherever enough detail or actual conversation is reported, one can see moral conflict as the pivot around
which the neurosis revolves. Here in these cases[11] one can view

the inner war of drive against drive, standard against standard, need against need, ideal against ideal, passion against passion.

A middle-aged businessman with a passion for submissiveness and succor that clashes with . . .

A housewife with a passion for superiority in masculine endeavors that clashes with . . .

A young medical student with a passion for ruthless success that clashes with . . .

A middle-aged businessman with a passion for sexual adventure that clashes with . . .

A businesswoman with a passion for stabbing intimate associates that clashes with . . .

A young housewife with a passion for phantasies about blood that clashes with . . .

A young man with a passion for beating the posteriors of other young men and horses that clashes with . . .

A young female university student with a passion for masculine decisiveness that clashes with . . .

A middle-aged businessman with a passion for promiscuity that clashes with . . .

A young office worker with a passion for violent rages that clashes with . . .

A reserve officer with a passion for self-preservation that clashes with . . .

A young man with a passion for sexual intercourse that clashes with . . .

A young woman with a passion for hating her mother that clashes with . . .

A young woman with a passion for self-effacement that clashes with . . .

Clashes with what? With the belief in every case that such action is wrong, evil, bad, immoral—in short, with the passion for righteousness.

An intriguing thing, this passion for righteousness, that sets itself up to rule over, to regulate, to govern all other passions. Says the patient to the psychotherapist, "What shall I do about my hatefulness—my hostility—my ugly disposition—my de-

pendency—my domineering—my sensitivity—my suspiciousness—my uncertainty? Something inside me tells me that it's
bad, that I've got to control it or get rid of it."[12] On a later
occasion the source of this ruling passion will be sought but already it can be recognized as man's arbiter of conduct, the
conscience.

It may be difficult to see why some of the passions mentioned
above should bring a person's conscience into opposition. Why
shouldn't a young woman hate her mother? Why shouldn't a
middle-aged businessman have his sexual adventures? Why
shouldn't a person keep his hatefulness or his dependency or
his suspiciousness? Not all of these things are immoral, are
they? Some of them seem to have nothing to do with conscience.

Regrettable though it may be, the answer is that a matter of
conscience for one person may not be that for another. What is
immoral for one person may not be that for another. What is
immoral is not the same for all men.

Take, for example, the passion for perfection. If the person
driven by this passion is unable to attain perfection, he to himself is evil. He proves his worthlessness and makes himself
guilty of failing his parents or God or his own ideals. Other
persons, on the other hand, might not admit the achievement
of perfection even in one sphere alone to be a matter of
morality. Or contemplate the case of an old man stirred
throughout life by a passion for independence. The first pension
check he received after being put in retirement precipitated his
suicide. As another example consider the scholar of ancient
Greece who, unable to satisfy a passion for impeccable transla-
tion in a passage of Thucydides, judges himself a failure in his
chosen task and collapses. Many other persons, including his
own colleagues, would not consider him the worm he took himself to be.

In some cases the moral conflict may be somewhat clearer;
for instance, in a daughter who conceals the fact of her
mother's adultery from her father. But in every example the

problem is moral in that the suffering person believes himself guilty. In him is the locus of immorality.

There may be and often is more than one moral problem involved in the neuroses. Confusion over several moral issues is usually present. In a single case there may be guilt over masturbation, one's duty toward one's wife, one's treatment of an employee, hatred of a daughter, homosexual tendencies, and so on. St. Fortunatus is reported to have cured a man possessed by 6670 evil demons. Or there may be involved only one conflict, one evil spirit—incestuous thoughts.

So Otto Rank, a star pupil of Freud, is correct in saying that "The neurosis has been revealed in its ultimate analysis as a moral problem." Carl Gustav Jung, another stellar member of the first psychoanalytic circle, is right, too, in a similar insistence. Still another—Alfred Adler—was on the right track in emphasizing the prevalence in the neurosis of feelings of inferiority and unworthiness. These conceptions of shame, guilt, inferiority, unworthiness, hang together, all characterized by a sense of failure or conflict about an accepted standard or norm. French psychiatry has had at least an inkling of the same fact; since the nineteenth century it has customarily referred to its work as "moral therapy." Earlier than this, the Spaniards of the fifteenth century, bearers of the Greco-Roman and Arabic traditions, worked with the same conception. In the Zaragoza asylum founded by King Alonzo V of Aragon "disease produced by moral causes was treated by moral means prudently managed." Possibly modern psychotherapists could have reached the point sooner had they heeded the writings of Robert Burton, who lived over three hundred years ago but is coming into his own only now. In *The Anatomy of Melancholy* he wrote that the "greatest cause of this malady is our conscience, sense of our sins, and God's anger justly deserved, a guilty conscience for some foul offence."[13]

The reasons that the moral core of the neurosis has eluded most modern psychotherapists are interesting and significant. The wide differences today in personal ideas of morality, discussed earlier in the chapter, offer only a partial explanation. There are other reasons which will have to be dealt with later. But because the fact has eluded them many psychotherapists deplore that people nowadays are still ashamed to confess to neurosis or mental illness. Existing studies of popular attitudes confirm this impression but to deplore the fact or to try to change it is futile.

A neurosis announces the presence of a moral split, of shame and guilt. If the person felt no shame or guilt he should not be in the psychotherapist's office. He would not be ill and the psychotherapist would be out of a job. This might not be a bad thing were it not, as will be seen later, that other consequences would follow which neither patient nor psychotherapist might relish.

Why but for the shame involved is such great pressure for the pledge of secrecy exerted by the patient and accepted by the therapist—a much greater pressure than on the ordinary medical examination or legal interview? In the auricular confession it is called the *sigillum,* a secrecy unto death. So important is it to their patients that some modern psychotherapists who are not physicians, lawyers, or priests swear secrecy although under the law they have no such right; they have not the immunity in court against divulging their knowledge that the physician or priest does. They promise secrecy because if they did not the patient would not talk. He feels guilty and ashamed. He does not want others to know. He does not want it blabbed abroad.[14]

It would seem that concrete modern evidence confirms what the scattered materials of history and ethnography could only suggest. The neurosis is a moral disorder. Out of the many, many dissimilarities that separate the various psychotherapies throughout time and space, this stable element appears. The person who brings his case to the psychotherapist brings a problem that is causing him great suffering and one that for him involves moral conflict, conflict between right and wrong, good and bad, a conflict over "oughtness," over standards or ideals which he has and cannot by himself change.

This last conclusion contains the first common element in psychotherapy that the comparative method turned up. Are there others?

CHAPTER FOUR

The Seat of Authority

Whether he is priest or psychiatrist, whether his patients come one or a dozen at a time, whether he heals in an office or under a plane tree, whether he dresses like a peacock or wears no clothes to speak of—in the psychotherapeutic situation wherever found—the psychotherapist holds authority.

Homer had a way of saying that the healer is a man greatly esteemed: "The healer is worth many men." Today one would express it differently and say that the healer is a man with high status or prestige. Homer's blunter way of putting it has the advantage of conveying that a man's status or authority is a comparative idea and depends on what people think of what he does. His position in the community, the real seat of his authority, rests on what they think.

Auctoritas is a good old Latin word. In English it becomes "authority," which means power based on esteem or respect. No other word carries its basic sense of power exercised over those who have willed its exercise. For this reason it will find its way to these pages again and again. Authority is not force or coercion. By definition it is a power that wants using, that is granted in order to be used, that has the support of those for whom and over whom it is used. In short, rightful power.

To be able to heal is to be able to do something of great importance, the Greeks thought, indeed of greater importance than the things most men do. Therefore the healer is worth many men.

Long before Homer saluted Podalirius and Machaon, his heroes of healing, the psychotherapist had achieved a typically high status. Ruder communities than those depicted by the Greek poet reveal the shaman in a post of honor. All studies of the medicine man speak of his authority—he is held in "veneration and awe," he inspires "utter confidence," "implicit trust" reposes in him, he "commands respect."[1] The priest of the ancient temple or the medieval church also had authority in his society. And in past ages whenever psychotherapy was practiced by medical men the healer received the authority that has been universally granted to physicians. This is not to say, however, that the authority of healers has been at a constant level at all times. History shows fluctuations. It is said, for instance, that the prestige of doctors declined in the Roman Republic. It is said, on the other hand, that the seventeenth century in Europe was a "century of aggrandizement of physicians." Even in its depths, though, the status of the recognized healer has been high.

In seeking the reason for the consistently great authority of the healer one should bear in mind the significance of Homer's words. The healer does something of the highest importance. Men value his services greatly. They dare not let him go, for they all may need him and need him badly. Pliny the Roman once said, "There might be a nation without a physician but there is not a single person who at some time has not resorted to some kind of treatment for his ailments." It is possible to go further and say that a nation without a physician has to all knowledge never existed.

Why man's health is not stable is a question related to the presence of evil in the world. But just as God has seen to it that health is a contingent thing, so has He seen to it that there is *pepsis* or *coctio* or the tendency of the body to recover its health, so that as a value the recovery of health is not paramount. Most men are usually healthy and, when so, other things are more important to them. These other values keep the healers from reaching the very pinnacle of communal authority.

Yet their position is often so close to the top as to be sometimes merged with the political and religious rulers of the community. Healers possess another attribute that expands their status. Their art is long and difficult to acquire. This has been the case throughout the memory of man. The training of psychotherapists requires different kinds of schooling and tests— fasting, abstinence, poverty, spells, hallucinations, celibacy, conjuring, sign interpretation or diagnosis and prognosis, special kinds of examination and instruction by superiors—but all demand great sacrifice and skill. So if the therapist has higher status than the cobbler or mechanic it is because of his more difficult training as well as his more important work.

In every political community there is a hierarchy of status that orders all customary activities according to importance for the commonwealth, and here, then, the absolute status of the therapist is high.

So far the authority spoken of has been that awarded the psychotherapist by the entire community, including the healthy as well as the sick. This is only a part of the healer's authority, however. Other factors come in sight as soon as one scrutinizes the relationship of the psychotherapist not to the community at large but to the patient himself. The following circumstances, which establish the authoritative nature of the relationship, are to be found in all known psychotherapies.

First of all, the patient is in grave need; the psychotherapist is not. The patient is suffering. It is true that for some persons there is a vanity of disease. A neurosis for them is the fashionable thing to put on or a favorite way of demonstrating that they have money to burn. But such persons the honest psychiatrist rejects at the earliest moment. Even the counselor who essays to handle the simpler cases of mental disturbance will not accept a patient unless there is evidence of stress. Thus a recent textbook on counseling advises that "One of the first observations which the wise clinician will make is [of] the extent to which the client is in a state of tension or stress. Counseling can be of help only when there is a certain amount of psychological distress."[2]

The psychotherapist cannot be considered to be in such straits. Only in a different sense can it be said that he is in need, a sense that the poet Rilke had in mind when he asked,

What will you do, God, when I die?
When I your pitcher, broken, lie?

The psychotherapist needs the patient as God needs man or as any man needs the materials of his calling. Without patients the psychotherapist would have to ply another trade but this is usually the case with any occupation. Without a demand for the services the job is obsolete. Today in the expanding market for psychotherapeutic services it is more likely that the therapist wants to get rid of patients.

In any case a single patient is but a part of the therapist's life whereas the problem the patient has rules his life. Disordered passions bring not only the dreadful pain of guilt but a train of evils so long that a man's life is intolerably burdened from one end to the other. If he is thus afflicted, how long does his health last? Strength, wealth, and reputation dissolve. He is soon down to living on the dregs of what life has to offer.

The second feature of the psychotherapeutic relationship is that the patient is ignorant whereas the psychotherapist is informed. The patient does not know what he should do about his disorder. He *says* he does not know, that he is helpless before it. He wants help from a knower, an expert, a man of competence. No theory of individualism or self-sufficiency can circumvent this fact. The man is at a loss, baffled, bewildered, bewitched, call it what you will. He wants help and he thinks he knows who can give him help. Without it he is lost. He cannot lift himself up by the ears.

Here lies buried his independence. He is weak now, poor, miserable, craving some sweet oblivious antidote for his anxiety. What anguish that word "anxiety" condenses!

In coming to the psychotherapist the patient asks that power be exercised over him for his own good. He makes a specific request for bondage. He confesses his ignorance and submits to the superior wisdom of the therapist. From this fact the other characteristics of the situation follow.

The patient expects to be obedient or passive while the psychotherapist is to be active, to tell him what to do, to play the agent to the patient. "That's what a doctor does," said one patient to his psychotherapist, "and a psychologist is a sort of doctor."[3] Now although he might in some cases, the psychotherapist does not necessarily speak more words than the patient or dance more steps or grimace more energetically. The puppeteer moves less than the puppets. Not that the patient is in any way as compliant as a puppet. Not even in the relation of hypnotist to subject is this true, as will be seen. The point of analogy is rather that the initiative is with the psychotherapist and he is expected to call the tune.

Furthermore, the patient believes that disobedience to the therapist carries a penalty; it will mean that he will not get well. He will believe this if he believes at all that the psychotherapist can help him. The psychotherapist, not being ill, is exempt from such a penalty.

In addition the patient is accessible while the therapist is comparatively inaccessible. Bearing the responsibility for more than any one patient, the therapist must make the ultimate decision as to time and place of treatment. This does not mean that the patient may not try to get all his time and care, or may not demand treatment on Sunday or at midnight at out-of-the-way places, but that, whatever he demands, he is, as in the other instances above, at a disadvantage. The patient proposes, the therapist disposes.

Finally there is the factor mentioned earlier in its general context—the community-wide authority of the psychotherapist.

When brought down to the level of the patient it takes on added meaning. Everywhere, as was seen, whether as priest, shaman, physician, or psychiatrist, the psychotherapist stands near the top of a pyramid of prestige. A recent and thorough study of the prestige of occupations in the United States[4] ranked physicians second only to high government officials. Recognition of such standing may well be the reason why psychoanalysts have insisted that their school be composed almost exclusively of doctors of medicine. Usually so deferential toward Freud, they have closed their ears to his unequivocal statement that whether a psychoanalyst be also a physician is a matter of no importance, that, in fact, to combine professional medicine and psychoanalysis is putting a ball and chain on both disciplines.[5]

Returning to the study of occupational prestige, the three jobs uncovered at the bottom of the hierarchy were shoe shiner, street sweeper, and garbage collector, but up at the top, next to high government officials and physicians, were college professors and scientists. One can see from this why, if the therapist in present-day America is not a doctor of medicine, he generally has about him the aureole of scientific research, a degree, or a university.

Translated into concrete terms, the prestige of the therapist insures that in matters of dress, achievement, language, income, education, taste, or manners the patient generally will feel he is dealing with someone of higher status.

Fortifying this arithmetical fact is the tendency of persons of high status themselves to seek as their therapist someone whose status is higher than their own. The rich man or the great man seeks the famous psychiatrist, if not Freud himself any longer, at the very least Freud's pupil. No study has been made of this heliotropism but it seems to be an everyday occurrence.

It may have been noticed that this description of the authority of the therapist vis-à-vis the patient has had nothing to do with ordinary notions of authority. It has not spoken of a man in uniform barking commands in Teutonic consonants. It has not mentioned the majestic throne of the monarch or the awesome mask of the medicine man or the wondrous tricks of the shaman, the cosmic dome of the temple priest, the baroque interior of the psychoanalyst's office, or the scientific bareness of the psychological clinic. Indeed it has not been necessary to speak of any one kind of person as a psychotherapist.

In the very logic of the situation the psychotherapeutic relationship is one of authority. Given a man who needs external help to fulfill a vital purpose, given someone else whom the first man believes able to supply that help, given that the first man asks the second for help, given that the first man believes that obtaining this help depends upon his obeying the second man over a period of time, given that the first man believes that the second will have or has his best interest at heart, then the second man has authority over the first. Once the person decides that he must have the help of the psychotherapist, everything that has been said follows from his need and his ignorance.

These pages have confined themselves to those persons who come to the therapist of their own accord but there are cases where the patient has been brought involuntarily—the delinquent boy ordered by a court, a child dragged by his mother, a criminal consigned to a mental hospital, a husband pushed by his wife. Such cases are most difficult for therapy. The handicap mentioned earlier in the case of Dora (Chapter One) was of this nature. Dora had been brought involuntarily by her father and as a result later broke off treatment "prematurely."

The obstacles are, first, that the patients feel no imperative need for cure and, second, that they have no respect whatsoever for the therapist. The weakness of the psychotherapist in the hands of the psychopath and the psychotic who present such obstacles is well known. The first seems devoid of conscience while the second seems to have reached his own private solution which he wants left alone. Neither of them, therefore, feels a need for the psychotherapist. Such persons, as Freud observed,

> turn from the physician, not in hostility but in indifference. Therefore they are not to be influenced by him; what he says leaves them cold, makes no impression on them, and therefore the process of cure which can be carried through with others . . . cannot be effected with them. They remain as they are.[6]

If no need is felt, the case is hopeless. If a need is felt but authority is not granted, the case is at best long drawn out, for the psychotherapist, using all the devices at his command, must make the patient look up to him. But when the patient appears with confidence and esteem already present, as is the usual case in the psychoneuroses, the task is easier. The situation then will be seen to contain all the characteristics of authority considered above. Ultimately, for a cure to take place, these common characteristics must be present whether there at the start or built up gradually through sheer effort by the therapist. The trappings of authority will differ, however, and this deserves a word of explanation, since in reality it is the trappings or signs of authority that many persons often object to.

The patient-to-be, in sore trouble, seeks aid. He selects someone whom he believes to have virtue and knowledge and skill in respect to his difficulties. The man with a secular education, prizing highly the symbols of academic learning, science, and medicine, looks to the degrees of M.D. or Ph.D., to the clinics, to the professional man's own rating of the professional as his guides to the best therapist. He then goes to the psychiatrist, to the psychoanalyst, or to the psychological clinic. But consider the poor man, the uneducated man, for whom the signs of authority may be an advertisement in newspaper or magazine or telephone directory, a shingle on a brick house, an ostensible degree—Psy.D. (Doctor of Psychotherapy), Ps.D. (Doctor of Psychology), D.S.D. (Doctor of Divine Science), or Ms.D. (Doctor of Metaphysics).[7] This man uses advertising as his clue; the other one, knowing of the medical and academic prejudice against self-advertising, uses as his clue the absence of advertising. Or it may be that the would-be patient puts no trust in secular healers and seeks aid from a priest of his religion. Jung once began an inquiry to find out which of the two—Catholics or Protestants—when in spiritual distress, resorted more to the clergyman than to the psychotherapist. The question merits being reserved for fuller consideration later but it might be instructive to present here the example of a modern religious cult as it engages in healing. Telling the story is a person who set out to observe those groups that the recognized religions shy at.

Every year early in the spring the same large poster appears in the streets of London. It portrays the head of a youngish man with curly hair; and it invites you to the Albert Hall on Easter Monday to attend three separate meetings: a healing service in the morning, baptism in the afternoon, and holy communion in the evening. The organizers are the Elim Foursquare Revivalists. . . .

The meeting was to begin at 10:30, and I arrived at the Albert Hall soon after 10:00. on a brilliant Easter Monday morning, to find a jumble of taxis, bathchairs and even ambulances in the street outside. In the crowd there were people on crutches, men and women with deformed limbs or with bandaged heads or eyes, mothers with sick children in their arms. . . .

The hall was filling quickly, and long before 10:30 there was not a seat left. The audience consisted mainly of working-class people. Many of them had come from Wales, from Yorkshire, from the Midlands, and much less Cockney was heard than is usual on popular occasions at the Albert Hall. . . .

The man whom ten thousand people from all over the British Isles had come to see and to listen to had mounted the platform quite unobserved. . . . The moment [George] Jeffreys [the founder and leader of the Elim Gospellers] began to speak the impression of impersonality disappeared. He came up to the microphone to say a prayer. . . . I did not doubt that the strong and sincere tone of the voice of Jeffreys was responsible for much of the veneration in which his followers held him. There was in it the reassuring note of fatherly advice and the attraction which we are told has its roots in the subconscious reactions of sex. A George Jeffreys with a high-pitched tenor might never have become known.

After praying, Jeffreys addressed the audience for the first time. He held a sheet of paper in his hand and said: "We have just received an answer to our telegram to H. M. the King. I will read it: 'George Jeffreys, Albert Hall, Kensington. The King sincerely thanks you for your loyal message on the occasion of the ninth annual meeting of the Elim Foursquare Gospellers. Private Secretary.'" The audience applauded. . . .

In the meantime the stalls were cleared in preparation for the healing service. The sick people descended into the stalls from all parts of the hall. They came down slowly one by one, many with the aid of relatives or nurses, others unassisted. Those of them who could kneel, knelt down on the floor; others remained in their seats, and a few in their bathchairs.

The climax of the morning had arrived. I was feeling excited: I had never seen any miraculous healing before. . . .

Jeffreys came down from the platform towards the sick, of whom there must have been some four or five hundred. He was followed by one of his helpers bearing a little receptacle containing oil, and by a few women who were there to assist the sick. Jeffreys approached them one after another, anointed their foreheads or merely put his hands on their heads, leant over them and uttered a few words. Though their eyes were shut they did not exhibit any signs of exaltation, and many of them had a faint smile on their lips. Others were sitting or kneeling, giving themselves up to the moment with such devotion that they had forgotten even to pray. Their inanimate arms hung down; their hands rested motionless in their

laps. Some of them had raised their heads and had
opened their hands as though waiting for God's healing
power to flow into them. Many remained in the same
position after Jeffreys had laid hands on them, but some
began to sway to and fro for a while, and had to be
helped by the attendant women. A few fell down on the
floor as if in a dead faint, sometimes after he had left
them.

While the organ played softly, the vast audience looked
down on the stalls. There was none of the morbid
curiosity that crowds generally manifest when confronted
with something outside their usual experience. They were
sitting quietly, many of them with tears running down
their cheeks; some prayed to themselves with numb lips,
others prayed aloud with clasped hands. The atmosphere
of faith that pervaded the hall was beginning to over-
power one's critical faculty. . . .

The playing of the organ had become so soft that the
steps of Jeffreys and his helpers walking from row to row
could be heard quite distinctly. Only when someone fell
to the floor was there any commotion.

In one of the farthest rows of the stalls there was a
woman in a bathchair, with a nurse at her side. I had
already noticed the woman once or twice. Her whole appearance suggested a class which was rather the exception
here. All through the morning she had been sitting motionless in her bathchair, but now I noticed she was half
standing in her chair; her face bright red and covered
with beads of sweat. She was raising her arms in slow
movements, performed with great difficulty, which suggested some odd gymnastic exercise. She exclaimed time
after time, loud enough to be heard all around: "I can
move them now, I can move them now." She went on
moving her arms in slow circles: and in her face there
was such expression of terrifying excitement that I had
to force myself to go on watching it. This expression suggested neither hysteria nor joy, but rather an awfully
intense curiosity and surprise. . . .

[Later] George Jeffreys was sitting on the platform in

a black gown, the organ was playing and hymn after hymn after hymn was sung. Jeffreys got up and asked people to testify to their healings in the years gone by, and voice after voice cried back from different corners of the hall, stating its individual case. I spoke to several of these people afterwards. They were workmen, artisans and small tradesmen, and it was difficult to doubt the honesty of their testimony. As I discovered later, hundreds of the most striking cases had been collected in book form, together with the original reports, and photographs of the subject.[8]

It should not be necessary to call to mind after this report that the claims to superior healing made by the various psychotherapies add up to a question mark or that a writer in the *British Medical Journal* could say not long ago, "Organic disease is what we say we cure and we don't; functional disease is what the quacks cure and we wish we could."[9] No one has ever been cured by what he thought was a quack, and men have been fleeced by real doctors as well as by quacks.

There are gods for the high and gods for the low. The choice each person makes reflects his idea of the valid signs of authority. The patient may find as he enters into psychotherapy that the therapist is not the person he expected him to be. It has happened that a person, making a telephone appointment with a psychologist and looking forward to dealing with a man of science in a white coat, backed out of the door at first sight of the therapist in a sport jacket and mumbled, "I thought I was going to see a *doctor*." The trappings that this person associated with authority were not there. True, there were other trappings—the person was a real psychologist, he had the degree of Ph.D., his office was in a great university, and so on. But these were as nothing compared to the lack of a white coat. No habit, no monk.

Not infrequently, of course, something like this happens; the patient quits; the authority is gone. One can entertain thoughts of situations where the would-be patient might suddenly be disillusioned on his first visit by the color or sex or habits of his therapist. What would a traditional Southerner do if he opened the office door and found a Negro there sitting behind the desk? What hesitations would a Nisei have on discovering his therapist was a woman? What would the educated man do if he saw the psychiatrist he was on his way to visit (this is a bizarre possibility) walking along the street during the noon hour with a sandwich board on which the "M.D." was prominently displayed together with an offer of free psychotherapy to all who needed it? Yet, having come, the patient so long as he willingly continues treatment shows that he believes the therapist has the good will and ability to help him. Faith remains unbroken. The pact is maintained.

Horace somewhere refers to his close friends as his "medicine," *dulce decus medicumque meum*. Rarely is it possible for a friend to serve as a psychotherapist. Horace was thinking of the way in which good and wise friends throughout life can keep one spiritually healthy. Ordinarily in the case of neurosis a friend is not of much specific help. For reasons which will be taken up later, one simply cannot pour moral woes into his ear. One tries to hide this kind of trouble from one's friend, who is apt to be more a curse than a comfort. For although one loves and esteems a friend, what superior knowledge does he have of moral conflict? He is no expert on such matters. He has no authority here.

A friend will not do. In the process of psychotherapy something frequently occurs that shows the inutility of friends, and at the same instant the utility of authority.

Pile up the authoritative characteristics previously discussed, let this relationship of suppliant and benefactor exist for a time, the patient is bound to arrive at a state resembling love. But this condition is not to be confused with the love of man for woman or woman for man, nor is it the love of friend for friend. It most closely resembles filial love, the love of child for father or mother. As a matter of fact it is so fully a repetition of earlier relations to parental authority that the psychoanalysts call it the "transference," meaning by that a transfer onto the psychotherapist of earliest sentiment toward parents. The patient may develop a burning interest in the therapist. He wonders, speculates, experiments, makes offerings. Everything about the therapist assumes importance—his family, interests, peccadilloes, and so on. The patient may become most agreeable, even pliant, and full of the praises of his therapist. He may feel queasy, tremulous, or awesome each time he steps on the office threshold, like a schoolboy before the door of the headmaster. In ways sometimes subtle, sometimes not, he curries and bestows favor. He is grateful, affectionate, and eager to do no wrong.

Illustrations from actual cases might make the phenomenon more familiar. In the example that follows the patient is speaking:

> Even while I'm sitting here, I have this terrific urge for you, I don't know why because, well, maybe there is a reason, there might be an emotional tie-up to you right now, but I have that urge to feel that well, you have so many cases, but yet, by God, mine's going to be different. Actually, I know darn well it isn't. My problems probably are repeated many, many times—ah—during the year. You probably hear them with little variation, and rationally and with my intelligence I know that it's silly to feel that way, and yet I, I urge myself to feel differently.

Somewhat later in the case:

> Did you read this article . . . ? I cut it out for you, I cut it out, isn't it funny? I didn't cut it out for anybody but you, and I have it at home. I'll have to give it to you. It's a very interesting article. . . . I've got to remember to bring it to you because I know you'll enjoy it. I tore it out and I didn't know why I did, but oh, now I know —for Mr. L. [the therapist] to read.

Still later the drama proceeds:

> PSYCHOTHERAPIST: [Our relationship is] really something quite different than most relationships.

PATIENT: Oh yes, and yet my—I couldn't say our—because certainly you haven't given me anything, so that it would be ours—but my relationship with you is fascinating. I enjoy it because it's so purely, uh, well, impersonal, asexual, everything, that's on an even keel. You're like a life buoy.

PSYCHOTHERAPIST: There's more constancy, somehow.

PATIENT: Oh, yes, and I enjoy being with you this three quarters of an hour and I walk out and I also think of you. I have no curiosity. Oh, yes, I do I have some curiosity about you, about your background, naturally, but not as vital as I would about somebody else, and in that respect, I mean this feeling I have about you seems to validate, or however you pronounce it, uh, this feeling that non-directive therapy is right and is good or else why would I have this constant, uh, feeling of security. I guess that is what it is with you. [THERAPIST: M—hm.] Whereas if it weren't right, why then the vacillations of my mind would make you a terrible figure, so evidently there is something. [THERAPIST: M—hm.] I had one dream about you. I don't remember what it was. It wasn't important, I don't think—you stood as a symbol of authority, I think, I guess at that time I was trying to think of your approval or disapproval. When I walk out of here, everything, which is the only way I can feel, the only way I can think, many times I walk and I think, well what did I tell Mr. L. now, because he laughed, and then a lot of times I walk with a feeling of elation that you think highly of me, and of course at the same time, I have the feeling that, "Gee, he must think I'm an awful jerk," or something like that.

In the second to the last interview the same patient reports a conversation with a friend just before going into the therapist's office.

I said [to Sally as we sat in the car], "Well, butterflies are beginning to fly in my belly, I guess it's time for me to go in." She said, "What! do you mean that you still . . . ?"

I said, "Yes, everytime I come here I have butterflies in my stomach."[10]

The connection between earlier figures of authority and the psychotherapist is not established entirely by inference. In the interview the patient may show in many ways that his actions are filial, sometimes even calling the psychotherapist father or mother. Here is a not unusual example of the past pressing hard on the present.

> PATIENT: It was a strain [to dream] keeping up a pretense of merriment with the brigands, and it is a strain here also keeping up this pretense with you—pretending to be a man when I don't feel like one.
> PSYCHOTHERAPIST: If you gave up the pretense what would you reveal?
> PATIENT: I would reveal that I was only a little child.
> PSYCHOTHERAPIST: Well, wouldn't that be a relief?
> PATIENT: Yes, it would, but I seem much too frightened.
> PSYCHOTHERAPIST: Why frightened?
> PATIENT: Well, it would be all right if I knew positively that you were going to pick me up and carry me. I liked being picked up, like the brigands. It was quite a thrill. But I can't say I felt secure, or relaxed, nor do I feel relaxed here. (Silence.) You see, it might have been all right. Perhaps, daddy would have picked me up, and carried me *provided I had never tried to be anything else except a little boy*. The trouble is that I have been pretending to be a man. . . .

Somewhat later:

> PATIENT: Yes, you are big. This is where I can be myself without having to pretend.
> PSYCHOTHERAPIST: And what is "yourself?"
> PATIENT: A little boy without any protection.[11]

One more case, this one as narrated by the psychotherapist alone:

His eyes on the distance, the patient said, "I was thinking of writing my aunt for a picture of Mother." Suddenly tears welled up and the patient threw himself sobbing on the couch. After ten minutes he grew calm and said, with great feeling, "Silly, but I feel as if my own mother were all around me here. It's something so familiar."

The emotional change in the patient was dramatic, he was ecstatically moved. Turning his attention to the therapist, he ordered her, "Tell me what is right about sex, possessions, religion. Talk to me as you would to an adolescent." He had never asked any opinion or advice before. When the therapist answered some questions, the patient rushed on to others, as if he were less interested in the answers than in the experience of talking. At the end of the interview, he said, "I know who I've been talking to—my mother! And I feel wonderful."[12]

Although the psychoanalysts were the first to make a study of the transference, the relationship always has been part of psychic healing. In numerous religions, past and present, where psychotherapeutic duties are the charge of priests, the penitent openly addresses the priest as father. Probably because of the primary importance of the mother in the nourishment of the child, the mother-kinship feeling in the transference often seems of greater importance than the father-kinship. This may account for the related fact that in many areas of the world male shamans and priests either impersonate or dress as women. Female attire was worn by ancient German priests, the priests of Ishtar, of Artemis at Ephesus, of Heracles at Cos, and by the priests of ancient Rome. Priestly robes, aprons, skirts, and soutanes are all of a feminine cut.

For the transference to occur it is not essential that an intensive or lengthy relationship be involved. It appears for example in the relatively brief contacts of the modern social service worker.[13] On a smaller scale it occurs in all personal situations with the slightest indication of an authoritative relationship.

A person is something to be taken account of morally, an

entity that can cause shame or mortification or pride. The sociologist Charles Cooley some twenty-five years ago attempted to form a law of behavior out of this fact by maintaining that a person is constantly changing himself in order to please others. What he overlooked was that the degree of change might be different, depending on who was superordinate and who was subordinate in the situation. The public-opinion polling interviewer has learned, often to his regret, that the persons whom he briefly accosts and questions frequently try to give him the answers they think he wants. Their answers might vary, for instance, when their interviewer is a worker or when he is a white-collar man. The interviewer himself does not change appreciably, but the one interviewed does.

How much more desperately does the patient want to please his psychotherapist, to know what is required of him, and to comply. The transference increases the authority of the healer, endowing him with greater knowledge, greater love, greater wisdom, greater power. This is tantamount to saying that the patient is in a state of heightened suggestibility to the therapist. Having imputed greater authority to the therapist, he is more willing to obey. The situation now fits clearly the definition of authority set down by Richard Hooker, the sixteenth-century theologian and politicist, in his work on *Ecclesiastical Polity*: "By a man's authority, we here understand the force which his word hath for the assurance of another's mind that buildeth upon it."

Thus the transference is on the one hand the result of the pre-existence of authority. Since the patient perceives the therapeutic situation as one of authority, it brings back to him and he relives previous situations of authority. And on the other hand the transference augments authority already existing. The reawakening of filial love increases the patient's willingness to conform to the therapist's wishes.

> *Where Love enters*
> *The dark despot Ego dies.*

Possibly paying homage to the present-day prejudice against the word "authority," almost all psychotherapists—even the hypnotists!—deny that authority plays any role in their own brand of healing. But, as said, when their ideas of authority are inspected it soon becomes clear that they mean different things in their use of the word. Thus a popular book on counseling goes so far as to declare, "Therapy and authority cannot be coexistent in the same relationship."[14] It turns out, however, that its writer thinks of authority as power over the individual in a solely military or legal or economic sense, as the power of the superior officer, the judge, or the foreman. One might add that the therapist has no authority in a musical sense either. A great violinist may go for help to the psychotherapist but not to brush up on his double-stops nor to run over Bach's Sonatas for Solo Violin. For such help he would go to an authority on the violin greater than himself.

Freud is more careful, as one might expect because of his own original work on the transference. When he speaks of suggestion he usually brings up hypnotism; when he speaks of authority he brings up Emperor Joseph II. It turns out that he thinks of authority as oriental potentates who walk into their palaces on crimson carpets bordered with bowing subjects. Yet the same Freud described (as quoted earlier) the impossibility of curing patients without respect for the analyst and in another place rightly held that age plays an important part in the authority of the therapist, "inasmuch as a young man under thirty years never gains that confidence of patients which is an indispensable condition for benefiting a patient psychoanalytically." But, as will be seen in a moment, his argument is more subtle and does not plead the complete absence of authority.

At this stage someone will object, "Why get embroiled with words? If someone else wishes to call something else 'authority,' why not let him? What difference does it make?" The first answer to this would be another question. "Would you call a lamb a wolf?" Words have meanings and these must be clearly stated and adhered to, if there is to be communication rather than intersecting monologues. Secondly, as indicated earlier, no other word means rightful power. Thirdly, the concept of authority brings together and clarifies the ideas of prestige, status, and suggestion. Lastly, subsequent chapters will show the concept to be a unifying one that illuminates the problem of mental disorder and opens up to it a fresh approach.

It must be admitted that the psychoanalysts do recognize in the transference a relationship of authority. A recent work on psychoanalytic therapy defines the phenomenon as one in which "the patient now entertains toward the therapist the same feelings and conflicts he had had in his childhood toward some person of authority."[15] Moreover they realize that without this relationship the patient cannot be cured. They nevertheless have been slow to point out the indispensability of authority, calling attention instead to two factors which are supposed to demonstrate its unimportance in their work.

One is the so-called negative transference. This term refers to the antagonism that the patient may exhibit in the course of treatment. The psychoanalysts see in this further manifestations of childhood relations with authoritative figures, and quite obviously the reliving of this part of childhood incurs not obedience to the therapist but recalcitrance, serving thereby to diminish his authority.

> Suddenly the patient flings the ash-tray across the room with such force that it shatters against the wall. Then comes screaming, weeping, and a flood of abusive language.
>
> ANALYST: What is the violent act you wish to do?
> PATIENT: Killing her. Giving mother a good hiding.
> ANALYST: Are you killing me as a successor to your mother?
> PATIENT: My wife and you are both in the same boat. Today I could have smashed your faces in.

To this thesis, though, a comment must be made.

Those who can recall their childhood will remember that, pleasant as life then might have been, it was not all smooth sailing. Parents cannot be indulgent always; they sometimes have to be thwarting. Children, for their part, are sometimes angry, hurtful, and disobedient, but they are in no position to be constantly non-conformist (a matter that will be treated more fully in later chapters). Parental authority eventually asserts itself and remains unbroken until a later date in the child's life. By and large the same thing is true of the psychotherapist's authority. Thus in the case immediately above, the patient continues:

> My poor head! Oh, doctor, do you really think you can help me? I am putting tremendous faith in you, although I feel unwell. I am in a terrible mess. Can you ever get me out of it? Here I am clinging to you, like I clung to my mother after that caning—clung to her and sobbed. I wanted to kill her, like I wanted to kill you, and here I am, clinging to you instead. Will it ever come right?[16]

If something like this does not happen, if positive feeling does not succeed the negative, if the therapist by his actions or appearance reminds the patient too much of the thwarting aspects of parents, either a transfer must be made to another analyst or the patient soon breaks off treatment. The positive transference must dominate the negative. Love must overcome hate.

The second point that psychoanalysts emphasize is their progressive attempts to eliminate the transference before the end of treatment. The procedure as Freud described it is to call into question at certain steps their own authority. Now the possibility already has been suggested that psychotherapists avoid the use of the word "authority" in deference to the current bias against the term. Many of their patients, of course, share this feeling. Therefore if the therapist in one way or another repeats, "I do not want to be an authority over you," he is not dissipating but increasing his authority by raising himself in the patient's esteem and affection. One example may suffice.

In the next interview, the fourth, the patient brought two pieces of news which she offered as if she were presenting a gift to the therapist. First, she had had intercourse twice without pain and with some pleasurable sensation, although as yet without orgasm; second, she had spent Sunday with her husband on a picnic instead of attending the usual family dinner. The patient was complimented and smilingly told, "You said that as if you knew I would be pleased." The patient laughed with some embarrassment but then admitted frankly that during the week she had often wondered if the therapist would approve of this or that thought or action, but she had also felt relieved that an adult she respected could approve of what she now accepted as normal feelings.

The nature of her relationship to the therapist was discussed with her; she now complied with what she thought the therapist expected of her just as she had been obedient in childhood to her ("puritanical") mother. The temporary nature of this dependence was emphasized.[17]

Now how has the psychotherapist done anything here but increased the patient's esteem? The next time the patient appears she will present the news less as if she were "presenting a gift to the therapist" because she knows the therapist sees through such conduct. Still she will present gifts, from now on in an offhand manner, reportorially, perhaps, with enthusiasm concealed, the beam in her eyes undetectable.

No, wishing will not make it so. There is one way for authority to diminish in psychotherapy, and that is for the patient's need to diminish first. It is this need to resolve his moral conflict that gives the neurotic his great suggestibility which one psychoanalyst styled "free-floating transference," and another, "transference addiction."[18] If the need is gone, so will be the heightened authority in the transference. Even so, the basic authority of the psychotherapist remains. Actually it may be that this general level has risen for the former patient. He has learned that he can be healed by the therapist, that so long as the therapist is there, somewhere in his office, reachable, he can always resort to him again.

> PATIENT: Well, tell me, Mr. L., uh, would you? How much longer do you think I ought to come here? [Laughs.]
> PSYCHOTHERAPIST: I don't know. Is this your last time or not?
> PATIENT: I don't know. Let's say it is, and uh, if I feel the need to come back and I would like to come back, why then I can call for an appointment, huh? And are you going to be very busy, I suppose, after the first?
> PSYCHOTHERAPIST: I'll see you if you call.[19]

The formula for saying good-by has been put thus: the patient "should not be encouraged to turn to the analyst at the first hint of relapse. On the other hand, he should have the assurance that if he really needs his therapist, he can always return to him."[20] In the case discussed earlier, of the patient bearing gifts, the therapist's final instructions make it quite clear that her authority is still there.

> With embarrassment, the patient confessed that she had worried some that her husband [who had had a single explanatory interview] and the therapist would be interested in each other and that she would be less important. When the therapist pointed out that the triangle situation was similar to that of child-mother-father, she accepted it easily and was interested in the ease with which a patient repeats childhood attitudes in the transference relationship.
> In the last interview she was encouraged to attempt a period [of not being treated] on her own, but was assured that she could return any time she wished. The similarity of this separation to weaning was talked over with her. . . .

Apparently the therapist is still unsure that the authority of the transference has gone. Otherwise why should she at the last interview have to speak of weaning? Authority remains, then, though somewhat less, perhaps, than during the full-blown transference.

It may be too early in the book to see this clearly but there seems to be something disturbing, something even unethical, about the open attempts of the modern psychotherapist to win the love of the patient only to try to destroy it later. It is a true love, this esteem in which the person holds the one who helps him in his time of trial, a love as true as for one's father and mother. Calculatedly to repudiate it is reprehensible. The theologian and philosopher, William Ernest Hocking, strikes at the same mark when he says of all this that, "unless attachment is sincere, it is a polite form of prostitution."[21]

This matter must be brought up again; it cannot be idly dismissed. Somehow it has disfigured now, and made regrettable, the truth in Jalâl-Uddîn-Rûmî's lines:

> *Where Love enters*
> *The dark despot Ego dies.*

CHAPTER FIVE

The Word of Authority

The poet T. S. Eliot once regretfully wrote,

And we know nothing of exorcism.

He was wrong. It is unlike Eliot to be fooled by the fanfares of modernity; nonetheless in saying this he capitulated unnecessarily.

Where did he expect to find exorcism? Where does anyone look to find it today? They do not look—that is the answer—they do not expect to find it. Even if they did look they should not find it, for they think of it in these words:

> *Ho! Ho! Ho! ye evil spirits*
> *Who live in the trees, ye evil spirits*
> *Who dwell in the grottoes, ye evil spirits*
> *Who lodge in the earth—*
> *We adjure thee by the sunne and by the moone*
> *Thou unclean spirits, thou cackling demons,*
> *Come forth out of this man!*
> *Go thy way, devils!*
> *We warn thee*
> *In the name of . . .*

No doubt this kind of exorcism will not readily be found in the cities today. One might as well search for the herb that goes with the words. It is to be dried out and ground to a powder, and used to be called *demonofuge*.

Language changes with the surface of things and the old

things continuously get made over. The same old devils sport a modern dress. They must be cast out with a modern vocabulary.

Nothing seems more prevalent in enlightened circles today than the notion that the psychotherapist does not moralize or tell the patient what to do. On the other hand nothing is surer than that the patient comes to the therapist wanting to be told what to do. Now either the first idea is wrong and the patient gets what he paid for, or the first idea is right and the patient gets cheated. Which is it?

In this case the patient gets what he paid for. Moral judgment and direction appear in all psychotherapy. For example, among the Colombian Indians,

> The sick man sends for the shaman (mama) to make full confession. He [the mama] then decides whether the sins are mortal or whether they may be forgiven and health recovered. This requires some judgment—the mama must decide from the condition of the patient, because he can become equally famous by telling a patient he must die for his sins (which on being so informed he usually does without much further delay), as he can by predicting renewed health and prescribing the formula for recovery.[1]

Here the judgment concerned the severity of the sins committed, and the direction, some might add, was either to live or to die, a direction not infrequently found to be within the power of primitive psychotherapists.

If the psychoanalysts published more of their cases verbatim it would not be surprising to hear one of them say to his patient, "Don't be so damned sycophantish!"—a phrase tingling with disgust and direction. Wilhelm Stekel's case, presented in Chapter Three, offers a clear illustration of moral judgment and direction. He agreed that for his patient, the cashier, to steal the bank's money would be criminal and directed him outright: "Give up your post as cashier." In another case quoted in the same chapter the patient said, "Tell me what is

right about sex, possessions, religion," and the therapist thereupon "answered some [of his] questions." Presumably the
answers given were moral judgments. To take a case not already quoted,

> Go to Reno. Get some rest and some sunshine. I'll see
> your husband, and if I can help him, you won't follow
> through with the divorce. If he's beyond my powers, get
> him out of your life.[2]

In spite of obvious examples such as these, psychotherapists
are almost as one in denying that judgment is expressed or
direction given in their own variety of therapy. Thus one school
of psychotherapy, somewhat extreme on this point, declares
that the therapist must exhibit the complete lack of any moral-
istic or judgmental attitude. A book on employee counseling
lays down as a rule of procedure, "Remain impartial and never
make moral judgments." A psychoanalyst declares, "A scientific psychology is absolutely free of moral valuation. For it,
there is no good or evil, no moral or immoral, and no what
ought to be at all." Freud, from whom they all took their lead,
rejects "most emphatically" the view that a psychoanalyst
should "force [his] own ideals" on the patient.[3] The reasons for
such repeated denials can be examined through illustration
from actual cases. Although the procedure will require the
presentation of many excerpts, it will at the same time demonstrate the inadequacy of the denial.

One reason first appeared in the previous discussion of the
moral core of the neurosis. The reason then was that different
standards of morality exist, so that what seems moral for one
person may seem immoral or unmoral for another. Thus the
extremist school of therapy above, claiming not to direct in
any fashion, is firmly convinced that it adheres to its own rule.
Because its own standards are so much a part of it, it cannot
see that others could disagree or could describe them as moral-
istic. Yet to one standing outside the charmed circle the bias
can be quite evident. A sociologist, after inspecting the work

of a representative therapist of this school, had a penetrating observation to make.

> It is interesting that in every single case [described as successful] the client always attaches himself to goals, or accepts roles, that would meet the hearty approval of any Methodist minister: Mrs. Land sees what harm she has been doing to her child, and decides to become a "better, more mature mother"; Barbara, with pronounced masculine trends, puts an end to her "intellectual" endeavors in favor of bobbing her hair, using make-up, going out with boys, and learning how to cook; Sally, who hated school, adopts a "more constructive attitude."[4]

Many other therapists of various schools, it is said, attempt "to improve the work habits" of their patients. Again this may not appear to be even slightly directive to those who subscribe to the kind of improvement aimed at, but to one who believes in *dolce far niente* it may be the rankest kind of moralizing. Or to the person who for one reason or another finds fault with the present economic system such efforts by the psychotherapist may appear as "goading" patients "to economic success."

The psychotherapists are like those persons who think that no one really wants war or that no one believes that war is a good thing. They believe the abhorrence of war is a natural tendency of the human mind. Only when they are confronted with the irreconcilable fact that whole ways of life, whole ideologies, glory in war, only then do they begin to see that theirs is a moral position.

COMMUNICATION WITHOUT WORDS

A further reason why psychotherapists have overlooked the moral direction in their work is the limited view that they have of communication. Recently a number of psychiatrists and psychologists actually have come to look at psychotherapy as a process of communication but for the most part have conceived it to be a matter of verbal exchange. A person communicates with every fiber—he blinks and blushes, he pales, snarls, twitches, nods, laughs and cries and wails, he hestitates, coughs, sits and rises, stamps, rages, kisses, caresses, stoops and steels himself.

By and large, the psychotherapists cannot be accused of neglecting the gestural, tonal, and other non-verbal aspects of their patients' acts. Generally they have followed laudably the instructions contained in the *Panchatantra:*

> *From feature, gesture, gait,*
> *From twitch or word,*
> *From change in eye or face*
> *Is the thought inferred.*

What they have not done is to watch carefully their own non-verbal communication.

Each morning they awake and begin to prepare themselves for their patients. They look in the mirror and see not the face of a boy eighteen to nineteen years of age with the fuzz of a peach on his cheeks but an unshaven face of middle age or more. What do they do to that face, how do they dress that body? Does the male therapist don a dressing gown, Bermuda shorts, or a double-breasted suit? Does the female therapist wrap herself in a tailored suit, a dress of baby's dimity, something sensual, or something "sensible"? Whatever it is, it is worn with an eye to communicating something to those to be seen during the day. In the office, where are the fresh flowers placed? on the desk? in the buttonhole? or are there none? Is there a couch here and who is supposed to lie on it? Age, attire, interior decoration—each conveys, and is known and used by the psychotherapist to convey, various impressions to his patients, and as much as he can he alters them to his wishes. But he does not make them the subject of technical papers.

The patient arrives and soon communication begins in earnest. The therapist, if he is typical and tries not to praise or blame, reins in on his own words. His gestures, however, may give him away. The psychotherapist in the succeeding case

said very little but at a certain point he moved his head in a
way that has conventional meaning.

> The patient said: "What trouble I have had! My hus-
> band drinks, you know. He always has been like that. He
> won't work. He did last year here at Alpha, then I got a
> job here, too, but he wouldn't let me ride in his car. We
> live 2 miles from —— and I had to walk those 2 miles
> each day to get the bus. I had to get up at five in the
> morning to get here in time. Then some of the men from
> —— who work here got after him; they shamed him
> so that he asked me to ride in his car when one of his
> riders quit him. He got going on with a girl who works
> here, though, and that's where he spent his money. We
> never got any of it. Women and drink, that's the way
> it's always been, so he's never been any good to me when
> he was working. I met her in the store one day, and I
> told her. I said to her: 'You've got five children, yet you
> run after my man.' I called her some names. He keeps
> pigs, you know, and I said to her: 'The pig you got for
> what you do for him is better than you are,' and I sort of
> spit at her. I said to her: 'Keep out of my sight, for no
> matter when I run into you, in church, in the store, any-
> where, I'll tell everybody what you are.' And if she sees
> me, she goes away fast."
> The therapist nodded.[5]

By this very nod has not the counselor said, "I believe your
story and I sympathize with the action you took against that
evil woman. Your action was justified"?

In the next case, too, the therapist says very little, yet at
a particular juncture he widens his mouth, crinkles his eyes,
turns up the corners of his lips, shows his teeth, and emits
conventional sounds of enjoyment.

The patient says:

> One day she [mother] grabbed ahold of the broom, I
> don't know what started it, really most ridiculous things
> would start these beating scenes, she'd get wild looking,
> you know when she isn't dressed up, she's very, not

sloppy, but she's not neat. To her, it wouldn't occur to her to get dressed up in the morning, put a little lipstick on, 'cause then she might look pleasant to the family. She'd get up in a vicious mean way and put on a dirty housecoat and slop through the dining room or the living room and sit down and make breakfast, an unhappy person, really, and—my picture of her, it's not a very pretty one, she wasn't pretty then—her eyes would crinkle up and the look would get stern and then she'd get a wild look in her eyes looking for the broom, the broom, where's that broom—and then beat me up and I'd run so this day she was looking for the broom and I ran and I said to her, "Mother, if you—" Of course I had my Aunt Sadie behind me. I would do anything that Aunt Sadie said, I said, "Mother, if you touch me, so help me God, I think I'm going to beat you up!" I says, "I don't give a damn! I've had enough of these beatings!" She said, "You wouldn't dare!" I said, "Oh, wouldn't I?" She said, "How dare you talk like that to me," and she grabbed the broom, I grabbed it out of her hand, and hit her so hard—I was a strong kid, I weighed a hundred and fifty-five pounds at the time and I lambasted it to her. She ran like a dog with its tail between its legs, screaming, ran into the bathroom, locked the door and screamed, "You mother beater, you!"

Therapist and patient both laugh. What a thing to laugh at! That man ought to be ashamed! All he is doing is encouraging that woman to have no love and respect for her mother. Imagine! Beating her own mother! And *he* laughs!

This could easily be the reaction of some simple soul, untutored in matters psychotherapeutic. To find someone able to perceive the direction and morality (or the immorality) of this therapist's gesture it was necessary only to produce (in imagination) someone innocent of the mother-hating tendencies of modern psychotherapy.

It is not to be expected that the psychotherapist is like an actor who can, if the plot requires it, lift either eyebrow at will or like an Indian dancer who has in the *mudras,* in the subtle movement of his fingers, a rich vocabulary. He can, however, both use and understand the language of gestures of his own society and within that language there can easily be a nervous, embarrassed laugh, a hearty, agreeable laugh, a wry, ironic laugh, and so on, which have meanings as precise as full series of words.

Another area of communication that the psychotherapist neglects is the sounds he makes that are usually not words in the dictionary sense—uh, uh-huh, m-hm, tsk-tsk, uhn-uhn. Interjections, "oh" and "ah" for example, often are used in the same way; as are "yes" and "no" in a corrupted pronunciation. Like gestures, they have meaning but their similarity lies probably in the greater variety of significances they can have and in their greater dependence on the context in which they take place.

In many published cases, for example, "m-hm" occurs with frequency.

> PATIENT: I'm always the one who bragged about the fact that although I was very complicated and neurotic that at least sexually speaking I was pretty normal and healthy and happy and could make the adjustment, so— up to a point, of course. And——
>
> THERAPIST: M-hm.
>
> PATIENT: And now, I don't really exhibit any anxiety about sex, but it's sort of like a stale cup of coffee, and— ah—is that normal, I mean should it come to a woman of 30? [Laughs.]
>
> THERAPIST: In many ways I take it that it hasn't been as satisfying.
>
> PATIENT: Well, of course not. I mean I want to enjoy life. I want to take—I mean it's like becoming color blind.
>
> THERAPIST: M-hm.[6]

What in words is the meaning here? A student of psychotherapy must know. He cannot be put off with the statement that it means nothing. Nothing is done by whimsey in science. That "m-hm" must have a reason for being there. Furthermore that meaning must be communicable to other scientists. The meaning must be taken from its elliptical form and put into sentence construction as a modern grammarian might require.

It is no accident that therapists who use these interjections most are those who maintain most strenuously that no moral direction appears in their brand of mind-cure. The ambiguity of these sounds in isolation, however, is lost when the full context of the case is inspected. The meaning then becomes quite clear, as it was originally to the patient, and, to take "m-hm" or a repetition as an example, it usually signifies to the patient: "I am not shocked or disturbed by what you are saying. I agree with you. I am on your side. That's all right. Keep on talking."

With the sounds decoded, the moral judgment appears. The therapist says in effect that what the patient is confiding to him is not immoral. Saying this is certainly making a moral decision.

Of course the meaning just ascribed to "m-hm" need not be always the same. It is simplicity itself to use such sounds and, by changing their inflection, tone, pitch, speed, cadence, or accent, to change their whole meaning. Often in training aspirants for the stage the instructor will demand, "Say 'oh' as though you meant 'I'm bored to tears.' . . . Now say 'oh' as though you meant, 'I'm glad to be alive.' " Or he may demand, "Say 'yes' as though you meant you agreed all right, but reluctantly. . . . Now say 'yes' as though you meant 'perhaps.' . . . Now say 'yes' as though you meant 'no!' " Such is the advantage of these words that they can so easily be given their meaning merely through the various qualities of the voice.

As a matter of fact many experiments done with the voice as transmitted by radio indicate that a person's speaking habits portray his personality with remarkable accuracy. Although listeners cannot describe from voice alone the height or weight

or hair color of the speaker they do fairly well in describing his
assurance, dominance, or authoritativeness.

DIRECTION WITHOUT COMMANDS

In claiming neutrality the psychotherapist has been seen to
neglect the meaning that his appearance and gestures and
surroundings may convey to the patient. Now it will be seen
that even his words suffer from lack of evaluation.

The following example of a case of hesitation on the part
of the psychotherapist may start the examination in the right
way. The patient has expressed the thought that she might
have in her a wide streak of homosexuality and the therapist
says:

> So there may be some—ah—some pulls in both direc-
> tions there against being feminine and also to prove to
> yourself that you are feminine.

And in the next interview, still in response to the thought of
homosexuality, the same hesitancy again:

> You think now you do realize that—ah—satisfaction
> has been greater for you where you were the predominant
> person.[7]

Why these fits and starts when homosexuality is brought up?
The patient can sense that the therapist is uneasy about such
perverse thoughts and she may wonder whether for him they
are taboo.

The practitioner might raise the objection that such little
things surely escape notice but if he did he would divulge that
he missed the point. It is not the little slips and accidents that
are important: they always occur. The point is that no matter
what he does the therapist's actions are understood by the
patient to be related to his problems. It must not be forgotten
that this is not just any type of relationship but a particular
type—between psychotherapist and patient.

In this special relationship is found the second reason for psychotherapy's blindness to its own moral direction. The first reason, it will be remembered, was its restricted view of communication; the second reason is its failure to recognize that the communication takes place in a relationship of authority. It might be advisable to invoke here the meaning in common usage of "direct." To direct is to point out to one the right way or road, to cause a person (or thing) to turn, move, point, or follow a course. Direction can be given by setting up a model to follow as Socrates did for his disciples and Christ for his. The Greeks called it education by paradigm. It can be done also by placing a person in a special environment where predictable influences will turn him along a certain course. This method is an extension of the atmosphere the therapist creates in his office. It also occurs, for example, in special schools for mentally distraught children and in mental hospitals and in group therapy where the therapist assembles a special milieu of troubled souls. The direction is built into the environment. It may be reflected, too, in the layout of a psychiatric ward, which may be constructed so as to form a semicircle of rooms, all facing the psychiatrist's office which, at the center of the circle, radiates to each room like the sun. The ensuing case presents an unusual form of environmental therapy.

> There was once a pretty blond who was attracted to a very rich man. They were both very happy until his family's objections against their marriage caused him to leave the city. The girl became very hysterical. When her neurotic behavior brought no results, she became so unhappy that she made repeated attempts at suicide. Every attempt was immediately telephoned to her lover and brought him back to her for a short time. It was a nuisance for everyone. His family feared public scandal and consulted the family lawyer and a renowned physician, and instructed them to spare no expense. The family would have liked to see her hospitalized, yet the physician and lawyer preferred to apply psychology. They

discovered that the girl was deeply devoted to her mother, and so created a large life-time annuity, of which one-third would revert to the mother upon the girl's death, except in the case of her suicide. This arrangement was carried through and restored her to normalcy. She later married another man.[8]

The case is worth citing because it makes its own limitations obvious. Therapy of this type depends upon a considerable control of the environment. Few psychotherapists can dispense large lifetime annuities to their patients. Environmental therapy generally requires the creation of a new world *in parvo;* this in turn involves large outlays of money and a nearly complete isolation of the patient from the larger world.

In both environmental and paradigmatic therapy the moral direction need not be given in words. The atmosphere whispers, "Be all that is good around you." It needs to be communicated by persons, surely, but not necessarily by verbal means. The range of cues pointed to previously work well the smile, the nod, the gentle touch. A fact that children first must learn in a therapeutic school is that "their life at the school is out of reach of their parents."[9] Henceforth they are to follow a new set of standards and those of their parents can be discarded. But these standards usually go unspoken; they are embodied in the milieu. Similarly Socrates did not have to demand, "Follow my way of life"; it was quite enough for him to demonstrate that no other life followed the path of virtue. He could add, "I do not teach my song save to him who comes with me."

These remarks are necessary because it is sometimes thought that if one offers himself as a model or if one structures a small new world one is not directing. But in effect the "renowned physician" said to the girl, "Thou shalt not take thine own life" and the director of the school said to his young wards, "Honor not thy father and mother." The moral direction is built into the model and into the new environment and whoever chooses the particular model or particular environment for the patient to conform to transmits the new morality and direction.

Furthermore the model must have authority—the person will not follow in the steps of one he does not love or respect and the patient will not fit himself into the new world until he loves and respects its builders. When, finally, one comes to review the psychotherapists' words themselves, one detects that this factor, the authoritative relationship, is overlooked.

There come certain times in a man's life when he is acutely sensitive to the acts of those he is communicating with. Such a time is the time of supplication. The patient, as the last chapter discovered, is a suppliant, no less than the *hiketes* of Asclepius. He is a seeker after aid regarding pressing moral problems. He wants answers. If the psychotherapist accepts the case he commits himself to addressing these problems. That is the patient's understanding and all psychotherapeutic communication must be analyzed in this light.

Ordinarily the patient does not need to be told whether to change his diet or to quit sleeping eight hours a day or even whether to marry or to burn. When the psychotherapist boasts about his restraint in such matters he is not to be exonerated. Unknowingly he may have laid down already the principles from which some one of those actions may follow. The patient's desire is for the governing principle, not the specifics. The particulars can be inferred from the general. Sometimes, it is true, the reverse can be done—the general inferred from the particular—but the other way is easier and faster.

What, then, has the therapist to say about the patient's moral problems? In the case above, of the therapist beset with "ah's," the patient was disturbed over the possibility of her homosexuality. She dared not ask openly about the therapist's own position; he had conveyed to her that he would not state a moral position. Therefore she had to utilize more subtle signs to learn that the therapist did not like homosexuality.

In another case the patient, trying to get answers to his moral concern with sex, says, "I don't know whether that's too

Freudian for you but I feel that sex is sort of dynamic and is the source of energy—for other activities too." The therapist replies, "Well now, I'd put it this way as to the way we can go at that. . . . Maybe it will be the sexual aspect; maybe it'll be something very different from that." Why did this therapist feel called upon to inform the patient that "maybe it'll be something very different" from sex? Another healer might have said simply, "Well, that's quite natural." Here is one who did.

> PATIENT: It makes me live and makes me keep living. Something about a woman—that thought comes out so often I know it's just an idea.
> THERAPIST: But there's nothing wrong with that thought. Why shouldn't you feel that way about a woman?
> PATIENT: Well, I should—I should, I suppose, but I'm . . . It just makes me—every time, it comes out. . . . It comes out so many times, that's all. I just have that idea. [Short pause.] Well, it is everything that keeps me going, that same thought and feeling.[10]

If the patient in these instances had no reason to listen closely to the therapist, one might believe that the import of these words would be missed. But he does have a reason, a good one. He is a prey to conflicting passions and disordered morality, and is there to have order restored to his soul. The observer, in searching for expressions of moral direction, is likely to look for the imperative form of the verb. He could spot easily the words of the confessor of Baron von Hügel, who when the baron told him of his hatred for someone commanded, "Down on your knees!" What he will not see, perhaps, is that in a situation of authority the imperative verb forms or normative terms like "ought" and "should" do not make adequate criteria.

First of all the assumptions present in the situation serve as silent communicators. The teacher in the classroom does not have to command her pupils to rise and go to the assembly hall. She merely has to say, "It is time to go to assembly." A simple statement of fact. No explicit command, no explicit norm, yet the class will rise to file out of the room. Similarly a father can say to his son either "Empty the trash, John," or "The trash needs emptying, John." One version uses the imperative verb form, the other does not. In either case John takes away the trash.

Secondly there exist an etiquette of respect and a style of direction that vary from hamlet to hamlet and from class to class. In the Old Testament God directs man with one language and in the New Testament with another. The Javanese squat to show respect; Americans stand. Both Thomas Jefferson and the high command of the Soviet Army found that titles of respect cannot be dropped. In America, where a long tradition of revolt exists against European forms of respectful address, a style of intimacy has grown up which is often taken to demonstrate that authority is non-existent. But the old forms have gone underground, appearing to the perceptive in nuances of tone and gesture, while yet the authority remains. The boss calls Jim Jim, and Jim calls the boss Joe but, when the time comes, that does not stop Joe from laying off Jim.

These matters can be very subtle, and the therapist must know what language he is to use with each patient. He is fortunate if he handles one class of patients and that one a class which he knows linguistically. Then again, he may have one patient, an assistant secretary in the civil service, whose chief directs him thus, "John, will you please see if you can get me those figures today on the Isham business?" Or another, a parentally nagged adolescent who, if he is not to walk off in a huff, must be directed thus, "What do *you* think of the idea, Leslie?" Or yet another, a workman, whose boss is accustomed to direct him thus, "Sam, get that damn machine cleaned up." Should Sam tomorrow get a new foreman, fresh from college, and be told by him, "Would you mind seeing if you could clean the machine, Sam, please?" he would think the new man effeminate or crazed and, in either case, would take a full measure of time in cleaning up his machine.

Some therapists in a drastic attempt to avoid the bugbear of moral direction have insisted on a repetitive style of psychotherapy with the rationale that if one merely repeats or rephrases the patient's communication one escapes directing him. Even this radical expedient is to no avail. Of course in practice they could not merely repeat; the patient would soon be looking for flaws in the acoustics and complaining of the echo. Out of necessity, then, they must omit certain things in their repetition of the patient's conversation. Moreover even those remarks selected for repetition cannot be reiterated verbatim; the patient would again be complaining of a ringing in his ears. Therefore the remarks selected have to be rephrased. Here again the therapists are in trouble.

If out of the patient's total communication—and this includes all the non-verbal ways he uses to express his feelings—the therapist rephrases certain things and omits others, the patient will obtain his cues from what is altered in his remarks and from what is left out.

Perhaps an example from a different but more familiar context would illustrate the results of a selection and omission of facts.

FOUND HANGED

> Oscar L. Rezel, Sr., 51, of 2113 S. Ludlow, a tool-and-die maker, was found hanged in the bathroom of his home Saturday night. His son, Oscar, Jr., 26, told police his father had been despondent over failing eyesight.

This item might have appeared at the bottom of the front or back pages of any metropolitan newspaper. It gets the smallest headline in the papers. In journalistic parlance it is known as a "filler." The story is told so as to make suicide the probable deduction. Of the two sentences in the story, one announces that a man has been found hanged, the other quotes his son as saying the dead man had been despondent. Although a coroner's jury had not yet held an inquest and pronounced a verdict of death at the man's own hand, the inference to be drawn is obvious. The words "in the bathroom" suggest that the man was alone when he died, the bathroom being a well-known retreat from society. The picture is clear: the man was alone when he met death, no one helped him rig up his execution, therefore he took his own life.

Note that many facts may be left out: what kind of material was about his neck, what it was attached to, whether any of the downstairs windows were open, whether the man's feet were touching the ground, whether the son told the police anything else. Note, too, that the newspaper does not say openly that the man committed suicide.

Where is the moral element in this story? Since in the United States at this time it is often said that suicide is no longer a sin against God, suppose instead that this event had occurred at a time when and a place where the ancient Hebrew view of suicide held sway. The Code of Jewish Jurisprudence concerning suicide sets forth that "There is none more wicked than one who has committed suicide, as it is said: 'And surely your blood of your lives will I require.' " Without contrary proof a man was not presumed wicked, and if therefore a person was found hanged or strangled to death, the act of killing was regarded, unless otherwise determined, as the deed of another person. The story might have appeared then in this fashion:

FOUND DEAD

> Oscar L. Rezel, Sr., 51, of 2113 S. Ludlow, a tool-and-die maker, was found strangled with a piece of electric cord hanging from a pipe in the second story of his home Saturday night. His son, Oscar, Jr., 26, told the police his father had no enemies.

By a new selection of facts, a new story emerges. This time, as the police obviously suspect, it is a murder story.

The psychotherapists who hold to a repetitive style will find

that their moral direction seeps in through the choice of words
they make in rephrasing, through their selection of the particular parts of the communication for repetition, and through
the parts of the patient's communication they omit.

An example of rephrasing:

> PATIENT: Sexually speaking—I don't know whether to
> bring that up. We're rather well mated. There's a little
> inhibition on his side, which causes me to have inhibi-
> tions, which I never had before. I mean they're not very
> large—ah—by inhibitions, I mean that he doesn't pre-
> vent himself from doing certain things which are normal,
> but he does them, but somehow in spite of himself. He
> has that feeling. He has never expressed it to me that it
> isn't good, you see, and that he really lost control of him-
> self. He won't ever tell me that, I know. . . . There's
> enjoyment on both sides, but it doesn't—well, it doesn't
> have that great thrill or drive that I had with Joseph.
>
> THERAPIST: All in all, it's satisfactory, but somehow
> lacking in some of the peripheral——
>
> PATIENT: That's right.
>
> THERAPIST:—refinements and adaptations of it.

Why did the therapist choose these nice words—"refinements
and adaptations"? Why not say "perversions and maladapta-
tions" of sex? Some persons, including the patient's husband
apparently, would consider such sexual practices to be that.
Choosing the words he did rather than the others gives the
impression that the therapist agrees with her moral judgment
about such acts and that her husband is a prig and a prude.
Later in the same case:

> PATIENT: In other words, he [her husband] makes the
> thing appear much smaller than it really is, and of course
> I can't accept it, and then I haul out some terms like
> "Freud says this . . . and Helen Deutsch says this . . .
> and so and so says that. . . ."
>
> THERAPIST: You differ pretty basically on your notions
> of psychological factors and you feel you have to justify
> yourself by drawing on authorities.[11]

The word "authorities," why use that? It is a word in bad odor these days. Why not phrase the last half of the sentence thus: "and the thing to do is to oppose unsupported assertions with the knowledge of those who are competent in this field"? When this patient first came to the clinic and was told that her therapist was to be Mr. So-and-so, she remarked how pleased she was, for she had heard of him. The interviewing therapist then could have said, "You are pleased because you feel your case will be handled by an authority." But no, he did not.

It is doubtful that any rephrasing or substitution of words can have the same significance as the original construction. Studies made of the questions asked by public-opinion interviewers show that if only the slightest changes are made in a question the results will be affected. If, for example, a group of persons were asked their opinion of the President or whether they thought he was going to be re-elected or whether they were going to vote for him or for someone else, their answers would differ from those of a comparable group for whom the question had been changed only so that instead of, say, "President Roosevelt," they were asked about "the President" or "Mr. Roosevelt" or "Roosevelt." This should not be a curious fact in light of the work done by Freud and Jung on the complicated influences that enter into a person's choice of words or numbers.

Moreover it can be asked of the case just cited, why did the therapist come in with the earlier comment, his pleasant one, exactly when he did? It could not have been solely because there was a pause at that point. There were other pauses and hesitations where he did not intervene. Why not come in one or two or three sentences earlier? Scrutiny of similar cases shows that the therapist sometimes is trying to repeat or rephrase a part of the patient's communication that occurred in the immediately preceding sentence or in a paragraph or two or four earlier. Why? What is the justification? Assuredly whatever the therapist chooses to restate will assume significance for the patient.

Also in those cases where there are many pauses and yet the therapist does not take up the conversation, what is the patient to think? Suppose the patient falls silent and the therapist remains so. The patient may feel that the treatment has failed, or that what he has just said is bad or that the therapist has become hostile to him. In the next case the patient speaks first.

> "In seeking for an alternative to teaching I have thought of a more practical occupation than gardening. With my savings I'd take a six months' course in domestic science. Then I would try to get employment as a housekeeper. Next to gardening I would like best to look after a house."
> "Whose house?"
> "Oh, perhaps some married couple who were out all the time and left everything to me."
> She becomes silent for several minutes. I do not speak. Finally she continues:
> "I suppose you are thinking that it ought to be *my* house. That I ought to get married."[12]

The therapist, be it noted, made no critical comment; the patient simply interpreted his silence as cricitism. Had the therapist given voice merely to an "m-hm," she would have taken it to mean "That's a nice idea," and would have continued with her fancying.

If instead of repetition or rephrasing or silence, the therapist chooses to ask a question, the same principles should be applied: why a question, why at this point, why not earlier or later, why this topic? It is just as easy to give moral judgment by question as by other means. To a woman complaining of the lack of romance in her marriage the therapist could ask, "You didn't think the honeymoon would last forever, now did you?" and he would be telling her that after a certain time romance is not an essential part of marriage, that she and not her husband is in the wrong, and that she should rest content with her lot.

Examples of omission also are easily found. One patient, for instance, insists, "I feel that sex is very fundamental in life and that the least a man can do is to be a good copulator."[13] He talks continuously of "sex," mentioning it explicitly in various forms like "sexual" or "sexuality" some fourteen times. The therapist during this entire interview and all subsequent ones simply avoids using the word "sex" in any of its forms—noun, adjective, or adverb. The closest he will come to "sex" is in using the pronoun "it." No wonder that shortly afterward the patient says, "Of course, I overvalue sex now." Two interviews later he also drops the word "sex" from his vocabulary.

Another example of avoidance:

> PATIENT: Of course [in a magazine article she had read] there was a discussion of the penis and the vagina and as I was reading that it immediately brought home one thing to me, how very uncomfortable I get at the word "vagina." The repugnance of the vagina is so deep-seated that every time I read the word "vagina" I feel it immediately and it's a peculiar feeling. I feel as if finger nails are scratching at the bottom of the vagina. Now isn't that peculiar, and certainly my, I never admitted it to anybody, I never had the occasion to say 'Oh the vagina makes me think of my nails scratching' but I always feel scratching, not going this way, but that scratching, like this, and that, the sharp nail at the bottom and it's a very uncomfortable feeling and I have that every time I read the word "vagina."
>
> THERAPIST: So you both reject the word and also feel a very painful sensation.
>
> PATIENT: Yes, I feel nails scratching, and I get very uncomfortable, you know. It's a peculiar thing, I can't get it out of my—every time, it never fails, it's a strong feeling, a scratching feeling going up with the nails, and I feel that it's tearing and scratching so as to become infected. So I suppose you analyze that, I could analyze that this way, I don't want the penis, and if the penis enters into it, it will scratch it and infect it, you see. So

it's the same old problem, the fact that you do sort of realize why you feel that way. Unless by repeating it and repeating it and constantly repeating it to you, there gradually will seep in the fact, the acceptance of that you see, not that I'm trying to accept the vagina or reject it, but accept the way I feel towards it you see which is what the ultimate end of this will be. And, ah, as far as penis is concerned I have no feeling one way or the other. I much prefer the sound of penis though I think it is an ugly sound too, "penis," with the word "pee," see? And "vagina," I think it is terrible. Every time I say it, I feel scratching, even if I talk about it now. . . .

She continues to speak of her horror of "vagina" and the therapist never mentions "vagina," not once! Why such reticence? Had the patient known only the obscene or four-letter word for vagina, would she have dared to utter it in the presence of her therapist? Contrast this case with one of a different school.

> THERAPIST: What was it you started to say at first, Tom?
> PATIENT: Well, that—isn't that nifty? Isn't that—what I was thinking was that that was pretty much of a—of big pleasure with an empty—with no satisfaction to it whatsoever—that's the way I look at it.
> THERAPIST: Masturbation?
> PATIENT: Well, masturbation and—I don't know what you'd call it——
> THERAPIST: Fucking?
> PATIENT: Cohibition [sic]? Fucking?
> THERAPIST: Yes.
> PATIENT: Cohibiting?
> THERAPIST: Cohibit and cohabitation. Well, that is a word that is used for it. Of course——
> PATIENT: Sexual intercourse——
> THERAPIST: Sexual intercourse.[14]

From these few cases one can imagine why different ideas of human nature emerge from different psychotherapies. One group by its diffidence about sexual matters imparts a similar diffidence to its patients; another group by its freedom imparts a similar freedom. The first school will contend that sex as a part of human nature is overvalued and the other will contend it is undervalued.

No one is saying here that the moral direction the patient gleans is always the moral direction that his therapist, wittingly or not, intends to give. Indeed a disadvantage of this kind of therapy is that its practitioners almost inevitably are unaware of the direction in which they impel the patient. Thus in the case of the "good copulator" above, where the therapist managed to avoid the word "sex" in his conversation and where the patient, sensing throughout a bias against Freudianism, says, "Of course I overvalue sex," the therapist congratulates himself on not being "judgmental" and actually believes that the patient now has learned all by himself that he overvalued sex.

When a psychiatrist or psychoanalyst says outright, "Don't be so damned sycophantish," he at least knows he is saying it and so does the patient. The therapists who use the repetitive and "m-hm" technique extensively are in their ambiguity like the oracles of old. "The Duke yet lives that Henry shall depose." What does it mean? Several possible things, but in the present case of modern psychotherapy it is the hearer of the oracle for whom no ambiguity exists whereas the oracle itself is not aware that it is making pronouncements.

Were not the patient in therapy like a mildly hypnotized person—submissive, yet because of it acutely aware of his therapist's wishes—were he instead like a repairman coming in to fix the office window, one could understandably object that moral direction is not greatly felt. But he possesses a child's uncanny powers of divination, especially in those moments where he is broaching, very tentatively, the subject of his guilt. Look for a moment at an interview which has none of the mutual expectations of patient and psychotherapist. An Englishman, an anthropologist, is trying to communicate with a Nuer, an African native.

> I: Who are you?
> COUL: A man.
> I: What is your name?
> COUL: Do you want to know my *name?*
> I: Yes.
> COUL: You want to know *my* name?
> I: Yes, you have come to visit me in my tent and I would like to know who you are.
> COUL: All right. I am Coul. What is your name?
> I: My name is Pritchard.
> COUL: What is your father's name?
> I: My father's name is also Pritchard.
> COUL: No, that cannot be true. You cannot have the same name as your father.
> I: It is the name of my lineage. What is the name of your lineage?
> COUL: Do you want to know the name of my lineage?
> I: Yes.
> COUL: What will you do with it if I tell you? Will you take it to your country?
> I: I don't want to do anything with it. I just want to know it since I am living at your camp.
> COUL: Oh well, we are Lou.
> I: I did not ask you the name of your tribe. I know that. I am asking you the name of your lineage.
> COUL: Why do you want to know the name of my lineage?
> I: I don't want to know it.
> COUL: Then why do you ask me for it? Give me some tobacco.

Compare the above scene with the following wherein the therapist has authority.

> PATIENT: . . . So, I on the one hand feel that it's [her little child's masturbation] perfectly normal; on the other hand I'm a little upset perhaps because of my experience

with it, in regards my mother, but also the reasons that Arnold [her husband] raised. So, I don't know what to do, and I thought I'd ask you for your opinion, since I think that you're an authority. [Pause.] I mean if she were your girl just what, how would you handle it?

THERAPIST: Well, I think the, I think the answer I would give there is I'm satisfied that people can handle such things in quite different ways without having difficulty, if their own attitude toward it is assured and I think——

The patient lets the "answer" pass but if the therapist had no authority in this case it is not inconceivable that the patient would have retorted, "Well, quit beating about the bush. Do you have an answer or don't you? Let's stop the stalling," or, "You poor man. You don't know what you'd do either, do you?"

The two interviews are poles apart of course, and the psychotherapist who fails to realize the effect of the authoritativeness of his communication is like Charcot, the nineteenth-century hypnotist, who thought his patients when in a trance could not hear him. The patient is so sensitive to subtleties that, were it the case now as it was once in Italy, he could tell from the frequency of active or passive verb forms used whether the therapist favored the active or passive role in his love life.[15]

The question, What happens to the modern therapist's rule, "Neither praise or blame"? can now be answered—it does not stand up. Psychotherapy is, as one patient described it, the last court of appeal. So whether the therapist says something or says nonsense syllables or says nothing it has meaning for the dangling patient, who will devour his words as rumors are devoured by an isolated army or a news-starved population. And whether the therapist directs politely or crudely, verbally or not, whether he holds himself up for imitation or manipulates the patient's surroundings, it is all *his* direction of the patient. A true king never bellows "I am the King!" Words can be sweetly placed and modestly directed, and the course all the more willingly followed for that.

CREED WITHOUT OATHS

There is a legitimate objection to be made about the way in which the cases in this chapter have been analyzed. It is not that they have been taken apart and used piecemeal to illustrate a number of propositions about psychotherapy. This is not a legitimate complaint, for if anyone should wish to consume the time and space similarly to analyze whole cases one could do so easily; the method has been given. But one verbatim case is often the size of a book, and here it was necessary not only to present more than one case but cases from more than one school. The real objection is rather that the full communication in any case cannot be recorded.

Existing cases even when published *ipsissimis verbis* leave out much of the non-verbal element which has been seen to be of importance. Some of them do indicate a few gestures that are partly vocal, such as the laugh, but the vast range of silent gestures is excluded. If cameras recorded the interviews photographically, there still would remain the problem of the angle of the lens and of the constantly changing focus of the patient's eyes from the therapist's nose, say, to the Braque painting on the wall, thence to the bust of Hippocrates.

Nor do present records take in the effect of the sense of smell. To an alcoholic the smell of liquor on the therapist's breath will convey many things. Also to a non-alcoholic patient or to a teetotaler such an odor might have significance, in some cases perhaps liquidating the therapist's authority. Yet the patient might indicate in no observable way that he had smelled alcohol and concluded what he did.

It is impossible, then, for any record of therapeutic communication to be complete. Perhaps for this reason therapists have complained of the tedium that afflicts them in going over published cases—so much of the record is not there. With these limitations in mind, it may be rewarding to approach the moral direction of psychotherapy in another manner, and that would be by examining the credos of the various schools. Having seen in how many ways the therapist influences his patient, one develops an interest in what the psychotherapist believes in, for it is this that he will most likely transmit, in whole or in part. In this context an examination of the creed of the leading school, the one whose tenets affect all modern psychotherapies, can serve as a specific example.

Since, as already pointed out, almost all modern therapies claim to avoid moralizing and thus to be scientific, their credos will not be couched in religious or ethical language. Their morality will be hidden in three separate compartments. The first is a comprehensive theory of personality that proclaims the true nature of the human being and includes as part of that true nature qualities that under previous theories were either immoral or unnatural. The second is a series of rules for conducting therapy that insures an influx of facts to support the theory. The third compartment is a technical jargon that gives new names to moral lacks or excesses and makes it possible to modify them while appearing scientifically neutral. So well is morality hidden that one ventures to predict that if psychotherapeutic creeds are translated into the language of the believer (as in the example to follow) the result will be shocking to many persons.

The Freudian credo (c. 1908) would fall into the three compartments thus:

> 1. I believe in Science the almighty, diviner of all things sensible, for of things insensible there are none, and penetrator of the mysteries of the universe and of man, who was conceived in an autoerotic, homosexual, sadistic, masochistic, exhibitionist, and incestuous mold, and for this suffered under parents, was crucified by the strictures of a misguided civilization, and descended into a living Hell of Neurosis, from which he will be taken by psychoanalysis.

2. I believe in psychoanalysis, the one true medicine of the psyche, *prima inter pares,* a therapy that requires the afflicted to talk to a healer of the faith, and in talking to lie hidden from a meeting of the eyes, to tell of his dreams, and to abolish all self-judgment.

3. I believe in psychoanalysis, a therapy that promises that nothing that the afflicted shall speak of shall be regarded as sinful and that, to insure this, requires that the afflicted shall be called a patient and his difficulties shall be known as clinical entities such as mental disease, maladaptation, suboptimal adaptation, neurosis, morbidity, infantilism, regression, malfunction, superego deficiency, personality deviation, hyper the one and hypo the other. I believe that henceforth all shall be tolerated save disrespect of Science. I believe that to him who has faith the unknown shall become known and Reason and Health prevail. If anyone has no faith in salvation, let him be pronounced forever incurable.

This creed, as fabricated, is no more comprehensive of doctrine than a theological creed. Many religious creeds, for instance, leave out mention of body and soul, and the above creed likewise makes no point of the familiar Id, Ego, and Superego. One should not expect a creed to reveal the entire faith. Nor should one hope that it will encompass the beliefs and practices of all who use the name of the creator. Creeds partly new and mostly old, schisms and splitting-offs, are all in the day's work of the student of doctrine.

Those who wish to see for themselves the original statement of the credo can go to Freud's published works. The *New Introductory Lectures* are recommended for evidence of the faith in Science and of psychoanalysis' relation to it. *Three Contributions to the Theory of Sex* and the *Introductory Lectures* propound the proposition that man is by nature polymorphously perverse and suffers under the Oedipus complex. *Civilization and Its Discontents* presents man as the victim of society. For the rules of procedure during therapy, the stress on talking and the dream, on lying on the couch, the abolition of self-censure, and the promise of no moral judgment, one should consult the *Interpretation of Dreams* and the *Collected Papers*. In addition there are books written by the faithful that summarize the beliefs of the faithful, and books by the not so faithful that show up the points of deviation or heresy.

That psychoanalysis has been a serious effort to turn much of existing ethics upside down can scarcely be doubted by anyone conversant with its facts and theories. What are some of the well-known proclivities of this school? Children are sexual, girls want a penis, boys fear castration, everyone is bisexual. The complex is explainable in terms of the simple. (Art, for example, is understandable as the resolution of the Oedipus complex.) The higher is explainable in terms of the lower. ("Religion, morality, and a social sense—the chief elements of what is highest in man—were originally one and the same thing," namely, the result of parricide.) The normal is a mere attenuation of the abnormal. ("The normal is a fiction. We know only the abnormal.") The civilized is the primitive after sublimation. ("Pity is a reaction-formation against sadism.") And so on. Freud once said that the fact that moralists thought psychoanalysis immoral while communists thought it reactionary proved that it was neutral. He overlooked the fact that both moralists and communists could be right in this case—the one in the sexual sphere, the other in the political arena.

As for the rules of procedure, the second of the three compartments, since the patient is put in an authoritative relationship where he is asked explicitly to talk and to eliminate his moral judgment, where he is asked to lie on a couch which permits him to escape the eye of the therapist, where he is encouraged to report his dreams (an area of his life for which he knows he is not fully responsible), where he is told that no moral judgment will be passed on his words or deeds—the patient finds himself in a situation redolent of childhood when his control of his passions was not at its peak. He will talk about those times, and since he need not morally condemn himself now—an authority has assumed that responsibility—

he talks especially about those times when the controls were in process of being learned via the family. This talk and these dreams, all products of a temporary lifting of the bars of moral control, are then used by the therapist as evidence of the true nature of man—a creature, locked in mortal combat with parents, laboring to crush his passions before the demands of a tyrannical civilization, and dragged down in his daily struggles by the dead weight of the past.

Finally there is the department of scientific language, which enables the acts and thoughts of the patient to be described not as bad or good but as part of a chain of cause and effect, as the symptoms of a disorder for which there is a clinical terminology. So long as this terminology is taken as sufficient unto itself and no questions asked, there will seem to be no necessity for a discussion of good and evil. The patient is maladapted or has a hypersevere superego? He can be treated without resort to moral direction. Treated, yes, but healed? That remains to be seen.

The major issue is that the analysts are not fully aware of the limitations of their findings, and the same applies to the other schools of psychotherapy. What they believe to be the true nature of man is not that but is the nature of man as seen in a particular kind of situation. This situation may be claimed to be the best now available for observing man but by no means are all the appetites and potentialities of man being watched.

And these rules of procedure that make up the therapeutic relationship, there is nothing in them that merits exclusive preference. Why should the patient talk? The words men say are one thing, what they do is another. History presents many kinds of psychotherapy that do not require talking or an anamnesis, and, remember, neither psychoanalysis nor any other modern therapy has demonstrated its superiority beyond question. Is talking required because it is so much a part of the Western world today, which is unable to share the sentiment, once a part of ancient Egyptian culture, that it is good to be properly and truly silent, that God loves the silent man more than him who is loud of voice, that the well of wisdom is sealed to him who can discover his mouth but is open to him who is silent? Even granting the use of talk, why then should the therapist tell the patient not to apply his moral discretion? Many therapies make no such requirement and yet, as will be seen, their patients talk about matters every bit as secret as those confided to the psychoanalyst.

As for the technical jargon, very little need be said beyond pointing out that it has a certain rate of attrition and change, that before long the words used acquire a stigma. Since they are used to cover up moral concerns and direction they sooner or later, like the term "neurosis" itself, acquire a moral tone. New words then must be substituted in order to keep the deception going. One often finds therapists boasting of and recommending a non-technical vocabulary but soon enough the words exchanged become the new jargon and in a matter of time gain the special ridicule reserved for an exposed deceit. Such, for example, has been the fate of one of the newer therapies whose stock in trade included originally innocuous phrases like "structuring" or "defining the relationship," "releasing free expression," "non-directive technique," "achieving insight," "accepting the self," "self-actualization," "the phenomenal self," "self-evaluative attitudes," "reflecting feeling," and "the internal frame of reference."

Although one should not discount too much the possibility of parallel developments, the influence of Freudianism on subsequent therapies has been incalculably great. Almost all of them subscribe to the creed—if not the whole of it, a large part; if not explicitly, then implicitly. Some dispense with the couch and ask the patient to have a chair facing them. Some speak not of maladaptation but of dysergasia. Some exchange the name "patient" for the name "client," hoping thereby to exchange a medical relationship for a business one along the lines of Marshall Field & Company's slogan, "The customer is always right." The extent to which the Freudian creed is incorporated by any other single therapy is unimportant here. If it is not one credo it will be another.

One school which currently enjoys a certain vogue among psychologists differentiates itself from psychoanalysis by claiming as its contribution to the true nature of man the ideas that everyone is an individual "whole," that the patient in therapy is solving his own problem himself by "accepting himself," that his problems are the result of his dependence on others, that he must differentiate himself from others before his "self" can "grow and mature." That these ideas are neither startling nor precise nor correct is irrelevant. Nor is it pertinent that this school obviously is trying to prove that everyone found alive is either a born individualist or a simple sort of democrat. It is relevant, however, that these ideas are communicated to the patient by all the means spoken of earlier in this chapter. Here for example is the way the patient is taught to say that he is an individual "whole."

> PATIENT: But I don't feel that the negative aspects of my personality are going to allow the intellect to turn the spotlight on the said key [to his feelings]. Well, that is the conclusion to my self-sufficiency. I'm going to enlist your aid.
>
> THERAPIST: The negative forces in your personality probably won't let you turn the spotlight on them, particularly as long as you regard them as something quite outside of yourself.

And again, somewhat later:

> PATIENT: Of course, I am—I mean, in a sense a person faces his feelings sort of *ipso facto* when he has his feelings—I mean, they bring themselves pretty largely into the realm of consciousness, and——
>
> THERAPIST: Sometimes he doesn't own them.
>
> PATIENT: I'm conscious of my feelings practically all the time—of my negative feeling. Well, you feel that the —that one obstacle in the way of cure would be to regard

the feelings as undesirable aliens rather than as worthy cripples?

THERAPIST: No, I guess that wasn't quite my notion. There's always a chance that they might not be aliens at all—they might be citizens right in your own country.

PATIENT: Well, they're fifth columnists, then.

THERAPIST: [Laughs.] You're not going to own them, eh? [Laughs.]

At the start of the very next interview the patient begins.

PATIENT: I got your point right after I left the office the last time. The notion came to me that all aspects of the personality should be owned—that is, should be regarded as myself. . . .

He continues in this vein, to which the therapist adds, "You feel that it is a part of you after all."[16]

The employment of "you" in the last remark should be noted. If one were to compare the proportion of "you's" employed by this school of therapy with that by another, one would find the former to be significantly higher. By a constant pushing of statements back into the patient's mouth he is made to feel that he ought to be and is deciding everything and directing himself. Here is a typical example:

THERAPIST: You feel perhaps *I* should know the answers, then.

PATIENT: That's right. Is it fair to an employer to go out and take a job that you feel, well, it may help you but it may not do very much good for him? (Pause.) Is it justifiable?

THERAPIST: You feel you might really be cheating the employer by doing that.

PATIENT: That's right. I've said that before. I know we've covered that once before. Uhuh. [Long pause. Laughs.] Well, what's the answer? Am I supposed to get the answers?

THERAPIST: You are wondering that, too, aren't you, whether maybe the answer is in you?

PATIENT: In other words, I'd have to make a radical change before I . . .

The therapist, like the Bellman in *The Hunting of the Snark,* might just as well have told the patient, "What I tell you three times is true."

When this kind of therapy is over one finds that the patient can ably parrot the therapist. Here is a patient reporting on his therapy six weeks after its conclusion:

> I was coming to see myself as a whole. I began to realize that I am one person. This was an important insight to me. I saw that the former good academic, job success, ease in social situations and the present withdrawal, dejection, apathy, and failure, were all adaptive behavior performed by me. This meant that I had to reorganize my feeling about myself, no longer holding to the unrealistic notion that the very good adjustment was the expression of the real me, and this neurotic behavior was not. I came to feel that I was the same person, something functioning naturally, and sometimes assuming a neurotic role in the face of what I had conceived as insurmountable problems. The acceptance of myself as one person gave me strength in the process of reorganization. Now I had a substratum, a core of unity on which to work.[17]

With this case and others in his pocket the therapist now can claim that he, too, has real evidence for his theory of human nature.

So it goes. Each psychotherapy operates with its own theory of human nature and each therapist finds that his cases prove his theory. But they do so because in the authoritative situation of psychotherapy the patient has responded to the therapist by becoming what he was wanted to be. He has been a good boy.

Very often the therapist gives moral direction beyond that contained in the ideology of his school. Not that he is acting *ultra vires* but rather the school's beliefs, unless finely elaborated, will not contain a position on minute or unusual questions. A patient may wish to know for instance whether capital punishment is justifiable and his analyst may warm up to the subject. Although psychoanalysis contains general principles from which a stand against capital punishment can be inferred, it has not made explicit its views on the subject. So one could distinguish, if necessary, the morality a therapist exuded as a member of a school from that as an individual therapist.

This has been a long and difficult chapter. It would not have been necessary to offer so many cases in illustration were it not that they help to put ideas in a concrete setting and also to show, as few studies do, that the psychotherapists are found to give moral direction in cases of their very own, in their own handwriting, so to speak.[18]

Perhaps one final case for this chapter would not try the patience too much. By contrast with the example of capital punishment just mentioned, the moral direction in this case is expressly a part of the school creed.

> PATIENT: Not only is there this fear of being in an intimate relationship with a woman, but I am also obsessed with the fear concerning that blasphemous thought. The reason for this seems to be that I had sold myself to the devil, merely by thinking this thought to myself. It is a fear of being possessed by the devil. I know it is rather absurd and based on the old theology. The devil seems to represent all that is evil or bad.
>
> The fear of selling myself to the devil takes my thoughts back to a dream I had at the age of 5 or 6 years. I was sleeping with my mother at the time. I woke up trembling very violently. I thought I saw a phantom fly across the room. It was like a flame, and yet it was like an imp grinning at me. It flew across the room and out of the window. I was scared to death.
>
> THERAPIST: What is the flame you would get if you were sleeping with your mother?
>
> PATIENT: Love of my mother, I suppose.

THERAPIST: What is the flame you would get if you were sleeping with a young lady?

PATIENT: Passion.

THERAPIST: Would you?

PATIENT: No, I expect I should be scared to death, and trembling violently, like I was in the dream.

. . . Now my main concern is this idea or obsession that I am possessed by the devil.

THERAPIST: Suppose you are?

PATIENT: That would mean that one would lose control of one's will.

THERAPIST: What is natural?

PATIENT: Do you mean that what I am afraid of is my own natural urge to live a normal natural life . . . ?

And during the next session:

PATIENT: Perhaps I am scared of a girl because I am terrified that my sexual feelings might run away with me, and I might not act rationally.

THERAPIST: What might you do?

PATIENT: I might love her too much

THERAPIST: What would that lead to?

PATIENT: My desire would be to put my arms around her, and tell her I love her. But I was scared.

THERAPIST: Does that seem so terrifying?

PATIENT: Well, I might lose control, and go too far.

THERAPIST: How far might you go?

PATIENT: Well, I might have sexual intercourse with her: that would be going too far.

THERAPIST: Would it?

PATIENT: Well, perhaps not as far as sexual intercourse. If that is the devil, perhaps he is quite a harmless devil. Perhaps the sooner I went to the devil the better.

THERAPIST: If that is all there is to it, why is there all this scare?

PATIENT: Apparently all this time I have been afraid of being possessed by my own nature. The thing I want more than anything else is to lead a normal natural life. Since coming to you I have understood that this fear of being sold to the devil is nothing more or less than fear of my own nature on the one hand, and on the other hand a preference for it, which I have thought was a preference for the devil.

The whole amazing thing has become quite plain to me. It is amazing how the obsession left me last night after that talk with you.[19]

This is exorcism at its best. St. Benedict, devil chaser, *effugator daimonum,* could not have done better. The victim is possessed of a devil. The exorcist, basing his incantation on the true faith, has but to catch the afflicted one by the ear and breathe into it, "What is natural?" and the devil turns tail and flees. In its place stands an angel—Sex—radiant in the glory of Nature.

Balm there may not be in the modern world but exorcism there is in plenty.

CHAPTER SIX

The Government of the Passions

"The stone which the builders rejected is become the head of the corner" (Psalms 118:22). Moral authority, an idea widely spurned by modern healers of the soul, is the crux of psychotherapy. The crystals that remain after distilling the multiplicity of therapies are not many. A bewildering array of brilliants dwindles down to a precious few: neurosis is a moral disorder, the psychotherapeutic relationship is one of authority, the therapist gives moral direction.

A logical objection to the significance of these findings might run like this: Although these three elements are present everywhere they are not necessarily the factors responsible for cure. It is possible that cure can be achieved in different ways. If all therapies have these three elements in common, it yet may be their differences that in some cases provide the cure.

A logical objection deserves a logical reply. First, that these common elements are accidental rather than essential is possible but most improbable. The comparative approach of the foregoing chapters surveyed the earth's psychotherapies through space and through time. It is difficult to conceive that these similarities could appear universally in such diverse settings and circumstances without being essential to psychotherapy.

Second, and more important, it follows from the nature of the neurosis that its cure can be effected only through moral authority. That is, given the first common element—neurosis is a moral disorder—the second and third must follow. Moral conflict or guilt can be resolved only by a moral decision and resolved only by one in whose righteous power the person believes. If no authority is present, as happens when the patient is a psychopath or when a friend tries to act as therapist, the moral dilemma cannot be broken. The would-be therapist can give all the moral direction he pleases, it will fall on stony ears.[1]

Without moral direction, how can there possibly be cure? Guilt can be removed only by some kind of moral intercession. The modern psychotherapist, as the last chapter disclosed, does intercede, primarily to say that what the patient thought immoral is not. In any case, modern or ancient, something morally wrong must be made right.

So though the trappings and language of authority never stay the same, the seat and the word are always present. The seat of authority may be no seat: authority resides in the eye of the beholder. The word of authority may be no word: the moral may never be worded but suggested and brought slowly by repeated images before the patient until it stays in all clarity, complete. Of these two things, the seat and the word, no psychotherapy can divest itself, now or ever, and yet be a therapy.

This means, of course, that the differences which each school holds up as superior and unique to itself are not the causes of healing. Instead it is the points of commonness that contain the elements necessary for what is generally held to be therapy. The next chapter has the task of carrying this proposition further. Before entering upon it, however, one should be better prepared.

There is this to consider. Why does moral disorder seem to shake the person to his foundations? Is morality part of his foundations? Is it inborn? If not, who or what is responsible for it? Would it not be better to spare the person the disabling guilt that results from moral disorder and thus, by eliminating morality, to remove at one stroke the evil of mental disease?

At various periods in the history of mankind these questions would have seemed like ninepins, set up solely to be knocked down with demonstrated proficiency. The world moves on, however.

> We must seek some consistent thread running through the weave of all civilizations we have known and preventing the development of all or almost all the people to a state of true maturity. What basic psychological distortion can be found in every civilization of which we know anything? It must be a force which discourages the ability to see and acknowledge patent facts, which prevents the rational use of intelligence, which teaches or encourages the ability to dissociate and to believe contrary to and in spite of clear evidence, which produces inferiority, guilt and fear, which makes controlling other people's personal behavior emotionally necessary, which encourages prejudice and the inability to see, understand and sympathize with other people's point of view. Is there any force so potent and so pervasive that it can do all these things in all civilizations? There is—just one. The only lowest common denominator of all civilizations and the only psychological force capable of producing these perversions is morality, the concept of right and wrong. . . .

It is a psychiatrist who says this. He continues:

> If the race is to be freed from its crippling burden of good and evil it must be psychiatrists who take the original responsibility. This is a challenge which must be met.[2]

Indeed it must. Today, apparently, questions like these are being seriously asked. Today also, fortunately, there is more knowledge at hand by which to answer them with assurance.

About the eighteenth century a view of man took hold that subsequently became part of several political philosophies such as the laissez-faire, the classical democratic, and the anarchist.

It assumed that man possessed an inborn morality. Voltaire for example spoke of "the principles of morality common to the human race." But the proponents of this view seldom called it morality; they called it Reason. Men could reach agreement and unity and a common life because they all were well endowed with Reason.

Similar to this view in one respect, although distinct in many others, was that of a group of political philosophers whose ideas had an even earlier origin. This group is usually known as the "state of nature" theorists. While they did not hold that man was gifted with an inborn Reason or morality, they believed that man in a pure state, in a state of nature, had motives which for one branch of these philosophers were mostly good motives and for the other branch were mostly bad.

This is not the place to go into a minute tracing of the fate of these schools. It is enough to note that the views that eventually struck root in democratic thought were offshoots of these thinkers. Men were born either with a Reason that would lead them to see eye to eye on the issues of right and wrong or with good motives that would move them together toward the beacon of righteousness.

While these ideas were incubating, a struggle was in progress against the hereditary kings and the established churches. The religious and political morality of the *ancien régime* had come to be stifling. Great sympathy would have been extended, on this account, to any theory of man that recommended leaving him to his own devices. The nature of man as propounded by the eighteenth-century philosophers and the "state of good nature" theorists (which last might be a fitting name for both groups) was of this kind. If man is born with a Reason or with good motives, the proper thing is to let him be. To interfere with him, to confine him in the strait jacket of morality, is to distort his life. The philosophies of education emanating from these views all lay stress on letting the individual alone to grow by himself. Morality, an idea identified with the old morality of kings and priests, came to be thought of as sheer restraint. And the democracies which were ushered in by these times fell heir to a vocabulary of violent iconoclasm—men would never be free till the last king was strangled in the entrails of the last priest—that in its milder form today still steeps in prejudice the ideas of morality and authority.

A fresh turn in the road appeared in the late nineteenth century with the coming of improved transportation. Certain men of means once again became men of parts. They traveled to more places and remained longer than Herodotus, the Greek *historicos,* ever could have afforded. These persons, when joined afterward by others of less means but more method, became known as anthropologists. In the same late nineteenth century the hypnotists and the psychoanalysts came to scholarly attention. They traveled, too, but their direction was backward, from the mind of the adult into the mind of the child.

Perhaps because they were recent to the scene the newcomers were swept along by the prevailing views of man's nature. The anthropologists found different moral standards everywhere: that fact was used to point out again that morality was unimportant. The psychoanalysts found that their patients' lives were confounded by the moral influence of their parents: that fact was used to point out again that moral influence should abdicate. In many instances such use of the facts brought out by their disciplines was not the fault of the anthropologist and psychoanalyst; in other instances, of course, they were culpable.

Actually these two disciplines have unearthed the materials that confront the view of man which has dominated the past few centuries, confront it and put it to rout. It is true that the "state of good nature" theory could have been disposed of without additional help, by picking out the flaws in its construction. One could have asked, How can you say the nature of man is thus when you are talking only of the adulterated product, the full-grown man in society? One could have asked, How can you say that all morality is restrictive when you are talking only of a specific and hated morality? Some political philosophers did ask such questions. Yet to find flaws was not easy except in retrospect, and it was especially difficult when the tide of ideas rose in opposition.

Furthermore there is in recent studies something new, something that makes a contribution beyond the questions raised by logic. The work of the newer disciplines not only routs the prevailing theory, it re-establishes the older Greek ideas of education and by dint of more evidence raises them to higher esteem. With new information in hand it is no longer necessary to speak of man in an imaginary state of nature. Man-as-he-is-born is a man of whom more is known now than ever was known of man-in-the-state-of-nature. It is this man on whom a theory of man's nature can be supported.

FORMING THE CHARACTER

Newborn man is an organism with potentialities. That is all that can be said for him in isolation. He has a divine spark but, unless fanned, that spark flies back to its Maker. He has needs or appetites but does not know what to do with them nor even what they are. It is part of the uniqueness of this organism that at his start he knows so poorly what to do for himself. His activity is diffuse, random, unco-ordinated, to say it in a word, unordered.

The "state of nature" theorists had given natural man credit for qualities he does not have: pity, compassion, brotherliness. Seeing the cut flowers in the vase, they forgot about the roots. They made the same mistake that Frederick II and many others before him made in thinking that the infant is born with a natural language—Hebrew, Greek, French, or some other patriotic tongue. The motives of new man, man-as-he-is-born, man uninfluenced by other men, are blameless, and just as surely they are praiseless. Man is born neither moral nor immoral. Only after he is touched by human hands does he get the chance to be good or evil.

Gradually he is brought out of this condition by the three most important communities of family, state, and religion. From them he learns what is right and what is wrong, he learns morality. He learns that he is expected to do right, he learns responsibility. The "state of nature" theorists, according to whether they held that man's natural state was good or bad, claimed that the influences of this unnatural state were restrictive or facilitative. But a psychological and anthropological examination of the influences that the community brings to bear on newborn man shows that they are not one or the other. They are restrictive and facilitative both.

The notion that moral standards are restrictive of freedom is a gross misunderstanding of the nature of morality. The community takes this bundle of life with its appetites and its faculties and tries to make it grow into an ideal form. Some of its activity the community blocks, some it ignores, some it encourages. Morality involves not only curbs and restraints but purposes and loves and ideals, not only restriction but also direction. A moment's reflection is convincing: a moral command has not only a side that says "don't" but also a side that says "do." The avoidance of bad behavior means the doing of good. Not to be dishonest is to be honest; not to be cowardly is to be brave and courageous. Morality is Janus-faced, and if it is conscience that says "no," it is also conscience as the mad poet Nietzsche insists, that can "say yes to one's self."

When brought together, these moral standards, these goals, and laws and crimes, sins, and loves and hates, constitute an interrelated system containing various elements, cosmological, eschatological, ideological. To say that they constitute a system is not to say that in the minds of most men they have a systematic shape. Some of these standards or beliefs are ordered, some unordered, some irreducible. They have an order or a system, however, in that all together they tell the person how to take his terrestrial journey. In the simplest terms they say to the man who is to become a political animal: *These* people are our kind, our brothers, therefore love them; *these* figures are the great ones in this world who help us to get what we need and desire, our common good, therefore love them and obey their laws; *this* is the way to show your love for them, this is the way they want you to conduct yourself.

Morality begins to be possible. As the political and religious system of beliefs of the community is unfolded to him, the new man begins to have purposes, things to do, ends to attain. Morality is the order given to the passions.

The reform demanded by the psychiatrist at the beginning of this chapter—to root out the evil of morality—tolls its own death knell. He could not have been more self-contradictory had he proclaimed, "Evil is the Good." Morality is itself the knowledge of good and evil. Whence his knowledge then that morality is evil? How could a psychiatrist or anyone else feel so strongly that something was an evil without firm ideas of good and evil within himself? It is the same error over again. One hates a specific kind of morality so much that one oversteps the bounds of logic by denouncing all morality.

Already some of the questions posed at the beginning of this chapter are answered. Yes, morality is part of the person's foundation; indeed it *is* his foundation and that is why when morality is disordered the soul itself is shaken. No, morality cannot be eliminated because if it were there could be no way of life, no movement toward the good, no freedom. No, morality is not inborn. But then if it is not, who or what is responsible for it, for the ordering of man's appetites and faculties? This question yet remains.

The beliefs and morals, the belief-system, that the new man acquires become what is known as conscience. The heart of the present problem is how conscience is formed, how this belief-system is "taken into himself," how these communal moral ideas become part of the self so that the self reciprocally becomes part of the community. At this stage of the inquiry the "state of nature" theorist gives way to another type of political philosopher, the "social compact" theorist, who interests himself in the inarticulated understandings of rulers and subjects.

In *The Leviathan* Hobbes, the great seventeenth-century English philosopher, wrote this interesting passage: "The desires and passions of man are in themselves no sin. No more are the actions that proceed from those passions, till they know a law that forbids them; which till laws be made they cannot know, nor can any law be made till they have agreed upon the person that shall make it."[3] Quite clearly, this is exactly the point, except that not only sin but virtue, too, is impossible without law. Asking now, When does man-as-he-is-born meet with the first application of law? one realizes that it has happened already, in the community of the family, with the first teaching of morality. At this time, as Thomas Aquinas would say, he makes his first decision concerning his last end. This original instance merits a closer examination. It may be regarded, if one chooses to use an older terminology, as the beginning of a continuously reaffirmed covenant. Who are the parties to it? What is their status? Who is the person that makes the law? What is the penalty for not agreeing to the law?

The parties to it are parent and child. Are they equals? Not at all. They are superordinate and subordinate, one the protector and provider, the other the protected and provided for. Not the child but the parent gives the law. He is the director or, to follow the etymology of the title "father," he is the spiritual infuser. And the penalty for disobedience? Ultimately, separation from the community of the family. Without the family the source of all gratification is gone, the orderly world drops into a bottomless hole, and panic and chaos take its place. It is a separation with the psychological meaning of death. This *The Political Community,* a work whose evidence is much relied on in this chapter, discovered. Repudiation by the community signalizes the visitation of every pain and terror, complete loss of the blessings of peace.

The salient characteristics of the persons who give the law or, as earlier described, who bequeath the morality of the community should be distinguished. They know right from wrong, their strength is great, they are concerned only with the common good. These qualities, it will be remembered, are the qualities of authority. In the case at hand these persons have power based on moral knowledge and physical force and they are esteemed for it and for their love of the common good. Note again that it is not power alone that makes authority but power *plus* an exclusive devotion to the common good.

Authority, then, is at the source of morality. Man is taken out of a state of nature by a set of understandings or by a covenant with an already existing authority. Accepting this authority gains him admittance to life according to the given system of beliefs, in other words, life within a community, first within the family, later within the great community.

Linking conscience to authority as this discussion has done may be somewhat perplexing. In light of the uniquely individual way the word "conscience" has been employed in modern times, a confusion is understandable. The role played by authoritative figures in the formation of conscience is determinant. Modern psychology with the aid of the backward-looking technique of psychoanalysis has rediscovered it by a process of uncovering in the mind layer after layer of persons —parents, teachers, priests, counselors, and leaders—whose morality, whose strength, whose knowledge newly born man needed and admired, and sought to unite in himself. Were it possible, which it is not, for psychologists to uncover the last layer and the last person, there would be nothing left of the man they set out to analyze but the empty vessel. In destroying his heroes man destroys himself.

In the development of new man's character the formative forces are figures of authority. The fate of the word "culture" shows what neglect has fallen to this principle of character formation. Originally culture meant the same thing as it does in the word "agriculture": the practice of cultivating. Applied to men, it meant the practice of cultivating character. Today it has been extended by the anthropologists to cover everything in a community including buttons, chipped stones, dishes, miscellaneous trinkets, and whatnots. This notion of culture is too vague to mean much; it conceals what is worth while or important. It is moral authority that teaches, that cultivates character, that deserves the name "culture."

The forms of direction that the early teachers of man use are similar to those used by later teachers like the psychotherapists. The model and its imitation are one form. Explicit communication in all its variety of etiquettes and styles is another. A third and one much more available to parents than to psychotherapists is environmental direction, in this case found chiefly in the atmosphere of home. Early teachers, like the later ones, utilize in varying combinations all these forms of expressing moral approval and disapproval.

In the twentieth century numerous educators and child psychologists have created a stir over methods of discipline and physical and moral restrictions of the child's freedom. They have even gone so far as to label certain kinds of physical discipline or unexplained commands as "authoritarian." These pedagogues usually make one or another of two common mistakes. Either they are misled by the "state of good nature" theories which instruct them to let the child grow alone like some weed; or they fail to realize that the expression of approval or disapproval (and one involves the other, just as the good the bad) is necessary to organize the personality.[4] To comment on the first mistake: Man-as-he-is-born has numberless potentialities for development. In what direction, in what image, is he to develop? If you leave him alone he will die. You cannot rely on age to bring him Reason, as John Locke, a prominent figure in the "state of good nature" school, suggested. The age he will reach will not be ripe enough.

To comment on the second mistake: Character cannot be formed by indulgence alone. It is logically as well as practically impossible to encourage some traits of character without discouraging others in man's repertoire of potentialities. A child can shed bitter tears just because his father's face reflected no sign of approbation. His parents as a policy may never have laid a punitive hand on him, perhaps being the kind who try always to indulge the child. In raising children one cannot seem perpetually good, a fairy godmother undisguised. One has to appear good *and* bad. There is a place for both expression and repression in the child's training. Because of the very gifts that make him far superior to animals, the being known as man has a capacity for great destruction, a capacity for evil. Call it original sin, if you wish; its other side then is original virtue. Every community tries early to preserve the things it cherishes by training out this evil and training up to the good.

The ways to train, to educate, to communicate moral favor or disfavor are many. One form, say spanking or physical discipline, has its peculiar advantages and disadvantages as does any other, say packing the child off to his room in solitary confinement or partial ostracism. The methods adopted are less important than the moral judgments they convey. Similarly with restrictions of bodily movement like swaddling; unless they result in disfigurement, in itself a matter of differing standards, their effects are usually unimportant beside the necessity for clear moral expression. The Della Robbia babies never suffered from their swaddlings.

The basic principles of ordering the passions then are three: good deeds demand honor and praise, bad deeds deserve blame and censure; moral habits must be built up early in life; and they must be imparted by figures of moral authority—persons upon whom others depend for this knowledge, persons who are believed to have the common good at heart. Every community has restrictions and facilitations that embody its ideals and every community must use figures of moral authority to impart these ideals to young and old alike. Virtue can be taught, but only by such persons and by the love they inspire and the suffering they must inflict.

FOCUSING THE SENSES

All this was known to the ancient Greeks, who made the greatest study of political education. What the Greeks were not fully aware of, and what modern anthropology and psychology have indicated, is the extent to which man is molded by his early guides, molded in ways of which the guides themselves are sometimes ignorant.

It now seems sure, for example, that the attendants of newborn man greatly affect the limits of pain and cold. Cold that is intolerable to Europeans without heavy wrappings is enjoyed by the Tierra del Fuegians with nothing but a pelt hung from the neck on the side of the wind.

As for pain beyond the imaginable endurance of modern Western men, here is an early account of certain practices among the American Indians:

> [The captives] displayed in the face of the most frightful torments a greatness of soul, a heroism, that is altogether unimaginable. . . . The prisoners sing their own great feats of arms and those of their tribes. Hurling curses at their tormentors, they try to intimidate them by threats, calling upon their friends to rescue or avenge them. They ridicule the executioners for not knowing their business, telling them how to apply the fire to inflict a bitterer pain, describing what they themselves did to prisoners who fell into their hands. If by chance they have ever dealt with a victim from the tribe of their captors, they enter into the greatest detail of the torments they inflicted, fearless of the consequences of such talk, which can only serve to enrage their tormentors. Though the sheer violence of their anguish makes them foam at the mouth or stare with the wild eyes of madness, they never utter a word of shrinking. The women are as heroic as the men. I saw one have two finger-nails torn out in my presence. Not a cry, not a groan! The most I could catch on her face was an imperceptible expres-

sion of tedium. Some of them laugh under torture,
take the whole matter as a jest, and amiably thank those
who have hurt them most.

This is not an account of one or two extraordinary individuals
but of the run of tribal members. Then comes the explanation:

> The savages seem to train themselves for such exhibi-
> tions from earliest childhood. Children have been seen
> to clasp each other with naked arms, with a burning coal
> between them, wagering as to who could stand it longest
> and with the least show of pain. I myself saw a child
> between five and six years old who had been seriously
> scalded about the body by a vessel of hot water being
> accidentally upset upon him. Every time his wounds
> were dressed, he would strike up his death-song and sing
> it with incredible courage, though he was suffering the
> keenest anguish at the time.

A few tests, not too satisfactory, have been made to ascertain
variations in pain sensation among persons of differing cultures.
The minimum pressure required in order to produce pain, for
instance, has been experimented with on Englishmen, Dayaks
of Borneo, Todas, and Papuans. The Englishmen are quicker
to feel pain. Renzo Sereno, a political scientist who includes
the West Indies in his compass, found there that the people are
so indifferent to the pain of afflictions like yaws and venereal
diseases that it is useless to instruct them in prophylactics and
simple health rules. "The child is reared," he reports, "in no
fear whatsoever of disease and grows up to be a parent unable
to educate his children in personal hygiene."[5]
Perception itself is affected by early trainers of sight. The
Torres Strait islander can detect a fainter red than can the
Englishman but it takes twice as much blue for him to see it.
The ordinary Westerner, listening to the music of peoples who
use smaller intervals, will think it out of tune, but he cannot
discriminate finely enough so that he can tell as they can when
they actually are playing out of tune on their own scales.

Much of training in perception is transmitted via the community's language. The language itself will embody the discriminations that are of value to the way of life of the community. A common language brings about a common perceptual field. A hunting community's language with its many terms for spears or guns will greatly differ from an agricultural community's language of plants and growth processes. Fishing communities make fine discriminations in marine life, desert dwellers do the same for sand topography, and arctic peoples make minute distinctions in the character and form of snow. The Tungus of Siberia have one name for a wild, and another for a tame, domesticated reindeer, one name for each age class, for a young female fawn, a doe with one fawn, a doe of three years with two fawns, and so on. The ordinary American can with luck distinguish between a deer and a moose and perhaps some one other, but he has a rich business language, as do the English, who along with the Dutch have also a rich water or sea language. In large communities with wide expanses of territory, perception will vary from area to area, as the city boy learns when visiting his country cousin who literally sees things in the woods that he does not. Anthropologists, too, often see things, such as a variety of vegetation, which the natives have never noticed, never needed, never named. A language shapes perception and in handing over a language the teachers of succeeding generations tell them what is worth while perceiving in the world.

Dietary preferences set in childhood are often the basis for the phrase to end all debate, *de gustibus non disputandum est.* Peripheral tribes in Utah and California (still under the sway of far-off pre-Columbian tribes of Mexico who ate a ritual breakfast of parched corn in sugar water, fruit, and boneless meat) eat a breakfast of Cracker Jack, tinned peaches, and corned beef. A French playwright on a visit to America, himself a drinker of wine and puzzled at the sight of grown-up Americans drinking so much milk, concluded that they must be unusually attached to their mothers. The effects of early formation of food tastes are persuasively expressed in this Southern Negro folk song:

> *Dem white folks set up in a Dinin' Room*
> *An' dey charve dat mutton an' lam'.*
> *De Nigger, he set 'hind de kitchen door,*
> *An' he eat up de good sweet ham. . . .*
>
> *Deir ginger cakes taste right good sometimes,*
> *An' deir Cobblers and deir jam.*
> *But for every day an' Sunday too,*
> *Jest gimme de good sweet ham.*

Just as the first teachers make the definitions of heat and cold, pleasure and pain, so do they administer balm to injury. If they recognize a hurt or pain as injury, if they do not say to the child, "It is nothing," they apply the salve, the swab, the soothing words; they kiss away the hurt, insuring its flight.

The later therapeutic effect of the materials used in family healing should not be understated. A mother in a community that sets great store by the healing properties of water may apply, with the accompaniment of melodious words of quick recovery, cool water to her boy's bumped head. An aqueous remedy in later life may carry with it the spiritual ministry of the early healer. The Bantu native, for example, is taught in childhood that the panacea for all evil or possessing powers is an emetic.

A native girl in the kraals described an attack of clinically typical Globus Hystericus, from which she suffered until cured by emetics. Some man is reputed to have put some of his urine into her coffee, which created a strong desire in her to give herself to him sexually. In struggling against this desire, it occurred to her that he brought her a mug of coffee from another hut. She then suspected what he had done, and immediately thereafter a lump came up in her throat and nearly choked her. The native doctor gave her medicine, and she vomited

SIX: THE GOVERNMENT OF THE PASSIONS 119

up a yellowish fluid, showing plainly the presence of
urine, and she no longer experienced the desire to run
after this man.

Much of the magic of primitive as well as modern medicine
can be thus explained and also much of the imperviousness of
one culture to the medicine of another.

> Just as the Balinese believe that foreigners are immune
> from the attacks of witches simply because they are of a
> race apart, so they believe that European medicines and
> the knowledge of white doctors, pills, liquids in bot-
> tles, and bitter or smelly powders, can be effective
> only to cure the people who invented them. Furthermore,
> the lack of showmanship of doctors, of dramatic hocus-
> pocus with which to paralyze the evil forces which they
> believe cause illness, leave them without faith in their
> curative ability.[6]

One tribe's medicine is another's ridicule, its snake oil if not
its poison. Offer cooling water or a mud poultice to the white
man and he is likely to say, "If you don't mind, I'll take an
aspirin instead." The primitive is not to be outdone in politeness. Offer him the contents of the white man's black medicine
bag and out of courtesy he is likely to accept. But the placebos
which have so great an effect on the civilized men who cut
their teeth on pills have no magic for the savage.

The amenability of perception and sensations of cold, heat,
and pain to early moral authority can be confirmed by the
phenomena of hypnotism. The hypnotic situation is an authoritative one that develops increased willingness to obey by
exploiting the existing filial relationship. If it is desired that the
subject be quickly hypnotized it is essential that the qualities
that the hypnotist communicates about himself closely match
those of the subject's early authorities. A good book on hypnotism will stress this point.

> The impression that the hypnotist creates in the eyes
> of the subject is therefore important, for the more closely

he symbolizes the powerful or benevolent parent, the more easily will hypnosis be induced and the deeper will be the trance. This explains why some hypnotists will fail and why others will succeed in producing light, medium, and deep trance states in the same subject. . . . [The subject's] responses are conditioned by his attitudes toward early authorities. Whether reactions are of defiance, compliance, surrender or contentment depends largely on the character structure the individual has developed out of early relationships with the parents. . . . The personality of the hypnotist and his ability to inspire faith and confidence is thus a determining factor. There are certain qualities such as appearance, eloquence and a kindly firmness which build up a desire in the patient to be hypnotizable, or which motivate him toward an inability to resist the hypnotist's commands. The reputation of the hypnotist, his reported successes in being able to hypnotize other people, also has a profound effect on the subject. One of the most potent influences is for the subject to see the operator hypnotize other people in a group. The old-time hypnotists had, at all times, one or more patients in a sleep-like trance in their waiting rooms for the subject to observe.[7]

If the hypnotist does not exude these qualities, quick hypnotism is impossible, although learning more through interview about the subject's early authorities and acting accordingly may bring about later success.

Utilizing this willingness to obey, the hypnotist then instructs the subject in one manner or another to banish attention to any but him. This reactivates the past even more quickly and deeply than the modern psychotherapist's instruction to eliminate all moral judgment. The world practically narrows down to two people—parent and child. The situation of newly born man is so nearly reached that the subject becomes able to control himself in the multiple ways open to him before the pattern of his early teachers set in.

Thus one finds that the hypnotist seems to be able to regulate all that was laid at the door of new man's authorities. He can produce, to use the technical terms this time, anesthesia, analgesia, thermoanesthesia, and paresthesias of the special senses, including photomata, parageusia, and parosmia. These facts suggest that all the hypnotist produces in the subject can be brought about if desired in the education of the child.

Some persons feel that hypnotism reveals nothing but the weakness and irrationality of man. Far otherwise. It confirms that man, especially new man, can control much more of himself and is therefore more educable than has hardly been dreamed of. A comparative study of the methods of transmitting belief-systems to the young would show that some communities have made use of hypnoidal states that permit the concentration of authoritative stimuli. The Papago tribe of North America, as one of its female members tells the story of her life, offers an interesting example.

> Early in the morning, in the month of Pleasant Cold, when we had all slept in the house to keep warm, we would wake in the dark to hear my father speaking.
>
> "Open your ears, for I am telling you a good thing. Wake up and listen. Open your ears. Let my words enter them."
>
> He spoke in a low voice, so quiet in the dark. Always our fathers spoke to us like that, so low that you thought you were dreaming.
>
> "Wake up and listen. You boys, you should go out and run. So you will be swift in time of war. You girls, you should grind the corn. So you will feed the men and they will fight the enemy. You should practice running. So, in time of war, you may save your lives."
>
> For a long time my father talked to us like that, for he began when it was black dark. I went to sleep, and then he pinched my ear.
>
> "Wake up! Do not be idle!"
>
> Then we got up.[8]

122 ERRORS OF PSYCHOTHERAPY

UPHOLDING THE GREAT LOVES

Thus for newly born man the Psalmist's words—"Who for-giveth all thine iniquities, who healeth all thy diseases"—point to his spiritual parents. These guides of the child have before them a choice which, could they but know it, would make them tremble. They can make their teaching so forceful that it becomes virtually a permanent, unmodifiable part of conscience. Among the tribes of Africa the boy is circumcised, and after an impressive ceremony:

> The old men warm their hands over the fire and put them to the boy's mouth while they are addressing him: "You must not use obscene language. You must never tell a lie. You must not commit adultery nor go after women who do not belong to you. You must always obey your father and respect your elders. You must never betray the secrets that you have learned from us to the women or the boys who have not been circumcised."[9]

Or the guides of the child can be less serious, less ceremonial, less firm, less horrifying, less forceful, and thus leave some of the morals they implant open to later influence with little or no guilt. In the one case what happens is that their authority is burnt in, so to speak; in the other their authority is merely impressed, left subject to change by later authority.

The morals, ends, and goals laid down in the first case be-come the irreducibles of conscience; those in the second case are often arranged as means to further ends and goals, and not as ends in themselves. The anthropological term "taboo" would be useful to cover the irreducible morals but is one-sided in its negativeness. Taboo might apply to "treason" but would not fit "duty." Piety and blasphemy, duty and treason, and a host of other forms of morality and immorality are defined early in the new man's life. Murder, incest, parricide, fratricide, certain foods and beverages are often proscribed. Frequently, too, the proper objects or directions of the passions set up for attainment include marriage, love, certain other foods and drinks, work, home, country, and God.

In history one finds that men have been variously thought virtuous if they were brave, courageous, and manly, or prudent, or just, wise or ambitious or pious or humble or rich or skeptical. If they chose one or another of these paths, was it because it was settled scientifically? Was it because incontrovertible facts and figures were collected? Could they choose now on such bases? Can they ever? The highest ideals, for example, of democracy, as well as the most routine habits, for example, of etiquette, are accepted and adopted not because a man's equal told him they were the right ideals and habits, nor because man believes everybody in the world believes them right, nor because they have been scientifically proved, but because man loved and trusted someone whom he felt knew more about right and wrong and with whom his best interests were uppermost.

As put earlier in general terms, the objects of love and the ways of acting toward them are presented by moral authority in the complex of a system of beliefs. Some are specially presented as objects to evoke a love that is great and constant. And when men love great objects in common they share a morality and comprise a community. Samuel Butler's literary skill caught this thought in one unassuming sentence: "If he has made me feel that he felt those things to be lovable which I hold to be lovable myself I ask no more." Men are bound together by the common objects of their love. A community is made up simply of men who love the same great objects.

Thus morality not only molds men's appetites and potentialities, but by binding them together makes it possible for them to rely on one another and to achieve their ends in a common life and an orderly world.

How much a man's morality should be subject to change or delegation is one of the thorniest problems that face the political scientist and the theologian. Obviously, in order to adjust to changing situations there must be a sphere of moral action that can be modified by later authority, but precisely how large a sphere and in what areas are things exceedingly difficult to determine. On some matters it is usually possible to say definitely that a moral directive should be imbedded in conscience, there to remain unquestioned or when questioned to arouse the severest pain of guilt. Two telling items, selected from similar ones that occasionally appear in the press, may be reproduced here.

BABY DROWNS IN TANK AT NEW HOME

The sorrowing parents of 21-month-old Harry Boyce, Jr., today took time out from the building of their new house in order to arrange the baby's funeral.

The little boy was drowned yesterday when he fell into a septic tank near the new house being built for the Boyce family at 1372 Rand St., in Talcott Twp.

The parents, Harry and Doris Boyce, now living at 4628 Monroe Ave., took Harry and his elder brother, Ralph, 6, on an inspection tour of their new home yesterday.

Leaving the boys to play in a sandpile in the yard, the Boyces went around to the opposite side of the house to watch the builders.

When they returned after a few minutes, Harry had disappeared. Ralph was unable to say where or how.

For hours they searched. Neighbors helped. Darkness fell. The Riverside Fire Department sent a floodlight truck to aid firemen from Talcott.

Eventually someone thought to look in the septic tank. The baby's body was there.

No one knew who had moved the temporary cover of the tank while Harry was near—or who had replaced it later.

The parents were at fault in their education of the older boy if they could even so much as suspect that he, if left alone with his little brother, could in a fit of passion do him grave harm. Without question most persons would agree to this. The injunction "Harm not thy brother" or, positively put, "Love thy brother" should have been burnt into his conscience.

Similarly for this shorter item.

THIS WAS ALMOST KISS OF DEATH

The Rev. Bruce Tilden forgave his wife today, but police ruled she must stand trial for assault.

Tilden told the court yesterday that his wife bent over his easy chair with her hand over his eyes, kissed him, and slit his throat with a razor.

Mrs. Tilden could give no reason for her act. Tilden will recover.

That a wife should be able without conscious provocation to cut her husband's throat while in the act of caressing him would also probably earn widespread reprehension. Such a wife could scarcely be said to love and honor her husband, let alone obey him. But apart from these news items, if anyone has the notion that nothing is so unchangeably right or wrong that it warrants being made an irreducible part of conscience, let him acquaint himself with the published and especially the photographed collections of the handiwork of sadistic and sexual psychopaths. There he may see horrors which he would excuse under no circumstances. He may learn something about himself.

These cases which arouse immediate indignation do not pose the stubborn problem for the student of authority. It is rather the problems of justice, of whether to abandon one's faith for another, of whether to join in a revolution or to oppose the successful coup d'état at the risk of slow death. These larger problems of the clarification of morality and law so that men can take courage in the right are problems that demand constant conscientious attention.[10]

Many persons do not understand what is required to build new man's character so that he will take courage in the right. They do not realize the implication of the great part of the studies done by psychoanalysts; nor indeed do the psychoanalysts themselves.

The man who is master of his passions is a slave to early authority. He therefore is a good or bad man only in so far as the morality that was burnt into his conscience was good or bad. The psychopath, for example, is master of his passions; unfortunately all those who guided and molded and channeled his passions worked to produce evil. The individualist or the self-legislator, the one who comes in for much praise from those who are on his side at the time, the one who sees the good way and follows without hesitation, he, too, is master of his passions. He is often one who is most skeptical and calculating about current authority; he is often one who says, "Do we really need to follow leaders? After all, we know they are only men and all men have clay feet." Yet he is also the one who possesses internal rulers stronger than the live rulers of his country. For him all men have clay feet, certainly, except those who set his course early in life and whom he now unknowingly obeys before all others. The Puritan, whose attitude toward all mortal authority was rebellious, paid obedience every day of his life to his internal masters of conscience. Cut open the man of character and principle and you will find inside him, like little statues, the good models—both human and divine—that he has faithfully followed.

The permanence of such teachings is undoubtedly greater than anything the hypnotist can construct. Although the parent can bring about all that the hypnotist can, the reverse proposition is not true. The hypnotist's influence increases the more he approximates the child's good parents but never is he fully identified with them. Even in the deepest hypnosis the subject retains a sense of the unreal. He is like a person absorbed in a drama, living the play in his heart yet knowing the while that he is a spectator. The hypnotist remains an external authority in that he cannot affect the irreducible, the morality that was burnt into new man. When confronted by an immoral command—be it to steal, to kill, to mutilate—the subject awakes, the trance breaks, the authority collapses. As he regains the mastery of his passions the subject once again bows to the law of his fathers.

This much can be said then. Some of man's morals are ordered as means to further ends, others are irreducible. Whenever traced, their ramifications lead back to authority, to the teachings of conscience, to the community goals. One can make a distinction between the directives of early authority and later authority, and say that conscience incorporates the teachings of early authority. One can say that later authority cannot conflict with the irreducibles of conscience. One can say also that to provide adjustment to a changing world there must be a sphere of moral action that can be modified by later authority. But one cannot say that conscience exists in man-in-a-state-of-nature or that it develops in any way except through authority. When Socrates heard a voice murmur in his ear, "Listen, Socrates, to us who have brought you up," when he listened and obeyed, he made his last political covenant with authority.

In a well-knit community a series of formal covenants occur that guide man from the state of nature into the state of family, thence into the state of community, gradually exacting more responsibility and granting more privilege. Anthropologists call these political and religious ceremonies the rites of passage. They mark formal stages in the acquisition of the community's system of beliefs. Once the person becomes a full citizen, though political ceremony and observance of tradition do not cease, participation now signifies a formal renewal or reaffirmation of the belief-system.

In these formal or ceremonial celebrations the presence of authority or its representative is unmistakable. The pact may be renewed or affirmed on other, less formal occasions, however, when the action toward authority is solely psychological in character. An explicit oath or pledge of allegiance to tangible or present persons is not necessary. Whenever in the acts of a man an alternative appears and yet he chooses the course of conscience or authority, his act becomes an encounter with authority and an affirmation of his unity with the community. Obversely, whenever he chooses to depart from the course of conscience his act is a breaking away from the community. This conclusion adds a new dimension to the theory of neurosis. As Immanuel Kant, the metaphysician of Koenigsberg, said, mental disorder represents the loss of the *sensus communis* and the establishment of a *sensus privatus*. Since morality guides the life of man in community, a disordered morality alienates him from his fellow men.

The relationships of parent to child and psychotherapist to patient recall two other relationships—ruler to subject and God to man. As just noted, when new man leaves the family he becomes a member of the greater political and religious communities. Now if authority and morality and healing are connected in the family, one should expect to find them together in the new authorities possessed by man the Citizen and Believer. And this *is* the finding. Indeed, had this study approached the subject of psychotherapy from another angle, by asking who throughout history have been the most famous healers, it might have come much sooner upon the fact that authority and therapy are related. For the greatest healers in the world have been kings and gods and their immediate representatives.

Rulers as far apart as the savage chiefs of the Tonga and Waldemar I, medieval King of Denmark, were known for their health-giving powers. In the Western world healing by the royal hand can be traced back clearly to the time of the Emperor Hadrian and reached one of its high points in England during the seventeenth century. The glandular disease known as scrofula was long called the King's Evil because of its peculiar quality of disappearing after the King's touch. Queens Elizabeth and Anne and King James II healed by touch. In 1633 Charles I cured a hundred patients in one swoop. His son, Charles II, was famous for his healing and, according to the statistical compilations of the age, he touched for cure during his lifetime one hundred thousand of his subjects. The French kings also were noted for their healing powers.

The therapeutic power of the kings of Europe fell away from them with the disintegration of belief in the divine source of their authority. They themselves lost confidence in their own gifts. William III refused to heal by touch. When crowds came to be healed he ordered them to be given a dole. One day, being practically forced to it by his advisers, he laid hand on a suppliant, saying, "God give you better health and more sense." Each French king, according to tradition, was to lay his healing hand on a leper brought to the court. The turning point in the power of the French kings occurred at the moment when Louis XVI, with the wretched man kneeling before him, asked one of his courtiers for a glove.

Louis XIV claimed the right of God; Napoleon claimed the right of the people. So divine puissance left the kings.[11] The power of healing, like the right to command, never was thought to reside in the secular ruler but was considered a gift of God to the royal lineage. Hence usurpers of the throne were not supposed to have the power unless they had a legitimate family connection. The idea, however, that the power of ruling was inherent in the people (sometimes the power was thought to have been given the people by God but not always) led to the decline of royal healing, though it has not yet fully disappeared where, as in England, there is popular faith in the monarchy.

The idea of divine or priestly healing, however, is of even greater importance and greater universality. The word "medicine" itself is based on the names of Greek healing gods, Medos, Mede, Agamede. All saintly healing reflects the belief that God can cure through holy men who are closer to His power and goodness. Jesus cured because he was the Son of God. "And devils came out from many, crying out, and saying, Thou art the Son of God. And rebuking them, he suffered them not to speak, because they knew that he was the Christ" (LUKE 4:41). Lourdes cures because it is a sacred place identified with divine intervention. All priestly psychotherapy too shares in divine power along with the great healing temples of the world such as those of Aesculapius and Imhotep, the Roman and Egyptian gods of healing.

There is one gesture by the therapist in political and religious healing that often plays an essential role—the imposition of hands. "And when the sun was setting, all they that had any sick with divers diseases brought them unto him; and he laid his hands on every one of them, and healed them" (LUKE 4:40). To understand the communication in this simple gesture one must remind oneself of two things learned in this chapter about the nature of authority and the plight of the sick in soul.

Moral authority is responsible for knowing or making morality. The parent is a giver of morals and law. The king is too, and so is God. The state, be it monarchy, aristocracy, or democracy, upholds in its laws a legal model that is part of a larger and more comprehensive moral model embodying the precepts of religion. Together, morality and the law, far from being solely prohibitive, furnish the pattern of a man's life. They give organization to his personality and purpose to his world, and make possible the community.

The plight of the mentally ill person is that for him the pattern is somehow obscure, conflicting, disordered. The world about him, too, has no meaning. How could a world without direction or purpose have meaning? How could a world without clearness of right and wrong have any meaning but an evil one? He had meant to do no wrong. It was just that he knew no steady standard to tell him what is noble and ignoble, and there was no way of finding out. And then came that fearful knowledge—he had done a great wrong. Others now seem not to have this turmoil. They are not like him. They can govern their passions. The beast in them is not too strong. They do not love or hate the same things in the same way. They do not even want to do the things he does. They have a pattern to live after. He is estranged from them, alienated from them, abnormal, stained with guilt, outside the pale.

The blessed touch of the hand from a knower or giver of morality brings the lost soul back to the community. It says, Your sins, whatever they are, we do not care even to know them, they are blotted out, God has forgotten them, you are one with us again, my son, see this hand, this touch upon you, it brings you back to us.

All well and good, this tactile communication, but what does it have to do with modern secular psychotherapy? Sometimes it has much to do, as in the following practice of a female therapist.

> If I say "I am cold," I mean that the temperature of my environment is low. If the schizophrenic says "I am cold," you can take it that she does *not* mean that—she may mean "something that matters to me is cold, deathly, and still, inside me," or alternatively, something like "I am utterly alone.". . . I just happen to believe in it and deal with that remark by cuddling the patient up close to me to convey that, although she could not have the intra-uterine warmth back, she could have close physical contact, which, as life goes on, more than replaces the loss.[12]

Contact or touch from a healer, then, may signify a rescue from isolation and a restoration to the community. This is new now—neurosis is a moral disorder and moral disorder is an estrangement from the community. Indeed it leads to a new theory of psychotherapy. Morality and law, it would seem, organize the personality. One cannot talk about cure without talking about morality and law and community, yet modern secular psychotherapists do it all the time. It is the right moment then to examine their ideas of what cure is.

CHAPTER SEVEN

The Four Walls of the Modern Healer

Like the strange person who crosses the dark streets of a dream, a hint has several times entered these pages: perhaps modern psychotherapists know not how to heal. They may even—but is this possible?—they may even aggravate the disorders they seek to cure. Then they would be sorry physicians indeed.

Among moderns the psychoanalysts have thought and written most about the process of curing. The principal theories of therapy have been developed largely by psychoanalysis. The other psychotherapies, whether they acknowledge their indebtedness or not, generally employ some variant of a psychoanalytic view of therapy. Of the many theories one can identify six of a major order.

These theories are not necessarily distinct. Some therapists hold to one of them, others use one or another emphasis without theoretical preference. Sometimes one theory has developed from the weaknesses of the other; sometimes one follows another chronologically in the history of modern therapeutic ideas; sometimes the six theories are variously combined in one mold, at other times they are used singly. The shortest method of presenting them, however, may be to treat each one as distinct, while giving at the same time fuller consideration to the two more important theories, namely, the fourth and sixth in the order to follow. In this way one can stipulate that whenever any of these theories are found combined, the same considerations will apply that apply to each singly. One thus can be assured that the many different combinations and special emphases found in therapeutic practice will not be slighted.

Oddly enough there is one theory which all writers on cure refer to as belonging to some other school than their own. This is the theory that health is reached if the symptoms of the disease are removed. No school claims this theory as its own but can find examples of it, if not in other modern schools, among the ancients or especially the primitives. A cure of symptoms is supposed to be most unworthy because, should the so-called underlying factors not be removed, the symptom will reappear, perhaps in its original form, perhaps in a novel shape. Thus a man whose symptom, a spasm of the masseter muscles of the mouth, was removed by treatment, newly developed a spasm in his left foot. Sometimes, however, an obvious symptom gives way to one less apparent. A woman whose symptom was attacks of asthma found herself rid of them after treatment but became greatly depressed, miserable, and irritable with her family. A girl afflicted with agoraphobia, the fear of going into the streets, was cured of it.

> She came in for follow-up and said she had had no recurrence of her agoraphobia. There was a change, however, in her appearance and personality. Previously she had been attractive looking with considerable sex appeal and complained that men were always being irresistibly attracted to her. Now she looked very plain, used no make-up and spoke in a flat voice instead of a throaty one. Her dress was unbecoming and she said that she could no longer find clothes that were becoming to her. She had one further complaint—boys were not interested in her and she never went out on "dates."[1]

These cases merely illustrate one of the theoretical difficulties of psychotherapy—separating the disease from the symptom or sign of the disease. But one thing can be depended on, that no therapist wishes to get the reputation of being only a temporary healer, least of all the primitive who, if he failed in his community, was not at liberty to start afresh in another city. There is no evidence to support the allegation that primitive or ancient psychotherapists as a class were merely symptom-removers.

Another theory of cure is that of catharsis. The idea is that the mentally ill person has something pent up within him and has only to let it spill out of his mouth, one might say, for relief to occur and cure to take place. It was only a matter of time, however, before psychotherapists began to ask themselves why the patient could not speak about the things he held inside him. The question led them to speculate that there existed some inner restraining force and to formulate a third theory.

The censorious internal agent named the "superego" (Chapter Three) became the stalwart of this theory. If the superego was too severe the patient could not talk about his problems, could scarcely acknowledge them. Onto this idea was added the concept of instincts or natural drives or needs. When speaking of these drives in an unmodified natural state, the psychoanalysts termed them the "id." If the superego was too severe (the fact that the patient came for treatment was usually taken as prima facie evidence of hyperseverity) it would suppress the person's natural urges and cause him mental torture. In trying to avoid this torture he developed the signs of illness.

So according to this theory mental disorder is a result of the frustration of natural needs, especially, as it turned out, the needs of sex and aggression. Therapy, then, would result in lessening the severity of the superego and allowing the needs to be fulfilled according to reason, which was called the "ego." A good example of a treatment based on this theory was given in Chapter Four, where the therapist attempted to lessen the severity of the patient's superego, which had been built up by a "puritanical mother." A slogan arose to express this theory: Where Superego is, let Ego (or Id) be.

This theory had several weaknesses. For one thing the idea of natural needs or drives of sex and aggression never achieved a clear exposition. Whether such needs were irresistible or merely insistent was left conveniently vague. Nor did the evidence for the idea reach an unimpeachable stage. The following case, for example, was reported by Stekel, whose own work on *Sexual Aberrations* frees him of any suspicion of prejudice against the theory that neurosis is due to frustrated sexual drives.

> I once treated a case of Quinke's disease (angioneurotic edema). The patient was a lady, aged forty, who suffered at intervals from extremely disfiguring attacks of edematous urticaria of the face and hands. For seven years she had been ineffectually treated at various clinics. One of her doctors recognized that the malady was psychogenic, and for that reason had sent her to me. I handed her over to my Dutch pupil Lingbeck, who discovered the following facts: The patient, a married woman with a grown up daughter, did not secure adequate sexual gratification in the intercourse with her husband, but did so in association with a lover. The attacks of angio-neurotic edema always came on after a visit to the lover, and were obviously a self-inflicted punishment for infidelity. (Fear lest the daughter might learn of the mother's misconduct was also a part-cause.) We advised her to discontinue the extra-marital relations. She did so, and the attacks of Quinke's disease ceased.
>
> At my instance, Dr. Lingbeck brought the case to the notice of the Medical Society. Its interest lay in the fact that it invalidated Freud's opinion that an adequate sexual gratification is a cure for neurotic disorders. Here the neurotic symptoms followed adequate sexual gratification, but ceased when the gratification was renounced. When this had been explained, one of the doctors voiced his objection: the case presentation was not suitable for the Medical Society. The results had been due to chance, and had nothing to do with science. This declaration was vociferously applauded.
>
> I intervened, and said that time would show whether

Lingbeck's inference and mine had or had not been "scientific."

The patient was seated in the ante-room listening to the rather heated discussion. Her natural reaction was: "These experts do not believe that my malady was caused by my love affair. Why, then, should I deprive myself?" That very day she phoned to her lover: they made an appointment, and she enjoyed herself in the old way. But within a few hours she had a distressing attack of Quinke edema, and came ruefully to consult Lingbeck. He and I were able to convince her that the illness was a conscience reaction. Now she permanently broke off the liaison, and was permanently cured. As to the last statement, I was reassured when I again saw her several years afterwards.[2]

Although one accepted the evidence of certain needs or appetites in man, this theory had another serious weakness. The psychotherapists' own data disclosed time and again that man's drives or instincts or needs could be gratified in numerous ways. This left them with the necessity to decide which were the right ways and this they—being scientists—could not do. One psychotherapist recognized the problem and illustrated it thus:

If, for example, the 17-year-old daughter of a National Socialist dignitary suffers from hysterical attacks as a result of repressed desire for sexual intercourse, this desire, in the psychoanalytic treatment, will be recognized, to begin with, as an incestuous desire, and will be rejected as such. So far so good. But what happens to the sexual need? According to the above-quoted formulation, the girl is "liberated" from the shackles of her sexuality. Clinically, however, it looks like this: When the girl, with the aid of the analysis, frees herself from her father, she liberates herself only from the toils of her incest wish, *but not from her sexuality as such.*[3]

Two methods were hit upon to cover up the moral decisions that had to be made. One was to give new names to what they considered the right and the wrong ways, the first being sweetly called "sublimation" and the second called variously "psychopathological" or "neurotic" or something equally bitter. The other method was to leave up to the patient the choice of ways in which to gratify himself.

Both these methods proved unsatisfactory. If a patient, say a homosexual, were to choose to retain his homosexual ways and yet feel greatly benefited by talking to the therapist, he should be considered cured, it was felt, or at least greatly improved. Yet according to the first standard the patient had failed to sublimate and so could not be considered cured; according to the second standard, although the patient had elected to keep his homosexuality, the therapist could not quite bring himself around to believing that the choice was a healthy one. Perhaps thinking of what the layman might say about such a notion of health, the therapist felt uneasy.

The fourth in this series of theories of therapy, one long favored by Freud, is superior to the others in several respects. It contained some of the ideas of the preceding theories but essentially was built around the idea of the unconscious. From the start psychoanalysts were impressed by the fact that the patient seemed to be driven by motives of which he was unaware. To explain this fact the analysts used Freud's theory of the unconscious, that events occurring in the past can have been banished from consciousness (by the superego) and yet can influence continuously the person's life. Further, the analysts found that certain events of the past were critical in that they permanently wounded the personality. Every neurosis, they discovered, had far down deep in the past a wounding experience of some kind which left a lasting and unhealing sore. When the patient in talking with his analyst uncovers or remembers such an event, the theory goes, he has gained insight (a word that became a technical term) into his problems, and soon thereafter the cure follows.

In this theory illness is the result of the memory of a critical emotional experience, banished from awareness but affecting the patient so that he acts abnormally. Therapy hinges on the patient's recovering this memory. Once aware of it, he can abandon his illness and act in the light of reason.

Before long this theory was extended into a concept of perfect health as full possession of the memories of the past. The man of true mental health was like an archaeological reconstruction or like the librarian's dream of having every book back on the shelves, no gaps anywhere. In effect this meant of course that no man could have real health unless he had been psychoanalyzed and that the opinion on psychoanalysis of any man, no matter how learned in the subject, if he were not himself analyzed, at best could be only the opinion of an intelligent layman. As in the mystery religions, the uninitiated could not hope to comprehend the mysteries.

The facts supporting this theory were important. They revealed that the past was not dead. They could have been used, as they were in the previous chapter, to prove false the "state of good nature" theory of man. No, they had to be used therapeutically. That is, they had to be used to make concealed moral judgments. The discovery in the patient's neurotic acts of links with the past were used to discredit these acts and to move him to abandon them. Instead of saying that the patient's ways of securing gratification were bad, they were traced to the past, described as being on various earlier levels (oral, anal, and so on) or subtly deplored as "infantile," "immature," or "regressive."[4]

Psychoanalysis and much of the writings affected by it embarked on vast criticisms of education, politics, and religion through what the logicians would call an *argumentum ad hominem*. Whatever other men were doing in the world, if it was disliked, could be traced to their infantile motives. If what others were doing was not disliked, no tracing of motives was necessary. But so much was disliked that the psychoanalysts became like the paranoiacs they sometimes treated—whatever was said or done, they stuck to the trail: what motive? what interest is served by the statement or deed? what purpose is

SEVEN: THE FOUR WALLS OF THE MODERN HEALER 139

pursued? They sniffed for motives in every chink and cranny. They forgot that the question was not, What are the motives? but in terms of its goal, Was the deed the right deed? In the rash of motives they were able to dig up, they forgot that the question had ultimately to be answered one way or another.

Upon this theory rests psychoanalysis' claim to an intellectual superiority over all other therapies. If another school does not reconstruct the past, its patients will never know the mainsprings of their action. Holding as it does that the way to health is to know all about oneself, this theory suits the modern hankering after knowledge, however indiscriminate. Furthermore one can be sure that this is the very theory that most psychoanalysts—if they did not begin to speculate on motives —would bring forth in objection to the theory here presented of neurosis as moral disorder.

Moral disorder indeed, they would cry, we have been waiting to say this for a long time. The moral disorder is not the one you point to but one that reaches down into the deepest levels of the personality, away back beyond the ages of five or six. *There* is the real source of the neurosis, in the conflict between superego and id. *There* is, as you insist on calling it, the moral conflict.

Sooner or later this important and influential theory would have had to be answered. It might as well be now.

One cannot say of any adult that an event in childhood resulted in unresolved conflict. The child, if he attained adulthood, must have come to some solution of his problems. No matter how dependent or shy, he must have been able to enter into relationships with other persons. No matter how rebellious or recalcitrant, he must have conformed to the family's minimal standards of restraint. He managed to live with his parents or other early authorities until adulthood. They did not imprison, kill, or abandon him. It is only in adulthood and with other adults that he can be said to have a problem. If the patient is having difficulty with other persons now, it is this difficulty and not his relationship to his mother that is most important. He somehow got past his difficulties with his mother but the current problems he cannot manage.

A man comes to the psychoanalyst. He is troubled by his passion to whip persons on the buttocks. The analyst after unraveling the patient's past finds that as a boy the patient wanted to beat his mother. This, the therapist would then say, is the real problem. But take another look at the case. The boy may have wanted to whip his mother but he did not, nor did he suffer intolerably from wanting to do so. Suppose now that he had lived in that certain social stratum of England which, if one is to believe Iwan Bloch, considered caning a remarkably good way to excite the sexual passion. In such a circle the urge to whip buttocks, far from being thought a problem, might have constituted a sign of belonging to the elite. The person, then, never would have had an insoluble problem, and the desire to beat his mother, if satisfactorily checked in childhood, would have been considered a normal transition to later adult sports and pleasures.

Another person comes to the psychoanalyst. He has struggled hard in life to get to the top. He always wanted to become the general manager of the firm. Or perhaps he always wanted to become the commanding officer of the regiment. Finally he gets the desired post. Then, curiously enough, he suffers a nervous breakdown and is forced to give up the position he coveted for so long. The analyst, rolling back the carpet of the past, learns that as a lad the patient had felt guilty whenever he tried to supersede his father, whether in the mother's affection or in gymnastics or drawing figures on paper. This, the analyst would say again, is his real problem. But once more the same objections can be raised. In childhood he did wish to supersede his father and did feel guilty about it whenever he succeeded in any way. Still he survived childhood, and how can anyone say this guilt was a problem unless he accepts some standard of moral manhood with which it conflicts?

Again suppose that the patient had lived this time in a hereditary aristocracy or a caste society where aspiring to the highest positions was treated with contempt. In such an event, if the person by some stretch of the imagination did go to a psychotherapist and told him that he aspired after an exalted position and then, when he might have had the plum, he had instead a nervous breakdown, the response would have been, "Well, what's your problem? You richly deserved a breakdown, didn't you?" And if, in even wilder imagination, the therapist proceeded to examine his patient's past, he would have said, "Obviously, by instilling this guilt in you, your father gave you good training. The Oedipus complex was properly resolved. If anything, your father was a little too lenient. You never should have thought of supplanting your betters."

So the therapist in a democracy passes one judgment, the therapist in an aristocracy passes quite another. Both base their judgment of the past on their belief of what their patient's conduct should be in adulthood. That childhood event which one culture might consider wounding or traumatic or a poor resolution of the Oedipus situation, another culture would consider excellent training. The standard of adult conduct is the key. With this realization the problem is brought forward again onto the current scene.

Even without realizing this, many analysts have begun to doubt the truth of their theory. They complain that a patient may have a fine intellectual appreciation of his problems, that he may know his past as only a man who has spent years under analytic tutelage looking backward into it knows it, and yet he is not cured. They cite cases where cures seemingly have occurred without lengthy retrospection. They look about for another theory.

The concept of the unconscious on which this theory is based comes in also for a share of the abuse. Persons troubled by a sense of sin done or thought will not want to talk about it, even to themselves. As a consequence they often probe the therapist's attitude thoroughly before they will confess to him the acts they believe evil. They want to make sure he will not be horrified. The modern patient might hesitate a long time before telling his therapist of a homosexual dream. If after lengthily sounding out the therapist the patient finally reports the dream, the period of hesitation probably would be interpreted as a period of unconsciousness of the dream and the minute of narration interpreted as the minute of insight or awareness. But in a land where homosexuality arouses less indignation the patient would have told his dream without hesitation because he knew in advance that the reaction of his therapist would not be horror. In the religious temple of Asclepius much less difficulty was involved in a male patient's reporting a dream of "lying with a boy." Sometimes patients will broach the subject in several versions, one worse than the other, until they are convinced that the therapist means what he says when he promises he will not blame them. Then they let out the true story. To assume that all this time the correct version lay in the patient's unconsciousness is unnecessary.[5]

Finally the idea of the psychologically healthy man as the one who has recovered by excavation all of his memories, if thought about seriously, cannot be long entertained. To recapture each memory of the past, even if possible, would require a lifetime at least twice as long as that at which the process of recapturing starts. If a person at forty commences to remember the past perfectly he will require forty more years in which to do it and nothing else. That superb chronicler Marcel Proust, who did a better job of remembering things past than any psychoanalytic patient on record, never got anywhere near a complete history, and of course had to find time in the present to eat, sleep, refresh his memory by visits to old haunts, and write fat books.

Moreover the psychoanalytic process of so-called free association, discussed in Chapter Five as rules of procedure, does not conjure up the past indiscriminately but works especially on memories associated with the conflict of passions in adulthood. Chapter Six brought up the point that some of these memories were consciously banished by the family by burning into the child's conscience the opposite commandment. It was the decision of the family that such evil thoughts or deeds had better remain dead forever, that the good and the healthy man is one who does not do or think bad things. Then there are all those memories of kindness, of tenderness, of joy, of devotion, which are unrepresented by psychoanalysis and its sour regurgitation of the past.

Another theory is that cure is achieved when anxiety is removed. There is little to recommend in this idea. In the main it is like saying that a patient is cured when he is cured. But the theory has been dressed up to appear less tautological. Thus some claim that the only way to know when anxiety is gone is for the patient himself to say that he feels better or cured. The weakness in this, of course, is that for one reason or another the patient may say in effect, Yes, I feel cured, my anxiety is gone; or, No, I do not.

A young artist in his early thirties came to a psychoanalyst for the treatment of a neurosis which had had its symptomatic onset before he was fifteen years of age. He was a man of outstanding ability, who had on several occasions been offered important positions in the world of art. On each occasion, however, his acute anxiety states, his fantastic compulsions, his neurotic seclusiveness and hostility, and his disordered psychosexual life, prevented his realizing his ambitions. When he came to the psychoanalyst he had been unable to work for nearly a year, because of a purely imaginary "hysterical" paralysis of one of his arms. As a result he and his family were on the verge of starvation. For many months he was treated without charge; and during the course of that work he was able to resume his craft. He secured a good position in commercial art, and he could feed and support himself and his children, and began to pay a moderate analytic fee. The larger part of his neurotic symptoms were reduced to negligible severity, although they were not completely removed. Indeed in the end the patient acknowledged that he clung to the symptoms which remained chiefly as an excuse for not pursuing again his earlier ambitions. Nevertheless, and in spite of his obvious improvement, after an unavoidable and premature interruption of his analysis this patient became hostile. Because the psychoanalyst had not turned time back twenty years to make him the infant prodigy which he once had been, he inveighed against psychoanalysis and the psychoanalyst. In his attacks he stressed only the large amount of time which he had contributed to his treatment. Furthermore, as evidence of his unimproved condition he pointed to the fact that he was still unable to realize his earlier ambitions. Naturally he did not mention the severe and crippling symptoms which had irradiated throughout his entire life, throwing him out of work and rendering him helpless and penniless, and of which to all intents and purposes he had been relieved by the analysis.[6]

On the other hand, a patient not wishing to disappoint the therapist may tell him of the set-in of improvement and health. It should be clear, apart from the merits of the foregoing illustrations, that though he must use the patient's statement about his feelings (just as the physician must in Galenic medicine) the therapist has to have other ways of judging the process of cure. One cannot have a therapy whose only test of cure is an examination or *scrutinia* where the patient to pass has only to learn to say, "Yes, you have healed me."

The theory of cure by the removal of anxiety faces its greatest obstacle, however, in the advanced mental cases, in certain types of psychotics. Tortured by passion upon passion, memory upon memory, sorrow upon sorrow, some of these persons flee the scene and build up for themselves a world, a whole new system of beliefs, where relationships with other beings are for the most part intrusions. By keeping out unwelcome persons from this private world they manage to rid themselves of the ever torturing guilt and anxiety that plagued them. They cannot be said to have anxiety any more. Anxiety appears when others try to cure them. But according to the "elimination of anxiety" theory, these persons do not need psychotherapy. This seems a paradox.

Some advocates of the theory, however, might argue thus. The theory applies only to the neuroses; a different standard must be devised for the psychoses. If this argument be accepted it signifies two things: first, that the theory is not comprehensive since it leaves out the psychoses; second, that the theory implies that there is a difference in quality between the neurotic and the psychotic. This latter proposition of course goes against the trend of modern psychotherapeutic thought.[7] Be that as it may, the theory has limitations in addition to these.

If one should ask the holders of this view, "By the elimination of anxiety, do you mean that man to be mentally healthy should have no anxiety?" they would answer, "Not at all. Everyone has anxieties but there is a difference between normal and neurotic anxiety. The neurotic's anxiety is greater than the situation calls for."

This is shifting the ground of the theory. Anxiety alone is no longer the telltale sign of the neurosis. Instead the situation or the environment has become the distinctive mark. With this alteration the sixth and final theory to be considered is reached. It is one that gradually is coming to be the most important of all and for this reason should be given some study. For lack of an adequate name it might be called the adjustment or reality view of therapy.

Mental disorder in this theory is considered an abnormal reaction to the environment or to reality or to social reality, each meaning about the same thing. The neurotic's anxiety is "more intense than is warranted by the environment" is the way Karen Horney, a well-known psychotherapist, phrases it. Sigmund Freud says, "The anxiety in regard to it [danger] is disproportionately great, greater in our judgment than it ought to be. It is by this excess that the neurotic element stands revealed." Disease, as it has been more abstractly put, is the interrupted "interrelation of the living creature with its environment. That interrelation can be expressed in one word, adjustment."[8] Cure by this theory would mean simply adjusting the patient to the environment or society or reality.

A sharp question presents itself. Who is to judge whether the anxiety or other reactions to the environment are maladjusted? One thinks of Nathaniel Lee, the English dramatist, and his sporting remark on being confined to Bedlam insane asylum: "The world and I differed as to my being mad, and I was outvoted." The psychotherapists, one may be sure, do not intend to submit the question to majority vote. The electoral procedure, among other reasons, would be too cumbersome. Then who is going to judge the crucial matter of whether the anxiety is "more intense than is warranted by the environment" or is "disproportionately great"? The answer seems clear from Freud's remark, ". . . greater in *our* judgment than it ought to be." By "our" he may be presumed to be using the possessive pronoun of "we psychoanalysts." It is the psychotherapists who are going to be the authorities for judging reality.

The theory is interesting because for the first time one sees the realization that some sort of direction of the patient is necessary. True, the psychotherapists will use terms designed to show that the adjusting process will involve not morality but solely knowledge based on facts. Thus they speak of their work as "corrective" or "adjusting" or "interpreting" or "clarifying" or providing "learning" (they do not say "teaching"). Nevertheless the notion is present that the therapists, since they are not in the patient's predicament, know something called reality better than he does. This notion raises yet another question. If the psychotherapists are to take the patient and make adjustments as with a setscrew so that he fits reality, then they must know reality. What qualifications do they possess for being knowers of reality?

One need not raise epistemological questions here and ask what grounds, what methods, the psychotherapists have for knowing reality, or why they have chosen these grounds and methods. It will be enough to accept their own pragmatic, empirical, sensuous conception of the world and ask them how in their own view they can claim to know reality.

A glance at the typical day of a psychotherapist is like watching a scene from one of Tchekov's plays. Himself a physician, Anton Tchekov had a genuine feeling for the lines spoken by his character, the physician Astrov.

> In ten years I have become a different man. And what's the reason of it? . . . All these years that you have known me I have not had one free day. . . . This life swallows one up completely. There are none but queer people about one—they are a queer lot, all of them —and when one has lived two or three years among them, by degrees one turns queer too, without noticing it. It's inevitable. . . . I've turned into a queer fish, nurse.

The modern psychotherapist leads a cloistered life within doubly soundproofed walls. Most of his patients are not too stricken to come to his door. Since the patient is ambulatory there is no reason why the therapist might not be invalided and yet keep on with his work. As his life is cloistered so is his timetable congested. Many a psychotherapist works from eight o'clock in the morning until nine at night seeing patients, nothing else. The bit of extramural activity he does manage to squeeze in is spent chiefly in the company of men of his own kidney—other psychotherapists and patients. And his patients are not drawn from all walks of life. In the main he works with one class of patients, often depending on whether he is in private practice, in a university counseling center, in social service clinics, or in a state institution, and often depending on his inclination or skill with particular types of patients.

His house sometimes resembles a city at peace hemmed in by nations at war, becoming a center of intrigues and rumors, a place for the exchange of information and the dissemination of whispers, hints, innuendoes about the goings-on of the many cliques of therapists and patients. This may seem an abuse but is almost inevitable if one confines oneself to treating the passionate problems of persons of similar means and circumstances.

At all events, though he find time to saunter outside, the extramural contacts of the psychotherapist are not much different from the intramural. About all he knows of the current environment is the conversation of colleagues and neurotics. From these facts alone one might say that what he knows of reality is based on his patients' ideas of reality, and since the patient is the one who is supposed to be maladjusted to reality, according to the theory of cure under discussion, it follows that in due time the therapist will take on a reality of like complexion. Can the psychotherapist enable his patient to negotiate the stream of life running past the office door when he himself, having hardly dipped his toes in it, knows little of its speed, depth, or direction?

The possibility exists that the psychotherapists learned about the nature of the environment or society or reality in their training or schooling. A perusal of their schooling, however, blows away this wisp of a chance. No one of them can say, or worse yet, would care to say, that like Avicenna, the Prince of Medicine of tenth-century Islam, he has read through the metaphysics of Aristotle forty times. If they are psychiatrists or psychoanalysts they had the typically narrow education of the medical man with its virtual omission of any special concern with society. To this may have been added courses in medical psychology and a training psychoanalysis. The latter, sometimes called a didactic analysis, a requisite for all psychoanalysts and most psychiatrists, is simply a psychoanalysis of the prospective analyst by an experienced, practicing analyst. As with all psychoanalysis, the candidate is expected to trace his development back to the formative events of childhood, overcome his "psychological" difficulties, and thus arrive at a better knowledge of himself as an individual. What such an analysis tells him about society or reality is anyone's guess.

The training of the non-medical secular psychotherapist is equally narrow. The fundamental knowledge required by the

American Board of Examiners in Professional Psychology of practitioners in the field of counseling involves psychology, tests and measurements, experimental methods, and statistics. Also included are the usual requirements of practical experience or internships in clinical work. An intern, it might be noted, means a person interned. If ever any education is listed that deals with environment or society or reality, it is relegated to an insignificant mention or a figurative footnote. How then are these persons to adjust their patients to something of which they know nothing? They themselves do not know where the market place is.

That their training and way of life are out of joint with the reality they are supposed to adjust patients to has not escaped the notice of some of the psychotherapists themselves. Writing in the *American Journal of Psychiatry,* one of them holds up a mirror that gives back a reflection as candid as that of Tchekov.

> We would all agree that psychiatry is the most isolated of the specialties in medicine. . . . Am I alone in believing that unremitting association with patients of unbalanced or deteriorated minds heightens any tendency a man may have to isolation from the normal give and take between intellectual equals? Where a superior few live long with an inferior many the stage is set for attitudes and social intercourse that will impress outsiders with a sense of constraint and queerness. Unless this tendency be counterbalanced by deliberate effort to consort as much as possible with a wide variety of normal human beings, psychiatrists incur the risk of being thought "queer."

The author of this statement is not alone, as he feared he might be. Another one, writing in the same journal, for example, advises the psychotherapist to "have other interests, a balanced mental diet, lest he suffer that particular prison psychosis from being too long immured in his ivory tower, or from having played too long the role of God in the lives of his patients."[9]

There is a Yiddish proverb that says, "Knock your head against the wall—but there must be a wall." The psychotherapist knows the four walls of his office, granted, but when he speaks of adjusting his patient to society or reality he means four larger walls and these, evidently, he does not know. Therefore not only will he be unable to make adjustments but he will be unable to say what is maladjustment.

Instead of the simple theoretical exposition given in the preceding pages, another way could have been chosen to demonstrate the inadequacy of these therapeutic ideas—by pointing out that no one of them has been found to be a common factor in therapies over the world in space and time. Many therapies have existed that made no use of the elements today alleged to be essential. To judge from the ideas of mental health of other times and places, it is not necessary, for example, to have insight into the unconscious or to find a key to past events or to have a balance of expressed drives over repressed drives or to extirpate anxiety or to have a catharsis or even to talk.

Now this is the way these theories of cure stand. Some practitioners in the field define cure in the vaguest, untheoretical fashion. Psychotherapy for them deals with "the patient's inability to conduct himself in a healthy fashion in his economic, social or cultural life" or psychotherapy enables the person "to live a free and constructive life" or to achieve "self-actualization." The majority, those who have been discussed in this chapter, hold to one or more of the six theories, either singly or in combination. Freud, for instance, used all six though holding a preference for the unconscious theory. At the present time the last three rank above the others in favor, with the very last, the sixth, becoming more and more the leading theory.[10] But as was shown, when subjected to scrutiny they fall flat, all of them. These trumpeters of reality, it seems, are bad musicians.

But, someone asks, does it matter that they hold different theories, does it matter that these theories can afford them little guidance in their practice, so long as they continue to work conscientiously and so long as the patients who leave their office feel happier?

The question is well put. In effect it says that there is a remaining chance, that with all the grandiose claims and theories of psychotherapy sagging under the weight of counter-evidence there is this one chance left, is there not? The psycho-therapists themselves, in their own hearts, bank on this hope too. When one of their numbers admits he has "never analyzed a case to a finish but hopes to some day"; when another says, cure has been "a very puzzling problem for the Center"; when a psychoanalyst declares in the throes of discouragement, "I have never yet seen a person cured by psychoanalysis"; when many of them return to their offices after a symposium on the question of cure where the conversation degenerates after a time to the old sniffing for motives—to hurling charges that those who press for the definition of cure are sadistic, while those who do not are masochistic—where the sense is one of oppressive futility; when despondent over all this, the psycho-therapist says to himself, What does it matter so long as I keep on working the best I know how and so long as I know that the patients who leave my office feel better?

Nothing is further from the intention of this study than to make a captious attack upon the honest and hard work of these men. Throughout, the ideas of such men, the ablest psycho-therapists, have been chosen for discussion whenever possible. It would be contrary to the purpose here to concentrate on second-raters. Every opportunity must be given to the best thinkers in the field. The problem of mental disorder is too serious to do less than that. So what of this last chance? Is there this consolation?

The question really asks whether psychotherapists, working as they now do and without regard to claims or theories, do good on the whole. In a way the question is curious because in their daily operations they have been most unwilling to calcu-late the effect of their work as a whole. In disregarding morality they disregarded the communal nature of man. They did not keep before them the simple fact that men are found together always, that their togetherness is not that of mere spatial proximity like dots on a map of population but rather that of moral beings in interaction, morally influencing one another. Man, the creature of community, remains in community by virtue of his morality.

If man must live in community his health must be found where his life is. He does not live apart from other men. For man there can be no idea of health in isolation.

Looking then at psychotherapy as the common enterprise of a community, one rubs one's eyes before an apparition. Scattered hither and yon are crews of psychotherapists busily at work receiving and putting out human material. Observe the thousands upon thousands of patients as they stream from the modern healer's four walls.

One man, formerly impotent, may be considered cured now because he can cohabit with a prostitute, though with no one else. His therapist did not think to remember that prostitution was illegal. Nor did he know of the Talmud's words, "He who has no son is dead." Another man, formerly impotent, may be considered cured now because he divorced his wife and married another woman with whom he could be potent. His therapist was not a Catholic. A woman, wanting a career but worried about its conflict with woman's duty, established by God, to bear children, may be deemed cured if she gains the insight that not God but her superego established that duty. Her therapist did not quote to her the lines García Lorca gave to a childless woman:

> Yes, I am offended, offended and forever humbled, seeing how the wheat grows tall, how the fountains never cease flowing and how the sheep give birth to hundreds of lambs, and the dogs, and it seems that the whole field is suddenly standing on its toes to show me its lovely dozing creatures, while I feel two hammer blows here instead of the mouth of my child.

Another woman, doing well at a responsible office job, may be considered cured when she comes to the conclusion that a tailored job and a tailored suit are not woman's true lot, that women should glory in their femininity and, as Henry James (a favorite of her psychiatrist) said, women need most of all a great deal of charm, an immense desire to please, and a wonderful collection of trinkets and dresses. Still another woman may be considered cured after it is clarified for her that the unconscious notion that her love affair with a married man was sinful was causing her needless guilt and anxiety. Her therapist, too, was unmindful that adultery happened to be illegal in that community.

A homosexual man may be considered cured if he accepts his homosexuality and is content with it. His therapist said it was natural, by no means a sin, and explained the "range of sexuality" to him by way of a drawing, thus:

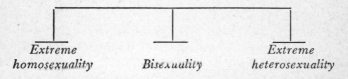

*Extreme
homosexuality*　　　　*Bisexuality*　　　　*Extreme
heterosexuality*

Another patient may be considered cured when he is able to have heterosexual affairs. His therapist once mentioned to him the time-honored belief, "And if a man live with mankind as with womankind, both of them have committed abomination," and furthermore, he said, having dabbled in Chinese philosophy, "the principles of yang and yin dominate the universe."

One man may be considered cured because he learned that he overvalued sex and undervalued sublimation. He now can quote for you: "Do you know what Krishnamurti says? 'I personally derive as much joy from touching the hand of a person I am fond of as another might get from sexual intercourse.'" On the other hand a different person may be considered cured because he came to realize that sex cannot be overestimated, being the vital drive underpinning all else. His therapist had remarked, "Yes, Voltaire hit it right when he said, *'Che sciagura d'essere senza coglioni.'* "

A wife overwrought by marital complications may be thought cured when she gets courage enough to separate herself from her husband, who could not realize, as her therapist did, that it is normal and biologically natural for women to be the equal of men in the home, in employment, in sports, and in politics. Another patient, a husband, was treated by a different therapist who believed that "a husband has got to be head of the household. If he feels secure in that, then he can share authority and responsibility."

One patient may be considered cured because he lost his rebelliousness (or his independence of spirit) and now can fill his place in society by holding down a steady job. His therapist's attitude was that bohemianism may be all right for some people but it is the mature and reliable workers who make society what it is. "I'll tell you one thing about the successful executive, or any successful man, and psychology will back me up on this," he once said. "He doesn't have the infantile idea of his superiors as being prohibitive or destructive but he thinks of them constructively as being helpful." The same therapist also held that a patient could not be thought cured unless he never had to resort to a therapist again. Another patient, a business executive, may be held cured because he no longer compulsively takes thought of the morrow (or of society's idea of success) but lets his family shift for itself, spits in the eye of the president of the corporation whom he always hated, and quits his position. (On the recommendation of his therapist he had read an article which quoted the head of a large corporation as saying, "I pay an executive fifty thousand dollars a year on the theory that he'll kill himself working in ten years.") "So spin your own wool," suggested this therapist. "Don't be dependent on others. Don't worry about what they think. Go barefoot. The Chinese coolies never get ulcers. Flaunt the demands of society if it cramps your true growth. Pursue your individual talent." He also held that it was perfectly all right for the patient, even months after his cure, to continue to visit him if he thus was enabled to tap deeper resources: the cure would be fuller and richer. "I'll see you if you call," he would tell departing patients.

Is it anything but clear that the moral directives that patients emerge with are conflicting?[11] Each crew of therapists, as one psychiatrist was not afraid to deplore, "each school of thought believes that it alone holds the true gospel and that its opponents are not merely in error but in mortal sin."[12] Like rival schools of toymakers, some want to paint the doll green, some to make it white, others red, some insist on gray. Not only each school but each therapist offers his own moral pirouettes and caracoles. If their moral directives conflict, how can the collective effect of psychotherapy in the community be good? A community is an organism and when its cells eat each other it dies. The tragedy of modern psychotherapy lies here.

These are not mere differences between societies. Everyone knows that when Gandhi fasted in India he became a hero but when a man does the same in America he is apprehended and a psychiatrist hastily summoned. The moral conflicts engendered by the healers of today are inside the community. If the basic laws in the community were thoroughly at odds the result would not be worse, for laws are only the explicit part of morality whereas morality embraces all that is alive in the law and much more that never gets written into it.

Few psychotherapists ever wonder what impact the patient's new standards will have on the persons he lives and works with. Most of them, even those who profess the reality theory, act as though each person is a self-contained unit or can or should live as one. Having no higher end than the individual happiness of a human atom, they might just as well direct their efforts to the discovery of the kind of drug, often entertained by writers of fantasy, that would keep a person in a state of constant delight until he dies with a happy meaningless gurgle.

Fortified by a new slant on morals, the patient emerges from the cloisters of the psychotherapist to rejoin the fray. Since he cannot avoid, in spite of the vociferous denials, a life of moral influence, he will infect others with his changed morality. Morals are not something to keep in your pocket or in a vault. Sometimes, in this loudly scientific age, persons go for so long without talking of them (or talk airily, instead, of "values," "norms," or "mores") that they fail to recognize that their every act involves a moral judgment. Morals are ways of life, not in a high-flown sense either, but ways of everyday life. Because the lives of men are woven together the patient's influence comes sooner or later to jar against the moral commandments given to another patient by another therapist. For as was seen, the criteria of cure and the practice of curing are not merely diverse but conflicting.

Suppose that a person of homosexual leanings learns in the authoritative setting of the psychotherapist (this one an ardent admirer of the writings of André Gide) that homosexuality is not an acquired vice but (as he read in the scientific article loaned him by the therapist), "according to our conception of homosexuality, it is a relative condition, just as dextrocardia and blondness are relative." He may emerge as one who flaunts his disease in the face of others, asserting that the Greeks were open about it, that the morally indignant should be rebuked for regarding it as a disease, that in reality they are reacting to their own hidden homosexual desires and seeking revenge on anyone who enjoys what they forbid themselves, and so on.

This person's influence will be various, perhaps enraging the man who feels that homosexuals are men who have sealed a pact with Gomorrah, or confusing the man who believes that no one's liberty ought to be infringed, or convincing the one who thinks the homosexual is only a butterfly trying to act like a man. To be more specific, what would this person's influence be on an employer or on a school board whose attention had been drawn to a scientific study which concluded that "the homosexual, not content with being a degenerate himself, must have degenerate companions, and the homosexual pedophile is ever seeking younger victims"?[13] Would either of them run the risk that this person's effect on others would be nil?

The influence of this flaunting of a disease also will meet, and theoretically it must meet, the influence of another patient of like disposition whose proclivities were regarded by his psychiatrist not quite as an evil but as bad habits which should be controlled as much as possible, as something to be exchanged for heterosexual relations (which alone were considered the mark of real cure), and if the exchange were not possible, as something that at least should not be broadcast. This man's influence may work in almost the opposite direction. He, who is trying to make no converts, who is trying to work and to marry, may hate the other for endangering his new standards and his job and his associations.

So the confusion of morals in the consciences of these two men is simply renewed in society. Although the two men, if they never collide, might be individually and temporarily happier, the community's moral conflict is intensified. Thus it goes in all the spheres where moral confusion is straightened out by the modern spiritual healer. Healers A, B, C, D, E, and F, issue standards to patients A, B, C, D, E, and F so that A clashes with B, C with D, E with F, each clash reverberating throughout the community like those balls suspended in a close series, which when the first is struck passes its impact on with negligibly diminished force to the next one and the next and so down to the end of the line.

If this process of the perpetuation of moral confusion seems somewhat unclear because of its indirect working, it ought to be recalled that human transactions take place in moral oxygen and that even the most superficial forms of contact—such as the purchase of a pair of gloves—are defined by almost innumerable conventions which enable one to understand, deal with, and rely on others. If someone is disrespectful by word or deed, for example, to an old man, you can allow the matter to pass, in which case you permit the villain to repeat his discourtesy in your presence; or you can immediately and publicly reprimand him for his unseemly conduct; or you can call him aside later and tell him he behaved badly; or you can strike him in the face at once and on the spot. Each action that you carry out is a moral one, each will affect him differently, and whatever the bodily risk to you, the last course, one dares say, will be the most effective in discouraging a repetition of his behavior. Which is merely another way of saying that the last course probably would best convince him that his type of behavior is viewed by many others besides yourself as reprehensible.

Or to take another example, which should make clear once and for all that the issuance of differing moral standards multiplies existing moral confusion: Assume that a patient A and a patient B have children. Further assume that the conflict this time is over the expression of hatred and hostility. A's therapist imparts this principle: "You certainly feel full of hate. Why? Don't you know the world is made up of well-meaning people? People are the same everywhere, more or less. These people all about you whom you can't look at now— you will find they're your friends. We're all your friends. We all love you. In fact it's the physician's love that cures the patient." B's therapist conveys this principle: "Don't be disturbed by your terrific dislike for people. The world is filled with hatred. Look at the international situation. People are full of hostility and aggression. Why feel so guilty about yours? Don't be afraid to express it. Out with it! You're not acting sadistically enough. You don't have to know someone well to hate him." Now as far as the children are concerned, what transpires? Quite possibly A raises his children in the way set by his psychotherapist, as in a garden; B raises his children as in a jungle. And there comes into being a new series of As and Bs whose irritant effects in the community will bring countless offspring into suffering to swell the coffers of psychotherapy.[14]

Moreover the patient with his immediate circle is not the only medium through which the psychotherapist spreads conflicting moral directives. Other media are used, in particular those of mass communication. The psychotherapist shows little reluctance to take to the air waves or the press. And of the making of healing books there is no end. The number of books of the psychotherapeutic variety alone, if thrown into the Potomac, would make a bridge from one shore to the other. The amplification of the psychotherapist's voice by such means gives it the authority of a Stentor and yet, though he blandly tell people how they ought to live their lives and to rear their children, his words are liable to all the failings and conflicts detailed in this and the previous chapters.[15]

When asked about mental disorder and the increasing difficulties it presents, the psychotherapist quotes figures, astronomical figures that burst the head by their very magnitude. One study reckons that "to treat only the estimated 3,375,000 cases in the country who wish to be treated we would need an army of more than 300,000 psychoanalysts." An English psychiatrist, looking back over his experience, says:

> No doubt some of you have done what I did many years ago in a flush of enthusiasm for the methods of analytic psychotherapy—which I still have. I took the most reliable figures and estimates of the number of neurotic or maladjusted men, women and children in Great Britain, say approximately three million, who were in need of treatment and worked out how many trained psychotherapists would be necessary to deal with the whole of this group spread over, say, a five-year period. The number of hours of medical time given to each patient was taken as round about twenty, a figure which is slightly below the prewar average of time given at the Tavistock Clinic. If you care to work out the figure yourself, you will find the result is somewhat horrifying and quite ludicrous. If you assume that the psychoanalytic method is the only one which gives good results, then the calculation becomes astronomical.

Today it is held that the demand is so much greater than the supply that established psychiatrists spend half of their time psychoanalyzing prospective psychiatrists.[16]

Apparently hell is empty and all the devils are here. On all sides the cry for psychotherapy is heard—in the factory, the school, the army, in charitable and social service work, in trade unions, in family and marital clinics, in hospitals, in religion, in business and government offices. Yet to no avail.

Without knowing it the spiritual healers of the time are working at cross-purposes. By sending individual patients out of the office not cured (for cure today is a mystery) but feeling happier, the total amount of moral confusion and conflict within the community is in no way diminished. It is truly written that if the blind lead the blind both will fall into a ditch.

It would be so easy to temporize, to say that scientific psychotherapy has gone thus far and made its mistakes but that now in light of full criticism it can push on to greater heights than before. Such a line would fit the modern spirit. To say it would be easy, too, but it would also be dishonest. So long as psychotherapy holds itself to its scientific role, narrowly or modernly conceived, it, tethered to its patients, will continue to stumble in the ditch.

With his genius impaired by a moral scotoma, Freud carried psychotherapy as far as could be done. The four of his brilliant students who broke away from him, Jung, Adler, Stekel, and Rank, were able to allow some small place in their therapeutic systems for the expression of moral ideas. But those who followed his steps were compelled to trace the same errors. Unable to acknowledge the moral disorder of neurosis or the moral order of health, they have had, all of them, to produce a therapy of toleration or, better, a treatment of toleration. Each stuck to the principle of not being shocked at shocking things, thinking thereby to preserve a moral asepsis. Tell us anything you want to, they advertised, we shall not think it sinful. They kept their promise, too. When the patient poured out his soul the psychotherapist by word and deed replied, "What is so bad about that? From the look on your face, one might have thought a monk was pregnant." This the therapist believed was maintaining moral neutrality. Obviously it was calling moral what the patient feared was immoral. For a fee almost all irregularities became regular. Shades of the sale of indulgences!

The psychotherapist became a merry-andrew, or as one patient put it, "Mr. In Favor." He befriended whatever the patient thought the evil side or the devil of his moral conflict. He was like the Jew in the old Arab story who, on being told by a Moslem attempting to convert him that "God wants you to become a Mohammedan but the devil won't let you," retorted with vigor, "In that case, I remain on the side of the stronger." Meanwhile his patients, both before and after treatment, wandered like poor Toms o' Bedlams given leave to beg across the countryside. Turned out into the reality that had broken them down before, they were still aliens in a hostile land. If anything, the reality had grown more intractable, with more and more persons falling under the category of neurosis and more and more psychotherapists coming forth to scramble their moral ideas.[17]

It was madness ever to think that under such conditions the health of the community could be achieved. Unable to admit morality, psychotherapists could not define health. So they became mystery-mongers, each peddling a theory of cure catholically vague enough to suit all comers and to enable all secular therapists to work under the one scientific accord: psychotherapy does not blame. No one of them could see that under this banner their collective efforts were not wholesome but harmful. There can be no doubt of it. In spite of a superficial smartness, modern psychotherapy, a hole-and-corner healing, is a failure.

It should not be thought that in this Freud or psychotherapy is alone at fault. If one seeks to correct the vision of psychotherapists so that they co-ordinate their efforts and cease grinding out confusion it will be clear that the remedy cannot be had in any of the social sciences. For instance, should prospective psychotherapists be made to take courses in sociology or in political science or anthropology? Should they read about Middletown or Greenwich Village or Yankee City? Would such training equip them to adjust their patients to society or reality?

The one who knows these fields and studies best, the social scientist himself, would answer no. He is too shrewd to say yes. Ask him if he himself knows enough of reality to fit someone else into its pattern, he becomes as coy as a dilettante coaxed to exhibit his talent. Though he is reputedly a specialist in social reality he will deny that he knows enough to fit any person to it. Furthermore, he will say, to want to adjust any person to society or reality is making a moral choice in favor of the status quo. Why should you want to adjust him? Oh no, you will not catch him redhanded, making moral decisions.

Well then, who is to help the afflicted soul? Who will bring him back to the community? Is he to be left comfortless? Is there no one to offer him a place of light and refreshment?

Religion, perhaps?

CHAPTER EIGHT

The Temple of the Religious Healer

Confession, one used to hear, is good for the soul.

Whether it is or not will be the burden of this chapter, for confession has been religious psychotherapy's favored instrument. Its pre-eminence indicates that religion rarely lost sight of the moral problem in mental disorder. Decidedly, confession contains the idea that the one who is to speak wants to speak of some wrongdoing. On this account the secular therapists, to whom the air of evil or wrongness is so repugnant, do not like to have their techniques of talk described as or even compared to confession. If anything, they prefer the word "catharsis," which was briefly discussed in Chapter Seven, but in the substitution, as so often happened, they failed to hide the moral undergirding of their work. Literally catharsis means a cleansing or a purging of the bowels. The patient, presumably, would not wish to be cleansed or purged of something good.

By no means is confession the only technique employed by religious healers. For example Chapter Three mentioned a case of temple healing which required no confession. In Chapter Six the healing touch of the hands was discussed. Here, too, talking was unnecessary. But it should not be overlooked that an understanding is present in all religious healing (Chapter Three) that the soul suffers from a moral disorder. When the person brings himself to the temple or before the religious personage the understanding amounts to a tacit admission on his part of a moral difficulty, amounts to a confession, in other words.

The prevailing religion today among the Indians of the United States and Mexico is the peyote cult.[1] An essential part of its ritual is the eating at nightfall of peyote, the button of the mescal cactus which seems to have the properties of a drug in that it may induce images. After the peyote is eaten and day begins to break, confession to a leader of the congregation takes place. The peyote worshipers believe that Earthmaker, their God, is good, that peyote is his medicine, and that whoever partakes of it will be able to free himself from the influence of evil. They further believe that a new convert should make a complete confession of the errors of his former life. The cardinal vices are thus to be vomited symbolically. One Indian, for instance, reported after confession that he felt as though he had vomited a bulldog, which he interpreted to represent his former stubbornness and pugnacity.

Crashing Thunder, a Winnebago Indian whose autobiography has been set down in writing, describes in detail the experiences prior to his own first confession. Long persecuted by the guilt of having once fraudulently told his people that he had had a vision and of having made a shambles of his life through drunkenness, living with various women, and even through implication in a murder, Crashing Thunder sets out uncertainly for a peyote meeting.

> I sat inside the lodge with them. One man acted as leader and we were to do whatever he ordered. The [ceremonial regalia] were all placed before him. I wanted to sit in some place on the side, for I felt that I might get to crying like the others [after confession]. I felt quite ashamed of myself.

Nevertheless he takes the peyote. Several meetings later:

> It was now late at night. I had eaten a lot of peyote and felt rather tired. I suffered considerably. After a while I looked at the peyote, and there stood an eagle

with outspread wings. It was as beautiful a sight as could well be observed. Each of the feathers seemed to have a mark. The eagle stood there looking at me. I turned my gaze, thinking that perhaps there was something the matter with my sight, but then when I looked again the eagle was still present. I then looked in a different direction and it disappeared. I looked around at the other people but they all had their heads bowed and were singing. I was very much surprised.

After another vision:

Then I prayed to Earthmaker, to God: "This your ceremony let me hereafter perform." . . . Again I prayed to God. I bowed my head and closed my eyes and began to speak. I said many things that I would ordinarily never have spoken about.

A third vision:

Suddenly I saw something. It was an object all tied up. The rope with which this object was tied up was long and the object itself was running around and around in a circle. A road was present in which it ought to have gone, but the object was so tied up that it was unable to reach it. The road was an excellent one. Along its edge blue grass grew and on each side there grew many varieties of pretty flowers. Sweet-smelling flowers sprang up all along its path. Far off in the distance appeared a bright light. There a city was visible, of beauty indescribable. A cross was in full sight. The object tied up would always just fall short of reaching the road. It seemed to lack sufficient strength to break loose from whatever it was that was holding it. . . . I looked at what was so inextricably tied up and I saw that it was myself. I was forever thinking of women. "This it is with which I am tied," I thought.

Not alone among half-primitive Indians but in Hinduism, Buddhism, Judaism, in all the great religions of the world, confession is found.[2] Generally speaking, in the beginning stages of a great religion or in sects or cults like the peyote just described, when the congregation is small and compact and has a sense of being opposed to the prevailing faith, confession is public. It is made before the assembled members of an intimate group rather than privately to a leader or priest. When a religion is widespread, encompassing whole cities, the sense of intimacy and militancy is diminished. In a public gathering the chances that shame will block the confessant in a public gathering increase; he feels the persons about him do not know his circumstances well enough to understand and sympathize with his failings. To maintain the institution, private confession must be inaugurated.

The well-documented history of confession in Christianity clearly reveals this process of change.[3] The New Testament refers often to the earliest forms of confession in the primitive church. They seemed typically to have a public character. "Confess your sins to one another, and pray for one another, that you may be healed," counsels James (5:16).

Tertullian, one of the early fathers of the church, instructed the penitent to observe all kinds of humiliation like fasting, groaning, weeping, falling down "before the presbyters, and [embracing] the knees of those beloved of God, beseeching all his brethren to intercede for him." Basil described the practice of daily public confession in the fourth century thus:

> Among us the people go at night to the house of prayer and in distress, affliction and continual tears, make confession to God. At last they rise from their prayers and begin to sing psalms . . . and so, after passing the night in various psalmody, praying at intervals as the day begins to dawn, all together as with one voice and one heart raise the Psalm of Confession (Psalm 51) to the Lord.

But around the beginning of the fifth century the practice began of writing out confessions and having them read before the congregation in order to spare penitents the mortification. Soon afterward Pope Leo I banned public confession entirely.

Apparently penitents were being kept from confession because of shame and also because of fear of being laid open to legal prosecution by an enemy, a further indication of how far religious assemblies had moved from the early intimate gatherings. From this time on, though with many local variations in practice, confession swung toward its private form, that between penitent and priest. The Fourth Lateran Council left no room for doubt:

> Every Christian of either sex shall, after attaining the years of discretion, faithfully confess all his sins to his own priest . . .

After these beginning words there followed the handing down of a number of decisions on matters that also had been unsettled in the previous centuries:

> . . . at least once a year, and shall endeavor to fulfill the penance imposed on him according to his ability. . . . Otherwise he shall both be withheld from entrance to the church while he lives and be deprived of Christian burial when he dies.

As the Lateran Canon decreed, then, confession became not only private but obligatory once a year on pain of separation from the church. The modern system of the Roman Catholic auricular confession dates from the time of this proclamation, A.D. 1215.

A confessional box, usually a small tabernacle of carved wood composed of three compartments, is located in the nave of the church. The priest is seated in the middle closet. His compartment is separated from the others by a grille or perforated oracle which at the disposition of the confessor may be completely closed off by a slide. The penitent in his compartment kneels on a bench, and when aware that the confessor is present and listening, puts his lips to the grating and begins his confession: "Bless me, Father, for I have sinned."

The history of Christian confession did not stop, however, with the reaching of this form by the Roman Catholic

Church. After the religious revolt that became known as the Reformation, public confession was reborn. The Wesleyan revival in England brought it back as an integral part of the Methodist movement.

The gathering at which public confession occurred became known as the class meeting. It developed out of the Organization of Bands, each band a group of five persons with one appointed the leader, who met together weekly "to confess their faults to one another that they may be healed." The number of members later established for each class was twelve but there was a tendency for the group to grow up to fifty. The leader of each class was regarded as its pastor, having direct spiritual supervision over his group. A traditional Methodist class meeting was a remarkable blend of nineteenth-century life in England and America with the spirit of primitive Christianity's public confession.

There they sat, twelve persons "having the form and seeking the power of godliness"; in the center, on the plain table, the leader's Bible; around it the circle of chairs, each with its occupant.

Generally the leader pitched the tune for an opening hymn: "All thanks be to God . . ." Followed prayer, fervent, from the heart, that the Spirit of God might be present, to expose the inmost thoughts and imaginings, and to inspire all to new heights of living, and after that the reading of a passage of Scripture, with perhaps a running fire of comment from the class leader.

"Brother Watson," the leader would demand, the reading done, "how has it been this week with your soul?"

Stammeringly, the lad from the farm just outside the village would rise to his feet. Words would not seem to come. At last with a mighty wrench, "I thank the Lord, well," he would mumble and sit down.

But the leader was not satisfied. "Praise the Lord," he would encourage, and then the probe would go on. "No wrestlings with temptations?"

"Yes." The lad's head might hang, but there was never any thought of holding back an answer.

"Did that old temper rise up again?"

"Yes."

"And did you win the victory?"

"Yes, thank God."

"Hallelujah, Brother Watson. Go on as you are, and one day the crown incorruptible will certainly be yours."

The next chair would bring a very different type of problem.

"Sister Lee, has the Lord been your support this week?". . .[4]

The Methodist class meeting has virtually passed away, and with it the reborn public confession. What is sometimes called public confession in Protestant churches like the Lutheran and the Presbyterian is really a general confession, a set form of words usually entitled the "General Confession" which the congregation repeats together. There is no personal rendition of sin or culpability but merely a blanket acknowledgment that one is a sinner, is penitent, and craves pardon.

We confess to Thee, our heavenly Father, that we have wronged Thee in so many ways. We have wronged Thee by what we have done and said and thought. We have not loved Thee as we ought. We confess that we have wronged one another. As children we confess that we have done so much that has hurt our fathers and mothers. As parents we confess that we have not always been understanding and helpful. We pray Thee for forgiveness. We thank Thee that Thou didst send Thy Son, Jesus, to make known Thy great love and Thy desire to forgive.

Lord, have mercy on us
Christ, have mercy on us
Lord, have mercy on us.

This is typically followed by a prayer of absolution by the priest for the entire congregation. In contrast to both the public and private forms the general confession pays no attention to the person's special problems.

It is not only public confession that has declined. Private confession, too, is now practically non-existent among the Protestant churches with the exception of the Anglican and the Church of Sweden (and Norway and Denmark). For the curing of souls this is a serious matter and leads one to ask why, if the churches proclaim an interest in the spiritual welfare of their people, they have lost this their principal remedy for spiritual conflict. William James, an extraordinary American psychologist, once puzzled over the same knotty problem. "The complete decay of the practice of confession in Anglo-Saxon communities," he remarked, "is a little hard to account for."[5]

A look at the criticisms of this essentially religious therapy may help explain its deterioration. Sharp points have been brought to bear against it from two quarters, the psychotherapeutic and the religious itself.

The sharpest criticism that modern psychotherapy has to make of private confession is that since the penitent has to think of his actions as sinful, he will be ashamed to speak of them. The criticism is most important because on it the psychotherapist bases also much of his so-called unmoral approach to therapy. The argument holds that if you declare in advance that you may consider the patient's actions to be sinful he will refuse to tell you of his trouble. In confession he refuses to talk of his real trouble, it is said, because he knows his behavior will be morally judged.[6]

Though sharp, this criticism is not telling, for no evidence is cited for the proposition. And there is evidence against it. First of all, as Chapter Three pointed out, feelings of guilt and shame, far from being absent, are prominent features of the person who goes to modern psychotherapists for help. What the psychotherapists call the "problem of resistance" and to which they have dedicated many learned discussions is just this phenomenon—the patient's reluctance to tell of his shameful deeds or thoughts. Thus the psychotherapists' own example does not strengthen their case.

Secondly, confessional documents show thoughts and deeds being spoken of no less frankly in church than in the sinless office of the secular healer. The psychotherapist knows of no actions of men which are unknown to priestly confessors.

Taking an example from medieval times when confession was not in decline, one will see that the kinds of sins encountered by confessors were similar to those encountered by psychotherapists today. The handbooks devised in the early Middle Ages for the use of confessors were called penitentials. They were designed to guide priests in prescribing penance for confessants and for this purpose they contained lists of sins generally met with by confessors. These sins were sometimes grouped within the headings of the Ten Commandments and at other times placed under such sections as "Of Greed," "Of Pride," "Of Lust," "Of Falsification," "Of Dejection," "Of Anger," "Of Dishonor to Parents," "Of Drunkenness," "Of Usury," "Of Fornication," "Of Matters Relating to Marriage," "Of Superstition or Magic," "Of Petty Cases," "Of Gluttony," and so on. If one wishes to find the sins often discussed as "sexual manifestations" in psychoanalytic cases, one has merely to look under such headings as Lust or Fornication.

OF FORNICATION

If anyone commits fornication with a virgin he shall do penance for one year. If with a married woman, he shall do penance for . . .

He who after his twentieth year defiles himself with a male shall do penance for . . .

Sodomites shall do penance for seven years, and the effeminate man as an adulteress.

He who often commits fornication with a man or with a beast should do penance for . . .

As for boys who mutually engage in vice, they should be whipped.

> If a woman practices vice with a woman, she shall do penance for . . .
>
> If she practices solitary vice, she shall do penance for . . .
>
> She who has a husband deserves a greater penalty if she commits fornication.

And these canons go on through instances and imaginings of incest, adultery, perversion, and others reminiscent of the work of sexologists of the late nineteenth century like Havelock Ellis, Krafft-Ebing, Hirschfeld and their twentieth-century carry-over, Kinsey.

Under such a heading as "Of Anger" one might find many of the thoughts and acts that the modern therapist would circumscribe with his heading, "Aggression." Under "Of Superstition" or "Of Magic," where many psychotherapists are inclined to put cure by faith or religious healing, such a question as the following might be found to be put to an adulteress.

> Hast thou done what some are wont to do? When first they learn that their lovers wish to take legitimate wives, they thereupon by some trick of magic extinguish the male desire, so that they are impotent and cannot consummate their union with their legitimate wives. If thou hast done or taught others to do this, thou shouldst do penance for forty days on bread and water.

Under "Of Dejection" and "Of Drunkenness" one could discover the cases nowadays treated as melancholia and alcoholism. However, for a number of these old headings, such as "Of Greed" or "Of Pride" or "Of Falsification" or "Of Usury," there are no equivalent modern cases, an oddity which will be returned to in the next chapter.

It would be strange indeed were one to find no sign at all of a disinclination to speak. In these handbooks a suggestion to the confessor sometimes appears for encouraging the reticent person. The priest is advised to say upon encountering "resistance":

Brother, do not blush to confess thy sins, for I also am a sinner, and perchance I have done worse deeds than thou hast. Therefore I warn thee in these things, since it is a habitual fault of the human race, as saith the blessed Gregory, both in falling to commit sin and not to bring out by confessing what has been committed. . . . We blush to confess at least in words, and in the presence of a man who is like to ourselves and perchance subject to the same passions. . . . Let us then freely confess what we have committed under no one's compulsion.

But it is hard to see that confession was lacking in what the modern psychotherapist considers frankness.

Another psychotherapeutic criticism is that confession, being an admission of sin, offers enlightenment to neither priest nor penitent as to the causes and circumstances of the sin. This simply is not the case. All the types of confession described above except the general form require the penitent to trace the history and circumstances of his acts. Even in the primitive form of public confession there is a discussion among the brethren of the causes and circumstances and the possible remedies for each confessant's deportment. In the Wesleyan class meeting the leader was under instructions carefully to inquire into how each soul prospered; both during and after confession a discussion took place of the conditions that led to the confessed acts, including recommendations for avoiding them. Penitential books as far back as the early Middle Ages reminded confessors frequently that they must carefully distinguish that "all persons are not to be weighed in one and the same balance, although they be associated in one fault" but that there must be a discrimination among cases. Among other things the priest was taught to differentiate

between rich and poor; freeman, slave; little child, boy, youth, young man, old man; stupid, intelligent, layman, cleric, monk; bishop, presbyter, deacon, subdeacon, reader, ordained or unordained; married or unmarried; pilgrim, virgin, canoness, or nuns; the weak, the sick, the well. He shall make a distinction for the character of the sins or of the men: a continent person or one who is incontinent willfully or by accident; [whether the sin is committed] in public or in secret; with what degree of compunction he [the confessant] makes amends by necessity or by intention; the places and times [of offenses]. . . . Further . . . "In judging be merciful to the fatherless as a father, and as a husband to their mother."[7]

One sees, too, that in the length and severity of penances given the confessor took into account the causes or circumstances of the act. A wife with many children who committed abortion because of poverty was to do a lighter penance than an unmarried woman who did the same to avoid shame.

As for the private confession today practiced in the Roman Catholic, Greek Orthodox, Swedish, and Anglican churches, the penitent is supposed not only to enumerate the deeds or thoughts that lie heavily on his conscience but also to state the circumstances under which they occurred and whatever facts or conditions might throw light on their nature. For his part the priestly confessor is supposed to serve the penitent as physician and teacher, to diagnose his difficulties, and give him admonition and advice concerning the correction of his faults and his future conduct.[8] So for the modern as well as for the medieval physician of the soul the prescription of the penitential book has significance: "For no one can raise up him who is falling beneath a weight unless he bend himself that he may reach out to him his hand; and no physician can treat the wounds of the sick unless he familiarize himself with their foulness."

It is more likely that what the modern therapist is objecting to in this instance is not so much the inability to get at causes but the lack of a theory of causes that conforms to his own theory of neurosis and mental disorder. But admitting this immediately puts the argument on a different plane. The Roman Church, for example, has a theory of a human nature as consistent and well elaborated as any school of psychology or psychiatry. If it has its flaws, so have the theories of psychotherapy, which were shown in Chapter Seven to be based on therapeutic interviews set up in a way to produce facts to support the theory. Also one could be more hospitable to the psychotherapist's theory of causes or of human nature if he were better able to demonstrate the success of the therapeutic work he uses it in. This surely would be an admissible claim but so far it has proved impossible to make.

The theologians themselves, however, can add other arguments against confession and these, too, should be heard. By far the great proportion of religious criticism has been against two features of auricular confession.[9] One of these is its obligatoriness. The Lateran Canon quoted earlier maintained that every Christian should confess at least once in the year. Now, unthinkingly, one might remark that confession once a year does not seem to be too much of an obligation in light of the thousand other forms of compulsion in everyday life. But one would probably be missing the point, and the point is easy to miss, for these religious criticisms of confession have been used in the seemingly endless battles of vituperation between Protestant and Catholic apologists. Consequently a short clarification of the nature of church membership may be necessary.

Every church has its rules of membership. If a person wishes to be a member of a church he has to follow these rules. They may be informal and few—for example acceptance of a simple creed or church attendance—or they may be formal and numerous—say participation in many sacraments. The forms for cutting off a member from the brethren, too, may be formal or simple, an elaborate excommunication or a mere general acknowledgment that So-and-so does not appear any more. Simple, complex, formal or informal, these rules exist and operate. If one objects that a person may be a Protestant without ever going to church or confessing a creed, the reply should be that a person may be a Catholic, too, under like circumstances. In the competition of these two bodies for members they have become quite willing to consider anyone whose parents were one thing and not the other to be ear-marked in some vague way for their own corral.

But if a person considers himself a member of a church, he believes in its doctrine and in general does not view it as restricting his freedom. So to say to a believing Roman or Orthodox Catholic that confession is a compulsion would be like saying to a Presbyterian that he is forced to believe in the Westminster Confession of Faith or to a Lutheran that he is forced to go to Holy Communion.

It is lack of comprehension of this fact that leads the Protestant theorist to say that confession cannot be worth while if it is obligatory. The answer is that the Catholic feels compelled no more than the American feels compelled when he is vaccinated against smallpox. In turn the Catholic can reply that the Protestant is influenced not to confess because every time he may wish to confess he must go through difficult special arrangements with his minister or priest. In this interchange there is a prime example of a point made earlier (Chapter Six): each side believes that the other's beliefs are restrictive of liberty, not realizing that their beliefs are what give both sides their own sense of freedom.

Perhaps it is not asking too much of Protestants and Catholics to agree on this one point, that if a man thinks he has gone a whole year without sinning he should confess at least to the sin of pride.

Apart now from consideration of any particular church, the idea that confession should be made at least once a year has two advantages which should not be submerged by the effusions of therapist or theologian. First, it takes away any stain of abnormality from the act of confessing. The one who goes to confession is in no sense especially sinful. Second, it can provide a system of preventive therapy by lifting away guilt before it accumulates to fearsome proportions. But more of these two considerations later.

The fourth criticism of confession is that in it the priest

must guarantee God's absolution of the penitent's sins, and to do this is not possible for Protestant clergymen. The flagrant example is in Roman Catholic confession where the priest at the end may say, "Wherefore I absolve you of your sin in the name of the Father, and of the Son, and of the Holy Ghost." (*Deinde ego te absolvo a peccatis tuis in nomine Patris, et Filii, et Spiritus Sancti*).

Certain it is that here again is a point around which Catholics and Protestants find it more enjoyable to engage in mutual vilification than in joint exploration. Though many may not remember it, John Calvin in the *Institutes of the Christian Religion,* the Protestant counterpart of Thomas Aquinas' *Summa Theologica,* provides open ground for ministerial or pastoral absolution.

> Here are three things, therefore, worthy of our observation. First, that whatever holiness may distinguish the children of God, yet such is their condition as long as they inhabit a mortal body, that they cannot stand before God without remission of sins. Secondly, that this benefit belongs to the Church, so that we cannot enjoy it unless we continue in its communion. Thirdly, that it is dispensed to us by the ministers and pastors of the Church, either in the preaching of the gospel; or in the administration of the sacraments: and that this is the principal exercise of the power of the keys, which the Lord has conferred on the society of believers. Let every one of us, therefore, consider it as his duty, not to seek remission of sins any where but where the Lord has placed it.

A Bishop of Durham in the seventeenth century, John Cosin, took occasion once to examine the agreements and differences between the Church of England and the Church of Rome. In the matter of the private and final absolution of penitent sinners he found agreement. At another time he had this to say: "The Confession is commanded to be special. The Absolution is the same that the ancient Church and the present Church of Rome useth. . . . If [a man] hath committed any mortal sin, then we require Confession of it to a Priest, who may give him, upon his true contrition and repentance, the benefit of Absolution, which takes effect according to his disposition that is absolved. And therefore the Church of Rome adds to the Form of Absolution *Quantum in me est, et de jure possum, ego te absolvo* (As far as in me lies, and to the extent of my lawful power, I absolve you)."[10]

This phrase *quantum in me est* is still used in the absolution of Roman Catholic confession. Moreover not only is there this reservation but also if there is no true contrition or repentance, if the so-called penitent does not feel genuinely remorseful and wish to reform, the confessor's absolution—it makes no difference how exalted the priest—is invalid. Repentance inside as well as outside is held to be necessary. Again, since both Catholics and Protestants are Christians believing that Jesus' mission was one of proclaiming God's mercy to the sinner who has faith and genuinely repents, what more would they have?

In fact the use of the phrase *ego te absolvo* is unimportant. Those churches that claim the Apostolic Succession, such as the Greco-Russian and the Roman Catholic and the Churches of England and Sweden, all tend to use a language reflecting the belief that their authority is a commission of Christ, handed to them in an unbroken chain of churchly descent. The unimportance of the language will be clear if these criticisms can be set aside momentarily for a look at what confession actually accomplishes.

"For him who confesses, shams are over and realities have begun: he has exteriorized his rottenness. If he has not actually got rid of it, he at least no longer smears it over with a hypocritical show of virtue—he lives at least upon a basis of veracity." This is the psychologist William James speaking. Pierre Janet, the psychotherapist, expressing himself more professionally, joins him: "Regular confession appears to have been invented by a genius of a psychiatrist."[11]

Why should confession work? Not all churchmen know the answer. Why should catharsis work? One of the early paragraphs of Chapter Seven implied that the psychotherapists, not knowing the answer, did not develop a theory of catharsis.

The essential part of confession is not that something bad is brought up and spilled out. It is not the telling of the sin that counts. To quote a previous page: "Neurosis is a moral disorder and moral disorder is an estrangement from the community." Then for a confession to be healing it must be made to one who represents the community. Still this is not sufficient, still the patient may thirst after health. The one to whom he confesses must make him whole by bringing him back to the community. Jung recognizes this necessary aftermath of a confession when he declares, "It is only with the help of confession that I am able to throw myself into the arms of humanity, freed at last from the burden of moral exile."[12]

It is in this way that the words "health" and "hale" and "whole" are related. One has neither wholeness nor health when separated from the community. The patient and the penitent must be restored by syllables or by signs, a touch of the hand, a prayer, an *ego te absolvo,* a sprinkling of clear water, or words that echo these: "I will forgive their iniquity, and their sin will I remember no more." The formula is not important. Whatever the mode, forgiveness is the promise and act of receiving the errant person back into the community.

What is the difference now between the psychotherapist's works and those of the religious healer? The one practices a therapy of toleration, the other a therapy of forgiveness.[13] The one says, "What you have thought or done is no sin, for sin does not exist"; the other says, "What you have thought or done is sinful yet you are forgiven." Which is superior, the therapy of toleration or the therapy of forgiveness? The therapy of forgiveness. And why? Because, first and last, it is truthful. It does not conceal from the person that the problem is a moral one.

The result of toleration therapy was evident in the previous chapter—a perpetuation of moral confusion. A toleration therapy degenerates whatever moral standards remain. A therapy of forgiveness contains its own moral law. It never lets the moral springs of action go unrecognized. It can declare boldly that pride is evil, it can be firm in saying that to dishonor your parents is bad, it can be just in holding that some things are not sinful—because it has a steady standard to follow. When applying this standard, all confessors, all healers, work not at odds but together. Thus does a therapy of forgiveness build moral unity. In short, a therapy of toleration corrupts morality while a therapy of forgiveness maintains it.

Yet is it not strange that this method of healing is gone from the Church? Even in the Roman Church it is on the wane.[14] Wherein lay the flaw? Many persons have the idea that for the Protestants it was a matter of voluntary abandonment, that reformers like Luther and Calvin were responsible because they demanded the abolition of confession. But they had no intention of doing away with confession. On the contrary, it was one precedent they wanted to retain. Calvin's teaching already has been presented briefly. The minister is by his calling "appointed to subdue and correct our sins." Ministers are said in Matthew 16:19, 18:18, to remit sin and to loose souls. A soul in distress should seek relief and consolation "by private confession with his pastor."

Luther's teaching is direct and crystal-clear.

HOW THE SIMPLE FOLKS SHOULD BE TAUGHT TO CONFESS

Confession consists of two parts: first, to confess our sins, and secondly, to receive the absolution of forgiveness bestowed by the confessor, as from God Himself, and not to doubt thereof, but firmly to believe that our sins are thereby forgiven in the sight of God in heaven.

What sins should we confess?

To God we are to confess all sins, even those that we do not recognize, as we do in the Lord's prayer; but to the confessor we are only to confess such sins as we know and feel guilty of in our hearts.

Which are they?

Examine thyself according to the Ten Commandments, whether thou art father, mother, son, daughter, master, mistress, manservant or maidservant, and see if thou hast been disobedient, unfaithful, and idle, whether thou hast done anyone an injury by word or deed, whether thou hast been dishonest, negligent, slothful, or hast otherwise caused harm.

I pray thee, friend, tell me a short form of confession. Answer. Say thus to thy confessor: Worthy reverend master, I pray you hear my confession, and declare absolution to me for God's sake.

Say thus: I, a poor sinner, confess myself guilty of all sins before God; in particular I confess to you that I . . . But if thou know of none (though this is wellnigh impossible), then mention none in particular, but receive upon the general confession which thou makest to the confessor before God.

Thereupon the confessor shall say,

God be merciful to thee, and strengthen thy faith. Amen.

Further:

Dost thou believe that my forgiveness is God's forgiveness?

Answer. Yea, reverend sir.

Then let him say,

As thou believest, so be it unto thee. And, by command of our Lord Jesus Christ, I forgive thee thy sins, in the name of the Father, the Son, and the Holy Ghost. Amen. Go in peace.

But if any are sorely afflicted in their conscience, or sorely grieved and tempted, the confessor will know how to comfort them with various words of Scripture, and how to lead them to faith. This is merely to serve as a general mode of confession for the simple folk.

Protestants cannot say that the decline in private confession among them was due to the express intent of the Reformers. The reason must lie elsewhere.

It was said above that religion rarely lost sight of the moral element in neurosis. It never failed to rebuke men for their sins. But the pastor who tries to heal souls by rebuking sin will soon learn that solely to blame is not enough.

The churches forgot the lesson of forgiveness, How they forgot it and why is beyond the reach of these chapters. Nonetheless they did forget it, as Protestant theologians in their writings over the past half century seem to perceive.[15] The intensity and haste with which the puritanical and pietistic strains of Protestantism attempted to change men's nature left no time for forgiveness of the flesh. In a fury also to loose themselves from all things smelling of the Roman Church— an ambition that did not impel the Reformers—they eventually let private confession fall into disuse. When they met with sin, in or out of confession, they were shocked, horrified, uncomprehending. Obsessed with man's sinful nature, they ignored the teachings of their masters. Men cannot live with their sin, they disintegrate. Nor would it have been of any use to try to hide their feelings from the penitent. Just as the psychotherapist, mightily though he try, cannot hide his feelings from a person whose senses are sharpened by desperation, so too will the clergyman fail. This is what the theologian Hocking has in mind when he says, "It is true that the moral element of judgment may be so far censorious as to inhibit the beginnings of confession, and this may be the temperamental disqualification of the Protestant clergy as a class as hearers of confession."

Perceptive secular therapists also have noticed this in their patients. "For the Protestant there is only SIN," says one. And another, "The pastor's hesitation strikes [the patient] as a traditional prejudice, which estranges them from one another. He asks himself: 'What would the pastor say if I began to tell him of the painful details of my sexual disturbances?' He rightly suspects that the pastor's moral prejudice is even stronger than his dogmatic bias."[16]

Usually when Protestant writers set out to consider the value of confession they praise it broadly for two minutes and then devote hours to excoriating the Catholic variety, leaving the impression that all private confession is vicious. The auricular confession of the Western world has been in experiment for over a thousand years. This certainly makes it worthy of careful attention. It would be most improbable that a thousand years of a healing ministry could be fruitless of psychological discovery. This confession has gone through numerous stages both to perfect itself and to conform to changing conditions. And one thing found in the literature of the experiment is the reminder, in season and out, that the confessor must treat the confessant forgivingly, mercifully, must pour oil and wine on his wounds. Protestant leaders, unwilling to learn from the more recent past, hankering rather after the primitive past, had to learn this lesson the bitter way.

The price they paid, though they do not know it yet, was the disappearance of religious healing and the rise of secular therapy. Men condemned of sinning had to seek forgiveness outside the church, so much hell was raised by pious little fellows. But men lost to the religious community will seek salvation elsewhere.

A priest has a church and a religious community to and for which he is responsible. A magician has an *ad hoc* clientele and is responsible to himself, a small god. Ages torn with discordant faiths breed magicians. In primitive communities that come in conflict with civilization this proves to be the case. Magicians rise to compete with the shamans. It is also the case in the Western world today. The numbers of psychotherapists and the claims of magical cures reach stellar proportions.[17]

But forgiveness is the unique possession of the community with its moral structure. Return unto me, it says, and I will return unto you. When this promise was not given, men had to find someone who would give it. They became like those Catholics who lived in the parish of a moral martinet instead of a fatherly confessor—they sought excuses to confess to a priest of another parish. Who would forgive them?

The medical men rose to the occasion. Some of these smart sons of Asclepius, sensitive of the need, invented new words and ailments for sickness of the soul. Medical men could not forgive, but their medical ailments had no need of forgiveness. The change was not wrought overnight. At first the penitents were unsure of their new confessors. Freud was so surprised when one of his early patients quickly began talking of sexual matters that he asked him whether he knew of his theories. The young man, in truth, had come across some of Freud's writings. Generally, however, when psychoanalysis started it spent much time explaining to patients that it considered nothing sinful. It called the patient's hesitation "resistance," and the length of time it took to convince him drew out the length of analysis interminably. Today the sinless idea is the best-known feature of psychotherapy and daily brings patients to the door. What Freud thought was hampering the acceptance of psychoanalysis, namely the public outcry against sexual tolerance, was really what in the long run brought in the business. This more than any other reason is why today many psychoanalysts find that they can use a shorter treatment.[18] The patient does not hesitate as long as he did before to confess his sins, to state his moral problem.

Jung, who is one of the few to have seen the clergy being ushered out, says:

> The wave of interest in psychology which at present is sweeping over the Protestant countries of Europe is far from receding. It is coincident with the general exodus from the Church. Quoting a Protestant minister I may say, "Nowadays people go to the psychotherapist rather than to the clergyman."[19]

The swing toward secular healing happened not because psychotherapy proved itself more successful—this it could not do—but because it removed guilt by toleration. People flocked to the priests of an outside parish, the secular healers.

Of course under the tutelage of medical men mental disorder changed. It took on body. If doctors of medicine were accepting guilt-consumed patients, what better way to be sure of acceptance than to present them with physical symptoms? Remember what was said especially in Chapter Six about the influence man has over his bodily condition at certain times, about the effect of man's early authorities on pain and perception and the like, about the similar effect of hypnotism with its analgesias and paresthesias, about that most ancient theory of the spirit's domination of the body. Then try to put yourself in the place of the wretched soul.

> I too have known a man who told me that he had often experienced these tortures, though only for a very short time, but so strongly and infernally, that no tongue can speak of it, no pen write of it—yes, that no one can believe it who has not himself experienced it. They were of such a kind that if they had increased and had lasted for only half an hour or even for only the tenth part of an hour, the man would have wholly perished and all his bones would have burned to ashes. . . . So there remains nothing for man [in such moments] but the naked longing for help and the terrible cry of fear and he does not know where to ask for help.

Would you not say, "Yes, yes, I am sick. The pain is in the bones of my left arm, sometimes, but it travels, and sometimes I feel I can't walk, it strikes my legs, and I can't sleep the pain is so unbearable." Or would you say, as did Martin Luther, the author of those lines above,[20] "At such moments God appears"?

One begins to understand why it is estimated today that 50–80 per cent of all persons who bring their ailments to clinics are considered psychiatric or psychoneurotic cases. One understands why a "new" branch of medicine called psychosomatic has been rediscovered. One understands why patients begin to acquire private repertories of disease which they play for their doctors with all the skill of virtuosi—first it may be a spastic colon with spitfire diarrhea, then perhaps floating-kidney symptoms, or a left-sided migraine combined with aching feet, facial eruptions of the rosacea complex, hypochronic anemia, difficulty in swallowing, neuritis of the left arm or fibrositis of the left shoulder. A very old Chinese proverb has it that the son of the good sorcerer is generally killed by demons while the son of the good doctor usually dies of disease. Today's children are sons of the doctor.

Uncounted numbers of persons, it is now being discovered, suffer from psychosomatic afflictions—that is, from bodily disorders produced by mental disturbances, including for example asthma, ulcers, allergies, migraine, essential hypertension, and "cardiac neurosis."[21] This should not be interpreted to mean that a new branch of medicine has been discovered, or that many illnesses were never before properly diagnosed, or that there has always been a fairly constant percentage of psychosomatic illness which is just now becoming recognizable. Rather is it that the new field developed because the cases appeared as symptoms of the times, a result of the "medicalizing" of psychotherapy.

The neuroses, it should be understood, are contagious. For this reason Plato wanted the demented kept at home and for the same reason military officers in combat must instantly pull out of sight the man who begins to crack. Neuroses are not infectious in the common medical sense. They are not transmitted by germs but by all the signs of human communication. The person of distressed mind is as suggestible as a woman pregnant for the first time, acquiring new symptoms and cravings with every new story of pregnancy she hears. In the days when Athens was loud and litigious about democracy Aristophanes described in *The Wasps* a mental case who went about scribbling on walls, "Lovely Ballot-Box." Neurotic symptoms follow patterns based on communicative proximity and can be traced by the neat methods of an epidemiologist.

With all the coddling of physical disease that goes on today, it seems the community will not be allowed to die without the prescription of the physician. Whereas one needs to know the religious beliefs of peoples of the past to comprehend their spiritual disorders, for the modern scene one needs a medical dictionary. As symptoms become more and more somatic the presence of the spiritual healer seems to be an anachronism, a hangover from some superstitious past. With the decay of confession no other good instrument was left. Clergymen concerned with the cure of souls then had to make a choice. Either they could hitch on to the wagon of secular psychotherapy or they could go on to prescribe the innocuous nostrums for mental disorder that have been the treasure of general practitioners since Hippocrates—fresh air, sunshine, rest, good music, good food, and all the other things that everybody dreams of getting enough of, someday.

The clergymen chose the former course.[22] Forward-looking clergymen today demonstrate their broad-mindedness by attending the lectures of the psychotherapists, lamenting only now and then that the therapists do not reciprocate. They write books showing how religion can survive the glare of psychotherapeutic facts. They frequently ask for co-operation between psychotherapy and religion, which is to say they beg the psychotherapists to give them some little chore to do in connection with healing. Also they complain that in his cases the secular therapist often snipes at religious belief, a well-justified but futile complaint. They are, however, of much comfort to the aged.

Against all this the beleaguered clergyman falls back on one defense. The truth is, he might say, that we cannot really use confession. Every man has the right to listen for himself to the voice of God, to say, "It is to me that God speaks, directly to me, not to the priest who thrusts himself between." Each man's conscience is supreme. If we use confession we must forgive, and who are we to forgive others? "By what authority doest thou these things?" asks Matthew 21:23. And so we ask, what authority do we have to forgive those who confess before us?

Modern religion, then, the house where people might find God indwelling, is cold. Healing is dead in the modern church. It has no peace to offer the strife-torn soul. The doors of the temple are closed.

CHAPTER NINE

By What Authority?

The one excuses and the other blames; the one plays, the other weeps. It is time for the turning point in the argument. Which of the two should heal?

First the psychotherapist—by what right does he heal? As a doctor of medicine or a scientist he has no right. He has no special knowledge of morality. Mental disease is a moral disorder. Moreover if he must make moral decisions and give moral guidance in his work, he is not a scientist in the present-day conception of the term. Then his current basis of authority founders, for he is respected for his science. All right, he is *not* a scientist. But then by what right does he set himself up to give moral direction? At one time he could say that his methods of curing were successful and that success entitled him to his healing authority. But under examination his success could not be demonstrated, and now that this claim is weakened, that authority, too, will begin to slip.

Well, someone might propose, the authority may take a long time to diminish; in the meantime the core of morality in mental disturbance has not yet been recognized; furthermore the clergy is not assuming the task; therefore the psychiatrist and the psychoanalyst and their co-workers might as well continue with their treatments. This justification will not be offered by psychiatrists and psychoanalysts, however; they will understand that it is unworthy of them. Dante put medical fakers and charlatans in hell. But others less bound by professional honor might make such an argument. It is similar to the last-ditch stand seen in Chapter Seven. This time still more force can be brought against it.

Who cares how the question is decided, whether the physicians or the divines should heal, or whether they should bury their differences or "collaborate," to use today's expression? Who wants to play Iconoclast or who Defender of the Faith? Whether the one group or the other tries to heal is unimportant, but please let there be healing. This there cannot be without truth for both the healer and the sick. The consequences of the existence of falsehood between the psychotherapist and the patient are what should make the physician admit, like his colleague in *Macbeth,* "This disease is beyond my practice."

Consider this: not only do the secular therapists not cure but in claiming for themselves the realm of psychic healing they have given rise to medicine-mongering. The medical or clinical view of psychotherapy makes for the appearance of medical or somatic symptoms and the sale of patent medicines. The extremes to which this trend has gone was not presented fully in the last chapter.

The conflict of passions in moral disorder leads to guilt, of course; guilt involves a need for atonement (or punishment, as psychoanalysts say); atonement, too, can be made in bodily ways. Today the strange phenomenon of a craving for surgery is prevalent enough to command attention. It is called "polysurgic addiction," and reveals persons going to the surgeon with one complaint after another for which there is no remedy but to cut them open, either remove or not remove some tissue, then sew them back up again until the next time.[1] Surely the penitents of less enlightened days never thought of this way of atoning for their sins!

In the campaign for scientific and clinical psychotherapy the reputation of the so-called prescientific ages has been given the worst possible blackening. One never hears of the milieu therapy of 280 B.C. when the son of King Seleucus was sick. Erisistratus, who acted as the psychotherapist, had all the women of the palace come into the room and pass before the prince. When his stepmother approached his color changed, perspiration appeared, his body trembled, and his heartbeat accelerated. Erisistratus recommended that he be allowed to marry his stepmother, which was done and the patient got well. One does not hear of the medieval case of the madwoman of Basil who continued for a whole month dancing in public. The magistrate provided a definite rota of strong men to dance with her in succession and without any intermission until she was exhausted and could no longer stand. She was taken then to the hospital where by degrees she completely recovered. Nor does one hear of the excellent moral therapy done in Arabic Spain of the fifteenth century. All that one gets as the picture of psychotherapy before the scientific dawn is Bedlam and the chain and the whip. The prison called Bedlam is gone today but what of the chain and the whip?

There is a complete modern approach to psychotherapy which so far has not been discussed because it claimed to work through means other than the communication of healer and patient, and because any earlier in the book its full significance would not have been appreciated. Furthermore, since it is a development of the medical and clinical conception of the psyche, it can be considered more pertinently here. In the Western world the approach stems from Hippocrates, who broached the idea that because one can sometimes find in the brain of a mentally deranged person traces of organic decomposition or damage, mental disorder is caused by so-called natural or biological factors. That organic damage to the brain or other parts of the body can cause odd behavior is beyond doubt but it is making an illogical jump to conclude from this that mental disorder itself is caused by organic abnormalities. The reverse is true, namely that mental disorder can, and in ages like the present often does, cause changes in the body. The autopsy is therefore of little value in tracing the etiology of mental disorder. It reveals the results more than the causes.

But the organic or biological view of mental disorder leads to the belief that in the body one can see all of the soul. Accordingly the psychotherapist begins a search for physical causes and physical cures.

In modern psychiatry the physical orientation has led to the use of shock therapy, a method based on the application to the patient of electricity or drugs (insulin, cardiazol, metrazol) that cause convulsions. The treatment is entirely modern. All its varieties are products of the twentieth century. Everything used is sterile and mechanized. There is no resemblance to Bedlam's dirty cells. The patient, however (already the dissimilarity begins to end), is strapped down, and the electric shock or drug injection given. At this moment one should resort to the description of a veteran observer.

> The patient may experience the seeing of flashes of light (stimulation of the visual centre), the taste of burnt matches (gustatory centre), the smell of phosphorus (olfactory centre), a widespread feeling of heat in the body (sensory area or ? the hypothalamic area), or, what is more usual, the patient may be conscious of movement in his body (motor area) which is objectively verifiable more frequently and easily than in connection with the other areas. . . .
>
> Examples of the aura as described by the patients were previously given and were summed up as "terrifying in the extreme." This fact is equally obvious when judged from an objective viewpoint. To plunge headlong through the ward window and thereafter betake an extremely hurried, unorthodox, barefooted and half-clad exit from the hospital in an endeavour to avoid "being roasted alive in a white-hot furnace" (the aura experienced) ; to scale with an easy facility in a matter of seconds on to the roof of the hospital (the repetition of which act took half an hour by his attendants) to escape from an aura which he could only describe as "an aghast shuddering"; or even the possibility of suicide rather than the experiencing of the aura, are but extreme examples of the

actions performed rather than submit to the cardiazol injections. . . .

Yet another point in connection with the aura is that patients are extremely reluctant to describe this and still more so to discuss it. Such descriptions as "like looking on God and Satan alternatively" or "like a great swell of water flowing over me" are only arrived at by dint of much perseverance on the part of the interrogator in the face of obvious reluctance on the part of the patient . . . —for instance, in the immediate pre-convulsion phase they may have exclaimed with a scream, "O God, my head!" Asked if they have ever felt anything of special note in the head as a result of the injection, they may confess after much coaxing and after considerable agitation that they felt "as if the skull bones were about to be rent open and the brain on the point of bursting through them." The above is an actual example of the steps one usually has to take before one arrives (frequently at the expiry of 15 to 20 minutes) at a fair description of the aura experienced, and to which their previous descriptions such as being electrocuted were but steps on the way to an acme of indescribable fear and terror, each ultimate aura arrived at being peculiar to each patient. . . .

And even the patients themselves will frequently admit that the aura experienced beggars even the description which they have given. It is something, they say, that never before have they experienced or even remotely conceived of, and, having said so, they state that it is on account of this that they desire treatment to be stopped, or inquire, as they eagerly expect the answer they desire, "How many more injections am I to have?"

These patients live in the constant fear of the recurrence of the aura. By further questioning it is eminently apparent that intimately bound up with this fear is the feeling of utter helplessness on the part of the patient while the aura is being experienced.

This feeling of utter helplessness seems to the writer to be of great significance, reminiscent as it is of descriptions of primal anxieties, and its objective presence is beyond all doubt. To hear a grown man (grandiosely convinced that his piano-playing must equal that of Chopin and his tenor voice in song surpass the mellow richness of Caruso) feverishly implore the aid of his mother (whom he knows to be dead for years) to rescue him from the dire terrifying predicament into which the cardiazol injection has plunged him; or to be frequently stayed by the appeal, as one turns to lay down the emptied syringe, of "Don't leave me, doctor!" (the doctor having been temporarily endowed with the attributes of the good mother) ; to hear an elderly woman, the mother of several children and who endured years of heroic toil amidst poverty to raise them, bemoan with despair how all is darkness and she the sole inhabitant of the darkness; to hear a frenzied and ear-splitting appeal from a woman to save her from being suffocated; to hear the despairing cry of another woman as she is falling, falling, falling through an illimitable inky nothingness: these few examples illustrate situations in which the patients are quite unable to help themselves.

The fact of the appeal to the doctor not to leave the patient in the midst of the aura, and other similar circumstances, such as holding on to one's hand or arm, immediately raises the question of transference, whether this relationship, either positive or negative, between patient and physician is established and, if so, to what extent it influences the improvement or recovery of the patient. . . .

The fear which the patient undergoes does not stop short with the completion of treatment or the dismissal from hospital. This fear is shown even when patients are examined months afterwards (e.g. to obtain an electrocardiograph check-up), when through the façade of apparent mental well-being there protrudes this feature of fear long continued. For when they are again asked to lie down on a bed (even though it be in a general ward of the hospital instead of a mental observation ward) to have an electrocardiogram taken, one again witnesses the same (though attempted disguised) behaviour as during treatment—reluctance to lie down, to undo a costume, roll up the shirt sleeves and trouser leg, or, when they are suitably arranged in bed, one sees functional tremors, detects markedly increased cardiac action, catches a rapid scrutinizing glance to see if there is a cardiazol tray in the vicinity, or a brave, resigned smile as equally devoid of amusement or mirth as their mental state is fraught with apprehension and fear. Indeed the question has been put usually in a feigned jocular manner, "Are you sure I'm not for more treatment?"

One even meets with cases who after dismissal from hospital have successfully transmitted this fear to their relatives, by, for example, a patient who utilized his waking hours by the detailed recounting of all his subjective sensations and experiences met with during active treatment, so successfully indeed that his mother complained of her "blood running cold" several times a day, and of her newly-developed reluctance to stir unaccompanied beyond the threshold of her house in the late evening.

Particularly is this state of continued fear apparent in cases who have "recovered" as a result of treatment and are waiting dismissal from hospital. Case 5, for example, despite her apparent well-being, had to be repeatedly reassured in reply to her frequent inquiries that she was due for no further injections.

In this connection, it is note-worthy that a normal [i.e., ordinary medical] patient with a physical condition is seldom so affected as to be continually referring to treatment which made him well, even though it may have been extremely unpleasant and distasteful.

This is the kind of cure of which a recent article on "Physical Treatment" says:

It is probably true to say that convulsion therapy now holds the field as the most effective single remedy in the whole range of psychiatry in relation to the number of patients deriving benefit from the treatment. Its uses should not be restricted to the mental hospital and any general hospital which is not offering the public this form of treatment is not discharging its responsibilities to the sick public.

But, says the scientist, "How does the treatment work? I think it is quite fair to say that we do not have the remotest idea."[2]

Now why do they not have the remotest idea? Is it because the patient's body and limbs are not left stained with blood? Sometimes the police use a rubber hose and there is no mark on the body. Have not these medical specialists had general practitioners send them patients with such a note as "He has silly, irritating obsessions; couldn't they be knocked out of his head with shocks?" Have not they had a parent or relative say, "He has been an awful nuisance; we have tried everything for him and are fed up; wouldn't a few electric shocks knock the nonsense out of his head?" And have not they offered the sick public, in particular their discharged patients, the benefits of this therapy only to find that they refuse to return voluntarily out of pain and fright? Come now, what is this treatment but a beating?

As physical punishment or torture it will have its effect on the patient. The chain, the whip, the alternating hot and cold plunges, all physical therapies, have made great claims for success through the ages. "By this method," says one seventeenth-century therapist, "the mind, held back by restraint, is induced to give up its arrogance and wild ideas and it soon becomes meek and orderly. This is why maniacs often recover much sooner if they are treated with torture and torments in a hovel instead of with medicaments." Failure is not the reason for abandoning such therapies. The reason is a moral one: the treatment is brutal.

This does not necessarily mean that the inventors or users of the convulsion method were looking for a substitute for the chain or the whip. The psychiatric fledgling studying the subject today finds that most accounts of the treatment do not speak of the effects above described. They usually say that there are no ill effects or discuss whether one of the various methods works better than another, electric shock better than drugs, for example. But one credible account of horror, only one, any one, should have been enough to spin experimenters and users around to face the fact that these diverse techniques all have as their one object a convulsion. Do they mean to say that a convulsion is a pleasant thing, nothing but a thrill on a large scale?[3]

It may be that patients even so should be subjected to the treatment but first the moral grounds have to be determined, and this the therapists have not done. The only grounds they present is that they want to eliminate suffering. But why do they say that the patient is suffering? He himself has not asked to be tortured; he has not strapped himself to the table. The kind of patients who suffer are the kind who come to the psychotherapist voluntarily—that is, the neurotics, not the psychotics. Indeed, running down history are many records of the happy state of most psychotics. One finds such cases mentioned in the writings of Aristotle, Heraclides of Pontus, Horace, and Dryden. Horace's case, a well-known citizen of Argos, berated those who called in the doctor.

> . . . *Ah! cruel friends! he cried.*
> *Is this to save me? Better to have died,*
> *Than thus be robb'd of pleasure so refined*
> *The dear delusion of raptured mind.*

Today unusual psychotherapists may admit this. In referring to the claim that such methods "diminish the sufferings of the chronically insane," one of them has this to say:

> But contrary to the belief held by the lay public and to some extent even by doctors, the greatest amount of mental suffering is met with, not in psychotics, but in neurotics. Over 50% of the inmates of mental hospitals are schizophrenics, the great majority of whom are emotionally indifferent, the maniacal patients are thoroughly

happy, the senile and other dementias vegetate in a
thoroughly contented manner; and the confusionals do
not know how they feel.[4]

Obviously individual happiness cannot be used as a justification for the physical treatment of these patients. So the problem of what constitutes cure intrudes itself once more.

As the matter stands, then, the procedure is immoral.
Though it is undoubtedly cleaner than the maligned practices
of bygone days, the treatment itself may or may not be as
brutal. Once one gets into the refinements of cruelty, one cannot say exactly.

Another unfortunate result of the medical or physical view
of derangement is its tendency to locate the malady in the head
or the brain or the mind. From this notion has evolved the
phrase *mental* disorder. But "mind," says the physiologist
Sherrington in a mood thoughtful and eloquent,

> Mind, for anything perception can compass, goes there-
> fore in our spatial world more ghostly than a ghost. In-
> visible, intangible, it is a thing not even of outline; it is
> not a "thing" It remains without sensual confirmation
> and remains without it forever. Stripped to nakedness
> there remains to it but itself. What, then, does that
> amount to? All that counts in life. Desire, zest, truth,
> love, knowledge, "values," and, seeking metaphor to eke
> out expression, hell's depths and heaven's utmost height.
> Naked mind.

The signs of neurosis can appear in body as well as brain.
A passion can be said to belong to the mind or the stomach or
the genitals or even, yes, even to the heart. Such attempts to
place derangement in the head recall the game that Michael
Faraday used to play with his schoolmates. He would stick his
head between the bars of an iron fence and challenge them to
say on which side of the fence he was.

It is more accurate to say that the disorder is not mental
or cerebral but moral and thus involves the whole man. It is

not a passion but a conflict of passions that causes the sickness. And the presence of this clash between the right and wrong passion entitles all moral disorder to the name schizophrenia—a split in the soul.[5]

To Freud's everlasting credit, he broke with the entire psychiatric slant and tried to get the patient to tell him of his grief. The secular psychotherapies that originated in his efforts and with which this book has been largely concerned have never succumbed to the lure of switches, straps, and injections. Thanks to his genius, these psychotherapies and not the others dominate the Western sphere. The one who could say that "to be alive is to the ego the same as being loved" would not be tempted by gadgets. Unfortunately Freud was himself a nineteenth-century medical man imbued with the glitter of Science and, though not one of the scratch-a-physician-find-an-atheist kind, he did have an antipathy for Jehovah. He never fully let go his hope of grounding his theories in biology and physiology, nor did he see the broader religious implications of his findings.

But now that the medical men can be shown to have no authority for healing, what about the religious claim? The curious thing of course is that here where there is a solid foundation there is also a denial of the possession of authority. The churches, while recognizing themselves to be deeply concerned with morality, fear to practice forgiveness. Without a daily ministry of forgiveness all the perfumes of Arabia will not bring healing back.

If the priest or minister takes the extreme position that the individual's conscience should reign supreme, the individual cannot be helped. Nor is there under this notion any need for a minister. To whom is he to minister? Himself? What is his calling?

God's silence has been often a trial to men. To circumvent it, however, by saying *Christus pro me* or God is mine, is in me, and is known to me alone, does not open up your ears to heaven. The result is a poor pretense at private hobnobbing with God, an only-child religion that hopes to woo God into a *folie à deux*.

You run about this earth, whispering and listening, and though the voice is there it is not there for you. In the end you crawl back to secular psychotherapy. And do not think your position is more independent before the small gods. Let the psychologist, one of America's best today, tell you how to go confess to the lay confessor: "If you can afford it, pick a trained analyst whom you respect, and enter into the experience humbly and without reserve, prepared to render up the whole confused welter of your being." You do not have to kneel but you may be asked to lie down on a couch. You do not have to bring frank-incense, your gold will suffice.[6]

All psychotherapy is evidence against the doctrine that man needs no provision for human moral guidance. The doctrine is certainly not true Protestantism. Luther considered himself a churchman by the grace of God. That was his vocation. He was called to minister and teach, to give selfless service to mankind, to mediate between God and man for his fellow men.

If one believes in an authoritative book instead of an authoritative apostolic succession, one yet must depend on men—to teach one to read German instead of Latin; to teach one what to read, the Bible and not the Koran; to teach one what parts to prefer to read, the New rather than the Old Testament; and so on. "The authority of man is, if we mark it, the key which openeth the door of entrance to the knowledge of the Scripture." And Richard Hooker went on to explain: "The Scripture could not teach us the things that are of God unless we did credit men who have taught us that the words of Scripture do signify these things."

The framers of the American Constitution were wise enough to realize that even a short document needs a body of select men to interpret it, and an unequal number of them at that, so as to guarantee a decision when the issue is tied. The written word never has been precise enough to dispense with the necessity for human interpretation.

Lawyers know this very well. Much of their prolixity is an attempt to avoid an ambiguous meaning. Thus they may write in a lease that the lessee should not mar, deface, damage, injure, or destroy the property. Yet judges are not on their way out of existence. To suppose that the written word in religious or secular law will do away with human dependence is a sandy illusion. Sooner or later in order to maintain the fiction it results in the retailing of falsehood.

Psychotherapy has already been caught in this predicament (Chapter Five) where to keep up the game of the invincible "I" it has been forced either to keep pushing the pronoun "You" at the patient or else to resort to outright deception. "Indeed," concludes an earnest therapist, the patient "must almost forget that it was us who put him upon the right track, and must find the truth for himself. So far does this instinctive distrust of everything instructional and authoritative go, that an insight already acquired by the patient may be once more imperilled if he is reminded that he got it from us."[7]

The doctrine of moral independence, it must be repeated, was not a creature of the Reformers who thought only of man's service to man. It is rather the infiltration into religion of the secular individualism of the Enlightenment. But it is just because of the belief in the sufficiency of the written word without human interpretation and emphasis that Protestantism has come to an ironic impasse. Having come to life with the proclamation of an absolute reliance on divine forgiveness, Protestantism finds that without men of the stature and confidence of the Reformers it cannot continue to proclaim this forgiveness. "And what they since have stammered," mourns the poet Rilke, "are only the fragments of your old name."

There is much that is vindictive today in the reluctance to help men by forgiveness. If the clergyman had no right to forgive, where did he get his authority to be unforgiving? For that is what he was whenever he drew back at confessed sin. His feeling toward those who still believed in forgiveness was one of envy. Nathaniel Hawthorne, who can speak for the Protestants if anyone can, was most fair to the Catholics, too, in *The Marble Faun.* One of his two main comments there on

auricular confession is put in the thoughts of a central character, Kenyon, who finds himself in Rome:

> For here was a priesthood, pampered, sensual, with red
> and bloated cheeks, and carnal eyes. . . . Here was a
> population, high and low, that had no genuine belief in
> virtue; and if they recognized any act as criminal, they
> might throw off all care, remorse, and memory of it, by
> kneeling a little while at the confessional, and rising un-
> burdened, active, elastic, and incited by fresh appetite
> for the next ensuing sin.

There is fear here, and envy. "Look at the X's" cry the Y's.
"They can sin and we can't." But who said they can't? They
can and will sin, shamelessly and uninterruptedly, and their
sins, red like crimson though they be, will be forgiven . . . if
they themselves can forgive. For to forgive one must love, and
he who loves much is forgiven much.

Hawthorne lent his words to a character who at the time
was in a morbid mood. "An imaginative man," explains the
author, "he suffered the penalty of his endowment in the
hundredfold variety of gloomily tinted scenes that it presented
to him." The other portrait of confession in the same book is
longer and more personal, involving the confession of Hilda, a
daughter of the Puritans.

> In the hottest fever-fit of life, they can always find,
> ready for their need, a cool, quiet, beautiful place of
> worship. They may enter its sacred precincts at any hour,
> leaving the fret and trouble of the world behind them,
> and purifying themselves with a touch of holy water at
> the threshold. In the calm interior, fragrant of rich and
> soothing incense, they may hold converse with some saint,
> their awful, kindly friend. And most precious privilege
> of all, whatever perplexity, sorrow, guilt, may weigh upon
> their souls, they can fling down the dark burden at the
> foot of the cross, and go forth—to sin no more, nor be
> any longer disquieted; but to live again in the freshness
> and elasticity of innocence.

"Do not these inestimable advantages," thought Hilda, "or some of them, at least, belong to Christianity itself? Are they not a part of the blessings which the system was meant to bestow upon mankind?" . . . If she had heard her mother's voice from within the tabernacle, calling her, in her own mother-tongue, to come and lay her poor head in her lap, and sob out all her troubles, Hilda could not have responded with a more inevitable obedience. She did not think; she only felt. Within her heart was a great need. Close at hand, within the veil of the confessional, was the relief. She flung herself down in the penitent's place; and, tremulously, passionately, with sobs, tears, and the turbulent overflow of emotion too long repressed, she poured out the dark story which had infused its poison into her innocent life.

Hilda had not seen nor could she now see, the visage of the priest. But, at intervals, in the pauses of that strange confession, half choked by the struggle of her feelings towards an outlet, she heard a mild, calm voice, somewhat mellowed by age. It spoke soothingly; it encouraged her; it led her on by apposite questions that seemed to be suggested by a great and tender interest, and acted like magnetism in attracting the girl's confidence to this unseen friend. The priest's share in the interview, indeed, resembled that of one who removes the stones, clustered branches, or whatever entanglements impede the current of a swollen stream. . . . And, ah, what a relief! when the hysteric gasp, the strife between words and sobs, had subsided, what a torture had passed away from her soul! It was all gone; her bosom was as pure as in her childhood.

And then:

"Absolution, father?" exclaimed Hilda, shrinking back. "Oh, no, no! I never dreamed of that! Only Heavenly Father can forgive my sins; and it is only by sincere repentance of whatever wrong I may have done, and by my own best efforts towards a higher life, that I can hope for

His forgiveness! God forbid that I should ask absolution from mortal man!"

But as was said more than once before, the *ego te absolvo* phrase is not a necessary part of confession. All that is necessary is some sign that the person recognizes to signify his restoration to the community, his redemption, in other words.

> The old priest shook his head. But, as he stretched out his hands at the same moment, in the act of benediction, Hilda knelt down and received the blessing with as devout a simplicity as any Catholic of them all.

The priest, the minister is needed. And right now he is needed to say to men that this is true, certain, and without falsehood—God does not lie when He gives His promise of forgiveness. This is as good news as it was in the days of the Redeemer.

The churches that believe they are carrying out Christ's direct commission and those that believe they are fulfilling His words and those that have the slightest knowledge of His short stay on earth, know what forgiveness meant to Him. Were He to appear among them today they would feel His reproach. For He would say to them, "What would you more, another crucifixion?"

Leave the clergyman to bemoan his deservedly outcast state. He had the knowledge but he had not the love. He therefore lost the authority to heal and now can be left to keep his museum piece, the church, in faithful repair. It is among the psychotherapists that one finds in rare instances a willingness to forgive. On the way to recovery one patient explained to her healer:

> You remember [she asked], when you once came to see me and I was in a wet pack and asked you to take me out? You went for a nurse and I felt very resentful because that meant to me that you were afraid to do it yourself and that you actually believed that I was a dangerous person. Somehow you felt that, came back and

did it yourself. That did away with my resentment and hostility toward you at once, and from then on I felt I could get well with you because if you were not afraid of me that meant that I was not too dangerous and bad to come back into the real world you represented.

The same psychotherapist has another case:

> The only sign of contact he gave to me or anyone was to indicate by gestures that he wanted me to stay; all that he said on two different days during this period [of a month] was: "Don't leave!"
>
> One morning after this I found him sitting naked and masturbating on the floor of his room which was spotted with urine and sputum, talking for the first time yet so softly that I could not understand him. I stepped closer to him but still could not hear him so I sat down on the floor close to him upon which he turned to me with genuine concern: "You can't do that for me, you too will get involved." After that he pulled a blanket around himself saying, "Even though I have sunk as low as an animal, I still know how to behave in the presence of a lady." Then he talked for several hours about his history and his problems.
>
> Finally I offered him a glass of milk. He accepted the offer and I went to get it. When I came back after a few moments his friendliness had changed to hostility and he threw the milk on me. Immediately he became distressed: "How could I do that to you?" he asked in despair. It seemed as though the few minutes I was out of the room were sufficient time for him to feel that I had abandoned him.
>
> His confidence was regained by my showing that I did not mind the incident. And for eight months of daily interviews he continued to talk.[8]

The days of the saint are not past. If ever there was saintly devotion, if ever there was a calling, this is it. Here is a saint to be found and not among the casuists who say they cannot forgive because they cannot pronounce absolution or who repeat by rote the theme of a dream gone astray—prideful independent man.

It is probably too harsh to call the bulk of modern psychotherapy quackery. It comes close to it, however, for quackery is an art or craft that pretends to be that which it puts on. Modern psychotherapy does not pretend; it is ignorant of its own nature. There should be some name for this phenomenon, an art or craft or discipline knowing not what itself is. Perhaps one should call it a "fawning science," for it apes science, much as Plato called quackeries "fawning arts."

Psychotherapy, the cure of souls, requires true art. What is more, the curing of souls is a divine art. The psychotherapist is the saint in spite of himself. He would throw up his hands in horror at this. Yet his protest would not be the result of false humility but of mistaken identity. Modern psychotherapy is unknown, itself to itself. Psychotherapists therefore are not successful. Still they are worthier than the divines and it is for them that all the trumpets will sound on the river's other side. A saint is not the one who puts on a halo but the one who says, "I come from Jericho with a wounded man."

These chapters in the course of their exploration have sustained a lengthy polemic. At times they may have seemed fiercely partisan. No excuse is necessary, for these healers today are more to be blamed than praised. But the time has come to put together some of what has been learned and, in the form of suggestions for a better psychotherapy, to clear the way for movement forward.

Universally, psychotherapy, as was shown, proceeds through the presentation of a moral problem to a person of moral authority who offers moral guidance. No one of these elements can be eliminated. The process distinguishes all psychotherapy. Yet both good and bad therapies are possible in this world, and the problem now is to set up the criteria for good psychotherapy.

The first step toward improvement, of course, would be the

recognition of the moral nature of the neurotic problem. One need not worry too much about this, though. It will come to pass.

Once it is recognized, attention is fixed immediately on the necessity for a speedy resolution. Moral tension if not resolved leads to the indecision, guilt, suffering, and separation which is neurosis. Neurosis if not tended leads to the formation of a new and private system of morality which is psychosis. A new and private system of morality removes the guilt and the conflict, makes the person happier but also alienates him from the community so effectively that he is not approachable through the usual forms of communication. He is cut off. The task is thus to give assistance at the time of moral conflict before the construction of a private system of beliefs, and if not then, as soon afterward as possible to forestall the growth of the hard shell of psychosis. Guilt ever accumulates in a widening gyre. Intervention must pierce swiftly through to the core of the moral problem before the soul cankers.

It would be simplest to call a system of psychotherapy that aims to intervene quickly a "preventive system" or a system of "mental hygiene." These two phrases are infelicitous, however; the first because it may give the idea that something should be prevented from occurring (and moral conflict cannot be prevented, as will be seen), and the second because it emphasizes two notions obviously inaccurate—mental or the mind, hygiene or cleanliness. Rather than these it is more reasonable for the system to have no name and to be incorporated in an institution that is charged with moral direction generally. Nonetheless the goal is the presence of moral assistance as soon as it is needed.

Continuing to turn a corrective eye on modern psychotherapy, one sees that the next step, a step of much greater importance, is the reconciliation of conflicting therapeutic standards of moral decision and judgment. Baffled by the use of terms like "normal" and "abnormal" in their search for the mystery of cure, psychotherapists do not realize that they are

grappling with Beowulf's vicious dragon. As yet they are unaware that at the end of the long corridor of their disputations,
in a handsome sun, there stands a man. The corridor is so
narrow and dark and the sun so bright that he can hardly be
seen.

Today psychotherapy works like this: here is a man, something is wrong with him, he says so, we believe him, we think
so too, we diagnose him as neurotic. To this concrete man we
apply our techniques—interviews, psychoanalysis, hypnosis,
tests, or electric shocks. After this we see some sort of a change
in him but is it good or bad, who knows? All we know is that
he is changed.

The patent fault is that there is no clear end in view. This is
not science. It is and remains guessing. Therapy, like any other
science, must proceed with an end in view. This end is the
standard by which progress (here, recovery or cure) is meas-
ured. When a particular man comes in to be helped he is not
cured at the time his tic is removed or his early love of his
mother uncovered or his silly obsession excised. He is cured
when the clash of passions within him is resolved, the moral
choice made, and the way to walk opened up.

To be able to heal, to be able to say, "This is the way you
should walk," the therapist must see the man in the sunlight,
who is not a normal or abnormal man, or even a false-faced
man adjusted to reality. He is a pattern, a model, an image,
the man of ideal character, the one of whom it can be said,
"There is no one more beautiful, more alive, more sympathetic,
more reasonable, more manly, or more perfect."

With this man in view therapy has foresight. It can see the
defects in the concrete man, can estimate the worth of its
technical methods, judge the desirability of the change it has
wrought in him. It has a scientific norm by which to measure
its work. It can lay its actions to the rule and conclude they
are good or bad. The ideal man will not be reached but the
concrete man will be helped one or two steps nearer and be a
better man for that.

The disturbing thing is not that the psychotherapist has no ideal in mind. With every moral decision or precept he makes he reveals one facet of his conception of right conduct. The trouble is he is not aware that he *has* an ideal and, because of this in great part, he contributes to an internecine war of standards of conduct which he calls criteria of cure.

The present mental hygiene programs of both private and governmental agencies are defeated by the same ignorance. One might suppose that since a state like New York for example has a unified mental hygiene plan, the guidance offered in its clinics would be unified too. Unhappily the state hires for this work, sometimes on a part-time basis, private practitioners in psychiatry, psychoanalysis, or psychology. It makes no effort to encourage them to unite their views, on the underlying assumption that mere mortals cannot interfere with Science at work.

Imagine now that all the practitioners in psychotherapy had got together in one grand conference. Further imagine that they had agreed on the ubiquity of morality in the neuroses and the necessity for concord in the moral directions they separately issue. In a proper mood of contrition they begin to set up according to the best-known principles a system of psychotherapy for the community.

Such psychotherapy, they would conclude, should ask no fees but should be supported by the community as a whole. Fees commercialize the help given, make the relationship temporary, contingent on payment, and no matter how they are graduated, operate to select certain classes of the population whereas the therapist should have a balanced picture.

It is better to have angels and no fees, they decide. The psychotherapist should be one who professes a life devoted to helping men, one interested in the assistance, not the vendability, of his work. He should be available at specified times and in emergencies be subject to call. And because of their own dedication to their work the therapists feel it would not be a travesty to speak of loving and being loved instead of "giving" and "receiving" love in the "transference." In fact the last term is no longer useful and no one goes through the absurdities of "breaking the transference."

The psychotherapist's chosen work proclaims that he upholds a life of service and devotion to others and does not want that devotion to be manipulated any more than he intends to manipulate the love that warms his patient's life, past or present. They are not, these psychotherapists, interested in a commercial love, wakened by payment, canceled by non-payment.

Jointly they would let it be known that they believe that moral conflict is something no one alive can hope to escape, that the subject of moral guidance is everyman. They themselves were in the habit of going for help to any one of their colleagues whom they respected. They thought the benefits of doing this were of inestimable value and they recalled that not only in the confessional of the Western world had a priest to go to confession himself but also that Freud had recommended that each psychoanalyst be reanalyzed at least every five years. While they do not hold that persons should be required to come in once a year or more, they believe it absolutely necessary for the health of both the person and the community.

They would let be known also their broad views of moral disorder. Persons, they would say, could come to see them either before or after the act that troubles their conscience. This provision for coming in before embarking on a dubious course of action would prevent counseling from being identified solely with cases of evil already done and would foster its selected end of general moral guidance.

Nevertheless the psychotherapists would not stress the point unduly. They expect most of their visits would be for acts already done and feared to be bad. Perhaps these acts were only thought to be bad, and this would be cleared up. In any case the fact that the problem was recognizedly moral would save much time in their work. The principle maintained is that men cannot help but fall sometimes into behavior that is not honest, fair, or just but if it is recognized as wrong and an attempt made to avoid future instances, the person is restored to the fellowship of the best. His fellow men regard him as so valuable, no matter how humble his station, and so bound to the community by ties of love and loyalty, that it cannot let him go. What is more, while some deeds such as murder and torture are so hideous as to separate any man from his community, there are other wrong acts whose character would be judged differently in different parts of the community, more severely in one region and less in another.

The reaction of counselors to this latter category of evils varies from town to town and context to context. They have a discretionary power, here, like the priest to whom a young Spanish woman confessed that every evening she stood nude before her mirror and admired her beauty. She asked him whether this was a sin. "No," said he. "It is not a sin, it is only an error." Thus could a degree of moral decentralization be achieved while yet the universal standard was maintained.

If the person wants to do something to make up for his wrongdoing, they encourage him. They have come a long way from the original psychoanalytic theory that the patient's need for punishment must be renounced and his inner court of justice denied. They know that a good man wishes to make amends for his bad actions. They know also that the refusal to recognize this leads to the polysurgic addiction, the psychosomatic sickness, the crime committed just in order to be punished—all in the spirit of the poet's lament:

> O God of our flesh, return us to your wrath
> Let us be evil could we enter in
> Your grace, and falter on the stony path!

They much prefer to let the person fulfill his need to atone by whatever good works he conceives of, be they but one of the "five hundred poor I have in yearly pay" of Henry V, or the founding of a St. Bartholomew's hospital, or a poem called the

Recantation. Plato said that Homer "never had the wit to know why he was blind," but Stesichorus, the Sicilian poet, "who was a philosopher, knew the reason why."

> And therefore, when he lost his eyes, for that was the penalty which was inflicted upon him for reviling the lovely Helen, he at once purged himself and the purgation was a recantation which began thus: "False is that word of mine—the truth is that thou didst not embark in ships, nor ever go to the walls of Troy." And when he had completed the poem which is called the recantation, immediately his sight returned to him.

The psychotherapists are further convinced of the desirability of good works because they have been informed that both Protestant and Catholic religions think highly of them. How did Luther put it? "Good works do not make a good man, but a good man does good works." He who has acknowledged his wrongdoing is of the substance of goodness and can do good works.

The psychotherapists would authorize the publication of special books, chiefly for their own use, to record their decisions and their wisest methods of handling cases. For they would not want to be caught as the Protestants were when Jeremy Taylor in *Doctor Dubitantium* said that they were left without guidebooks on the perplexities of conscience. Protestants were driven to Roman confessional manuals for help with their difficulties of moral decision, as in the days when there was no smith in Israel and men had to resort to the forges of the Philistines to sharpen their axes and mattocks. From these special books it is clear that in the matter of techniques the psychotherapists are pliable.

Unless there were peculiar reasons against it, their practice would be to let the person enter the room, in which there was a bench and a screen. Behind the screen or partition would be the therapist, who would then ask whether the person preferred him to remain there or to appear face to face during the visit.

The person could sit, kneel, or lie on the bench, or stand. He would not be required nor asked to take tests or to give his name, age, education, income, and serial number.

Sometimes the visits would be long but sometimes, especially in the presence of the overscrupulous in conscience, the psychotherapists would follow the practice though not the words of the priest who used to say, "Be brief, be contrite, be gone." In each case the visit would be terminated by the therapist. If still behind the screen, he would say, "That is all now." Then, whether behind the partition or not, he would add these words: "You have done well. Good-by." It would be the custom, too, that if the therapist were before the person, he would rise and extend both his hands to the other.

An effort would be made to rotate psychotherapists every five years not only from city to city but from province to province. They as a body had concluded that there was no necessity for the person to have the same therapist all the time. Having begun to think of themselves as the representatives of the community, they justifiably felt that the person in his visit would sense that he was not talking to a collection of individual kinks and quirks.

Nor would they worry whether the person was telling them the truth. They would know and teach that when men in a conflict of passions do things they believe they are not supposed to, guilt will descend on them like a cloud of soul-consuming grief. If this guilt were not acknowledged, in time it would be a man's undoing. Unrelieved guilt, they say, is the mind-destroyer.

If presenting a serious problem for which this short form of moral counsel did not suffice, the person would be recommended to go to one of the special schools maintained by the therapists for difficult neurotic and psychotic cases. Here the variety of treatments would be more in evidence. Music, baths, dramas, great silences, striking architectural innovations, hypnotism, dances, and a host of other modes of healing would be used. The one unbreakable law would be that no technique could be applied that might in the short or long run violate their ideals of character.

The psychotherapists in these schools on the average would be older and have much experience in seeing the evils men undergo when their guilt stays unuttered. They would be trained in observing the various forms that symptoms take, in learning the meaning of these symptoms, what conflicts they are trying to express that cannot be expressed verbally, what private new worlds are being built bravely and tenaciously within the breast of many a tortured soul.

Their main purpose in learning the patient's history would be to find the language of authority through which they could communicate with him. In the early days of course, they would be very much aware that most of their patients when young had been steeped in schools that taught an aversion to seeking moral help. Yet they would never resort to the easy expedient of falsehood. They would never tell the patient that men should not seek aid when troubled or that their own counsel was not such aid. They know well that each person reacts differently to direction, and that their task and their skill are to find out how best to express it so that it would seem to the patient to be the exercise of that just auhority in which they believe their work consists.

In these schools they would work long and hard at the problem of restoring their patients to living again in the community. It would be a most difficult problem. There would be unsolved issues both as to how and to what extent the return should be accomplished. In attempting to solve this and their other problems they would make use of the monthly reports sent in by each counselor. Here in these schools would meet each month those groups of therapists called the "councils of conscience" which would have the duty of recommending changes in practice from time to time.

The next problem on the agenda is to discuss what qualifications are to be set up for counselors and therapists. It is quickly agreed that no premium is to be put on medical schooling. Apparently the psychotherapists have had their fill of the pathophobia that disfigures the nation.

But at this point in the conference, which has been marked throughout by a great sobriety and willingness to let minor criticism give way to major principles, a young man stands up to be heard. He is recognized as a young doctor who has gone through one of the best known training schools for psychiatrists. He has made a brilliant record in the behavioral sciences and has just finished an internship in a state hospital noted for its advanced work in shock therapy. Evidently he has waited long and impatiently to speak, for he can hardly contain himself. "My God!" he bursts out. "Are you all crazy? This is not psychotherapy. It's religion! And these visits, what are they but confession! And this ideal character, it is nothing but the imitation of a Christ!"

The meeting falls into an uproar. On all sides wrangling and shouting break out, the chairman cannot maintain order, and the conference is disbanded.

The young man is right.

CHAPTER TEN

The Vision

Take each school of psychotherapy separately; it is a redemptive system, designed to relieve guilt. Take them together; they are a snarled mass of conflicting moral teachings. Take them separately, tune them together like the strings of a lute, harmonize their knowledge and ideals; they become a religion.

This transubstantiation is worth further thought. Daniel Defoe once wrote a two-volume opus called *The Complete English Tradesman.* In it he declared that "a Tradesman behind his counter must have no flesh and no blood about him, no passions, no resentment; he must never be angry, no, not so much as seem to be." If Defoe could sit down and spell out the specifications for an ideal character, anyone else should be able to do the same, is it not so?

No, it is not as easy as that. When one tells the psychotherapists that in their floundering about for criteria of cure they are seeking an exemplary man, one has not given them as much help as possible. In fashioning this ideal there is yet a law that cannot be violated. Community is the natural order of man. An ideal of man must place him in community with other men.

Defoe himself realized some of the difficulties he would have with his man of trade:

> There are men who have, by custom and usage, brought themselves to it, that nothing could be meeker and milder

> than they, when behind the counter, and yet nothing be
> more passionate and choleric in every other part of life;
> nay, the provocations they have met with in their shops
> have so irritated some men, that they would go upstairs
> . . . and fall into frenzies, beat their wives, kick their
> children about like dogs, and be as furious for two or
> three minutes as a man chained down in Bedlam; and
> when their heat was over, would go down into their
> shops again, and be as humble, as courteous, and as calm
> as before; so absolute a government of their passions had
> they in the shop, and so little out of it.

Unless one believes that the ideal man should beat his wife,
kick his children like dogs, and foam at the mouth for two
or three minutes, the image here needs correcting at least.
Defoe had more success with another more famous character
of his, Robinson Crusoe, who lived all by himself.

Though one add to this ideal the polish of later years and
describe it as a character fit for economic achievement, independent, loathing idleness, thrilled by the challenge to subdue
and develop the earth's treasury—even so one sees that the
conception never quite got around to embracing man's relation
with other men, man in community. This ideal man does not
know how to live properly with other men.

During World War II it was possible for psychotherapy in
some areas to measure its cures quite successfully but only
because it had a partial ideal man to use as a model. Therapy
was successful if the patient again could get into his submarine
or fly his plane in combat.[1] The virtues of the fighting man
are unquestionably important and should be maintained in
men who are to strive for a great common life. Yet to hold
that these should be the only virtues would neglect the man's
life with the other members of his community.

One must visualize how he should live with others, not alone
customers or wives and children, but tradesmen, wholesalers,
retailers, priests, farmers, musicians, senators, poets, parents,
and teachers. One must consider also how each of these can

share the ideal and how all can work together to reach the ideal. It is not essential to have a great detail like that established by age-old tradition in China, fixing the hierarchy of the womenfolk of a mansion, circumscribing exactly the rights and duties of all, from the seventh concubine to the old grandmother of the husband. On the other hand it solves nothing to say that the ideal man is a hunter and hawker and everyone should learn to hunt and blow a horn and carry a hawk. The threads of the ideal should run through each occupation or station in life and color it with the same purple and gold.

Observing the various modern psychotherapies, one does see embryonic ideal characters. Since none of the therapies, however, tries to present clearly its ideas on the subject of an image of a man, it is impossible to sketch them accurately. Any brief characterization that could be made would probably caricature their model men. Apart from this, though, and apart from the conflict of these ideals in different schools, there remains the fact that each fuzzy model man is designed with little thought of having him live with others.

In setting out the criteria for an improved psychotherapy the last chapter raised two requirements—a system for speedy assistance when needed and the creation of an exemplary man toward whom all therapies might strive. There is now this third and last requirement that the ideal man must fit in community with other men.

At last the question of where rests the ultimate responsibility for healing nears an answer. To heal, one must teach what men's relations should be to each other. To give an order to the passions, one must have a model of order in the community. The government within must be patterned after a government without.

That the secular therapists as they are now trained have not this capacity is clear. In their criteria of cure, in their ideals of man, they have succeeded in connecting nothing with nothing. The psychotherapist must admit he is a stranger here himself, no less than his patient.[2]

Those responsible for knowledge of the connectedness of things within the community and the ordering of them toward the highest good are the statesman and the theologian. It is their job to take the apparent war between truth and truth, demonstrate that it is only discord between opinion and opinion, and yoke them both in peace. The communities they represent, the political and religious communities or the great community, take in all of man's life. Theirs is the task of raising and holding before men's eyes the vision of the ideal community. Only they have the tradition and the training to do this. Theirs is the duty.

It may occur to some to ask how it happens that, to know what the therapy of the soul is, one needs to know the common ideals, yet for the therapy of the body such knowledge is unnecessary. As a matter of fact it merely seems that such knowledge is unnecessary. The criteria of cure of the physician of the body are also subject to morality and law. There is this difference, however, that the standards of the proper development and working of the body usually have a wider basis of communal agreement. For example if a person is brought in a comatose state, the doctor has a problem of decision. There exist over half a hundred possible causes and an almost equal number of remedial procedures to apply. Yet he goes right to work to try remedy after remedy until one succeeds or until further efforts are useless. The point of morality does not hinge on the indecision involved in a plethora of remedies but rather on the absolute reliance of the doctor on the community's desire that this person be brought out of the coma. The sureness of this sentiment can be vivified by supposing that the doctor, wishing to experiment on what would happen to comatose patients if no remedies were applied, therefore applied none.

In an area not so securely settled by uniform morality the doctor's real indecision increases. Recent medical investigations seem to indicate that about one half of all natural abortions reveal a malformed fetus. The signs of an oncoming natural abortion can often be seen far enough in advance by the doctor so that he can take some action (make up, for instance, a presumed hormonal deficiency) to prevent it. Should he? Or, if a pregnant woman has a heart lesion, should she have her baby or not? In these cases the physician is unsure at present of the standard because the community itself is. Sometimes he is controlled by law in these matters. The state may forbid him to procure an abortion on an unwilling mother physically capable of bearing a child without risk to herself. But if the mother is willing or if the risk is present and the mother wants no abortion, the physician's own moral sureness may have to tell him what to do. Then his decision may depend on whether he is Catholic or Protestant, as will the patient's.[3]

There is the example of aid and comfort to the enemy. Plutarch says that, when sent for professionally by the King of Persia, Hippocrates declared, "I will never make use of my art in favor of barbarians who are enemies of the Greeks." Also questions about which potentialities of the body are to be developed are matters of communal standards. A community may have an ideal of health and beauty that calls for tall men. In his book on *The Courtier*, a Renaissance ideal of man, Baldassare Castiglione said, "Then coming to the bodily frame, I say it is enough if this be neither extremely short nor tall. . . ." The form of the body desired in men as in horses will vary from one part of the world to the next, if one part loves a sedentary life, another an agricultural, and a third part a warlike life. In one region the experts on nutrition may study ways of getting stouter and heavier and in another the way of getting thinner and lighter, and in large communities embracing diverse occupations and pleasures they may have to study both problems and others besides.

It is appropriate for an age that has difficulties with its therapy of the soul to believe that a therapy of the body is a matter of individual or scientific decision. Any standard—even one that merely says, "You cannot send the stomach here, the heart there, and the guts somewhere else"—is admired by one who has none himself. The age forgets or does not know of the great moral conflicts that were fought for centuries not only by laymen but by doctors among themselves. And it forgets those times when Martial's story is repeated with glee, the one about the man who dreamed of a doctor and never woke up.

A man "in hand and foot and mind built foursquare and without a flaw" is the one Simonides, the old Greek poet, sang, and the one Masaccio, the young Italian painter, painted. Without such a goal not only psychotherapy and medicine are impossible but so is the development of character or, as Chapter Six entitled it, the government of the passions. For any community such an ideal is necessary.[4] It is not ectoplasm nor does it thrive in a rarefied atmosphere. The passions are directed and arranged by morality and law, which form the structure of the vision as a great temple parallels the cosmos.

It is not startling then that, were a system of psychotherapy to be built by having all secular therapists, in a carnival of hope like that of the last chapter, agree to harmonize their divergent criteria of cure, it would emerge as a religious enterprise, an *imitatio Christi*. If the psychotherapist complains of being called religious, he will have to be told that that is the danger of his calling, his *risque du métier*. It is religion that has said all men are brothers ever since the birth of mankind.

Religion's duty is to lead men into communion with one another and with God. Morality, the ideals of right living, is its concern. Politics' task also is to bring men together and to lead them toward the common good and therefore law, the younger brother of morality, is its concern.

Those who know most about the community and the way it can cohere and attain its ends should be its authority or its teachers in the governing of the passions.

So it may be. Yet if in a well-ordered community the authority of law and morality has reared the child to manhood, where do disorders of the passions come from?

The answer is and has to be humble. Mortals—and the category includes earthly authority—do not know everything.

They cannot choose but err. Men are not yet gods, the world is not yet at rest.

When religion lets a man say, "God is mine and is known to me alone," without condemning it as pride, the sentence can change to "God is mine and I am God and belong to nobody else." Pride, that vice that escapes the owl's eye of the psychotherapist. Science, which is only another name for knowledge, has come to symbolize this pride. When one reads of "Science's conception of the universe" this should mean nothing more than man's conception of the universe. The eye behind the telescope or the microscope is still an eye of but mortal scope. Behind that eye man cannot get. For "Science" with or without capitals, read "man" in small letters. Science today is a synonym for pride when it should be a synonym for man's accumulated learning.

No better illustration can be found than psychology, which along with other social sciences has taken over the arrogance of an earlier vintage of physical scientists. The student of politics when he meets a statement like the following may admit to its directness and exuberance. "The question is, therefore, a quantitative one, How much and what kind of limitations shall we impose on the craving mechanism which is biological man?"[5] But he cannot fail to be annoyed with its lack of perspective. "Poor human nature!" once wrote the novelist George Moore, "when you pinch it in one place it bulges out in another, after the fashion of a lady's figure."

The psychological theories of psychoanalysis led many persons to make statements about the restrictions of civilization on drives or instincts and about the necessity for alleviating them. But as Chapter Seven took care to point out, all psychotherapeutic interviews (and, for that matter, all psychological tests, questionnaires, and experiments) put the subject in an extraordinary situation which itself was presupposed by an already existent theory of human nature and which produces facts to fit the theory.

There is something lopsided about a psychological theory

of human nature that does not explain that a man can be sick because he is a Protestant and was not brought up to live in a world without a God of forgiveness; that a man can be sick because he is a Jew and was not brought up to live in a world that hated Jews; that a man can be sick because he is a Catholic and was not brought up to live in a world of competing impersonalities. "Is there any significance," asks a wide-awake psychologist, "in the fact that fancy-priced practitioners have never acknowledged the profit-motive, the immorality of greed, robbery, and exploitation?"[6] Sloth does not seem to be a vice in common use nowadays but what of Pride, the first of the deadly sins? Finally, there is something askew in a theory of human nature that seems to have no place for the idea that man tries to be good, has a passion for righteousness so strong that it takes him often through a vale of suffering and sometimes to the heights of nobility.

These items merely point to gross omissions in a psychology based on a view of man in closed quarters, so to speak—man as seen in the ghetto of the psychological experiment or the psychotherapeutic interview. How narrow is this glimpse when compared to the broad expanse of man in history. All psychological experiments put man in strange settings and thus prejudice the results. Not much experimental knowledge of man can be got without his co-operation, and his co-operation has its reasons. The experiments of history or the panorama of men living in community, often less subject to such limitations, can be used to give suggestions, balance, facts, and evaluation to modern psychological attempts to learn more of man's nature.

Yet granting the acceptance of this oft-repeated and seldom followed recommendation, there will always be part of man's soul left unknown, there will always be the secret workings of the spirit. True, men are all made of the same paste. They are subject to certain rules prescribed by their own nature. But from the instant of birth they are subject also to the controlling and freeing influences of the community. There is no way of

getting around and behind these influences to see man's drives
or needs or instincts in the raw. They can merely be gauged
roughly at later stages.

Whatever may be the theory of biological needs or appetites,
no community has restricted them voluntarily to the point of
exterminating its members en masse. In addition nearly all
appetitive theories of man include the possibility of substitute
gratifications for raw desires. In these theories the substitute
needs can grow through combination to be more powerful than
raw needs—as when a man dies for his country (violating the
familiar need of self-preservation) or when a man vows sexual
abstinence (violating the familiar need of reproduction or
sexual union).

The result of course is that it becomes nearly impossible
to extract from the entanglement any but the simplest needs—
man must eat, drink, move about, and so on. For such a
formula, however, no elaborate psychology is needed and no
elaborate psychotherapy has precisely pinned down man's
cravings.[7] Indeed there is no psychology of man as such. Man
as man is unknown. Psychology can only study the products,
the incipient beings, of particular religious and political communities and there learn that, whatever the original nature
of man is, these men in these communities at these times show
a wide range of passions. Which of these passions pertain to
biological needs and which to needs developed and encouraged
by the community cannot be said.

To claim therefore that certain acts are compulsive or in-
voluntary in order to excuse those acts (as psychotherapists
frequently do in courts of law) is unsupportable doctrine.
Both sides of the conflict of passions must be regarded as voluntary. In Chapter Three, for example, where a list of typical
cases of warring passions was given, it was not possible to say
which passion was based on raw drives and which on trained
or educated drives. The businessman's passion for submissiveness and succor clashes with another for dominance and independence. Which is the need here that is ineradicable? The

housewife's passion for masculine endeavors clashes with another for feminine pursuits. Both these patterns have been offered her by the confused education that brought her up; neither one can be said to be based on biology. And so on through the other cases, including those involving the passions of sex. One passion must be judged wrong and the other right, according to the ideals of the community.

Still, because it is obvious that man is a desiring creature, it is necessary to provide in any community the means whereby some relief can be offered. Sympathy must ever be extended to the plaint that the mastering of nature is hard beyond all hardness. This is where the flexible remedy of forgiveness steps forth.

Man being a desiring creature who lives in community, his wants and his sight are fused. In viewing his world and himself he at the same time half perceives and half creates. He can be sure of what he sees but never sure of how much he does not.

Mortal authority is not infallible. Must it be in order to be authority? It need only be as close to the truth as man can get. The secular healer can scarcely repress a snicker when he hears of the "faith cures" of kings and saints but the people who were sick knew as simply as they knew that the sun makes the birds rise that they had to go to the moral authority of the community. Today one's intelligence is thought to increase with the strength of one's professed disbelief in everything. In the army or out, upon the command "Eyes left," one is supposed to counter-cry, "Why left? Why not right?" But it is now as true as always that to disbelieve in something is to believe in something else.

Forgiveness in psychotherapy, in the curing of souls, allows authority to judge and yet reconsider that judgment without imperiling, in a fast rush of certainty, the moral standards of the community. It allows man to question whether his light is not darkness and yet to walk by the light he has. To guide men's morality without forgiveness is prideful. To guide with forgiveness is humility. Because his remedies are and must be earth-hewn, man must say loud and clear, "Right and wrong," and add soft and clear, "Forgiveness."

For the political scientist there are two facts that serve as guides to the health of the community. One is the amount of crime in it and the other the amount of neurosis and psychosis. They serve judgment on existing law and morality. When the figures shoot upward, they warn that the ideal of man in community is somewhere out of plumb.

No land is known to exist without crime or derangement. It is the reflection of man's inability to make for himself a perfect community. Most of the time the political scientist can trust religious psychotherapy to bridge this gap between the existent and the ideal. His main task is that of the statesman—to know the community and to hold up its highest good. Hence he cannot himself engage in psychotherapy. But he trusts religion to know that the neurotic is one who feels estranged from the community. He trusts the curer of souls either to tell the neurotic he is not alienated or, if he is, to try to bring him back. For his own part he likes the saying of the caliph Ma'mûn: "The best life has he who has an ample house, a beautiful wife, and sufficient means, who does not know us and whom we do not know."

But when he sees the cold mist of delirious disorder crawl across the window and creep under the door, he must go out himself to discover the truth.

What he finds has already been told. The link between therapy and political and religious authority is snapped. Secular psychotherapists have no idea of what to teach, have no knowledge of what to bind and what to let loose, have no unified conception of their community or their dependence on it. Religion has given up the task except to add to the confusion. Practical theology, which was the clergyman's main effort to learn about and help the whole community, has given over its work to the social scientists. These good men dull, in turn, have split up into bailiwicks, without relationship to one another, without leadership, and without moral acknowledgment or responsibility. The political scientist begins then to look more deeply for the sources of trouble.

Where, he asks, is my trusted servant, Education? Under the social sciences he finds it. Paying homage to nothing but an abstract conception of itself, education, too, the real therapy of the body politic, is floating on a raft tossed by every crosscurrent of pedagogical whimsey. "Education," he calls, "don't you know me?" "Certainly I know you," responds Education. "You are the student of the political community, which is just an association like any other association. There are the denominations, the learned bodies, the improvement clubs, and the technicians' societies, the bowling groups, the matrimonial agencies, the labor unions, including the butcher, the baker, the candlestick maker, and there are some others I forget. Anyway, your community is one like them, no more important, no less." Then Education springs a few barbs. "Oh yes, your field, too, is one of the social sciences. And I am not your trusted servant. You're just like Agrippa's dog, trying 'subtly to maintain all other sciences are vain.' "

It is true that politics now finds itself one of the social sciences without a position of leadership. But it wants the social sciences and psychotherapy to have a dignity and value they never could have as fawning sciences. They themselves never cease to talk of integrating themselves, yet that cannot be done without leadership. Unless they are reborn as moral disciplines their help for the problem besieging the world will continue to be negligible.

It is true that many who call themselves political scientists teach and write only about the machinery of government. Yet fewer political scientists than the members of any of the social sciences are prey to the practice of saying they belong to a science professedly unmoral, and these few have generally mistaken power for authority. Fewer still have forgotten that the political community includes all associations, that the members of all groups belong to it, know they do, and want to in preference to all and any other group, and that this can be said of no one other association. And a few political scientists still know that the political and the religious communities make up the great community.

It is not too late for political science. It has a long tradition behind it with which it has not yet fully broken.

Psychotherapy is not the only method of governing the passions. It is the heal-the-breach method. It exists because of man's imperfect knowledge of man. The positive aspects of man's knowledge, what he does know and dream of, are expressed in his education. If psychotherapy is the sign of man's weakness, education is the mark of his strength.

Education is a process of forming character, the ordering of the passions. Character is formed by teachers who teach the government of the passions by holding up for imitation the ideals of man and community embodied in morality and law. Morality and law contain both the ends and the standards the community has learned for holding together and moving toward its ends.

What has happened to education is similar to what has befallen psychotherapy. It has first of all tried to divorce itself from all political and religious ties and to call itself neutral. The political ties it has not succeeded in throwing off but it pretends that it has. The religious ties, though, are gone and most of the moral teaching of religion are gone too.

"Moral education is impossible," says the philosopher Whitehead, "without the habitual vision of greatness." Education, so called, has no vision of greatness and therefore forms no character. Instead it talks of "personality," which denotes a self casually acquired, subject to alteration without notice, disintegrating on petty misfortune, a self as splintered as a secret agent's, always prepared to change identities though never secure in any one. Character is not a whimsical penciling but a clean engraving. If it appears today it is the result of education not in the schools but in the family, where religious tradition still warms the hearth with its embers. Education

228 ERRORS OF PSYCHOTHERAPY

must have a morality or a law to transmit or it, too, will have no teaching around which to form character.

There is a general theoretical relation between law and morality. Law concurs in all morality but retains for itself the command or prohibition of certain external acts. It says, Be Honest, Do Not Steal. It is a standard of minimum morality. It takes motives or thoughts into account but chiefly to determine the background of actions. To the state the motives of a St. Francis or a Marquis de Sade may be the same but the different acts of the two are what lets rest or calls in the arm of the law. An unlawful act must have followed the unlawful thought or else the law takes no direct steps.[8]

Morality, however, is a judgment on all thought and action. It can say not only, Do Not Steal, but also, Do Not Covet. It is more detailed. It offers a fuller picture of the ideal, going into fine shadings and colors, things too subtle for the law, too insusceptible of proof or too burdensome of administration. It prescribes all virtues and represses all vices.

Traditionally the chamberlain of the inner life of man has been religion. This does not mean that the state cannot do or has not done the task but rather that it is unused to the problem. The state upholds the minimum standard to allow men's reaching for the maximum. It is a minimum only in terms of the number of rules it contains—their importance is definitely not minimal. The law may embody some of the highest and firmest moral principles a community has. The church, while involved in this vital minimum, exhorts to the maximum. It, too, can and has assumed the task of directly restraining external acts.

The two spheres cannot be separated neatly. The state will consider intent or motive in a crime; the church will consider criminal actions immoral. The law, though admitting the impossibility of including morality in its standards, sustains all morality. It knows that morality controls action. With his political authority the judge uses morality constantly to fill in the spaces of the law. Morality, while recognizing the lack of detail in law, realizes that only a small portion of the community's standards need be made explicit in order that all morality be given the opportunity for expression and change.

Because the state acts on the infraction of the vital minimum it must seem less forgiving than the church. To it the statements of reforming psychologists often betray a lamentable ignorance of the purpose and problems of law. "An expert on criminal psychology said Thursday," reads a news item echoing a common thesis in psychotherapy, " 'Many of us want to murder but few of us do. . . . The only essential difference between a lawbreaker and his fellow man is that the offender acts out what others suffer.' "⁹ What, one might ask, about the little difference there on the floor, the man with the hole in his head? He used to be a live member of the community.

Such criminal psychologists should learn by heart the maxim of Cosimo de' Medici. It is brevity itself. "States are not governed by paternosters." The state considers the offender in such cases to be a born devil on whom nurture has not stuck. In order to protect his fellow men it must put him away from them, must excommunicate him. The church, however, has greater freedom in this matter. It can forgive and rest more assured that its work is going well.

The essential reason for this difference in the state and the church is that the former, because it deals with external acts, deals with those persons on whose conscience the vital minimum was not profoundly enough engraved. The criminal is often unrepentant. The state thus has on its hands not only a person whose conscience in that respect is deficient and who therefore must be at least partially excommunicated for the safety of others but it must also reinsist for all the rest on the undisputed existence of an educational standard. It must enable all teachers to say, "This act is bad. Do not doubt it. The community's law punishes it."

The church in its psychotherapy deals with cases where conscience is strong enough usually to prevent external criminal acts, where the person recognizes his own wrongdoing enough to confess at least a moral quandary, and where the morality involved is apt to be less necessary to the maintenance of order and hence more flexible.

The state, however, can and does use forgiveness. Almost all political rulers, including democratic chief executives, have a pardoning power. The judge himself has a typically wide discretion in the application of sentence. To a much larger extent than is ordinarily thought his decisions are based on considerations not to be found in the law as written. Even written into the law are provisions for leniency toward the criminal who confesses his wrongdoing or in other ways manifests his repentance.

A political community cannot live by formal or written law alone. The law contains only those prescriptions and injunctions which for one reason or another need to be stated. It is not necessarily true that the law bothers only with moral rules that are likely to be violated in action. It may also uphold moral principles which it repeats solely because of the desire of men to proclaim their ideals. But the ramifications and interrelations of morality are too numerous, too intricate, and too flexible to be all embodied in law. The law of the state therefore depends on the existence of morality.

As just discussed, the church in the Western world has been the custodian of morality. Religious teachings of morality once permeated family, school, and adult life. With the coming of the separation of church and state, the church lost its middle ground in education—the school. In so far as religion was taught anywhere, it was taught in a separate bin, distinct from political education.[10] The Reformers had passionately proclaimed that there could be no separation between the duties of the religious and the secular life. Once the rift between religious and political education developed, religious teaching seemed to have no relation and indeed had lost its relation to the moving world.

In fact these two communities, the political and religious, are so important and so intertwined that for one to act in its teaching as though the other did not exist was in effect a teaching against the value of the other. Omitting religion from education meant that as far as the state was concerned religion was stone cold dead.

There are persons, to be sure, who think that not only the separation but also the slow death of religious education is a cause for rejoicing. To the political scientist there is nothing exhilarating in it. With the collapse of religious teaching to the young, religious training in the family was delivered a blow from which it is still reeling. The religious ideals that remain in the family today resemble cut flowers, beautiful, perhaps, but without roots and without duration. This is the reason the psychotherapist finds it so easy to convince his patients that their morality is parent-made, not God-made. The enlightened parent nowadays, when transmitting a moral standard to his child, is reluctant to say that it is a rule of God. Unless it is also a law (whereupon he can say with surety, "It is the Law") he does not know exactly what to say. He therefore usually transmits it without reason. So, when the psychoanalyst in his humming about the patient's past, accuses, "You got that idea from your father," the poor patient does not know enough to say, "Yes, of course, but he got it from God, and through my father and all before him, so have I."

The political community is left with a morality that is but the perfume of an empty vase, to use the historian Renan's phrase. Since the state, for reasons already discussed, cannot incorporate all morality into its laws, it must either devise ways itself to teach morality or soon find that it requires more and more laws that need more and more enforcement.

The incredible amount of neurosis today results from the withdrawal of religion from moral teaching without the substitution of another institution to assume its task. The impact has been felt also in the widespread distrust of political leaders. If men have no common moral background it is difficult to trust them with any power. Under such conditions the political problem of who will guard the guardians, *quis custodiet ipsos custodes,* becomes insuperable. No machinery of checks and balances and counterchecks is able to substitute for the early moral education, the formation of character, in the community's rulers. Without religion a righteous government is not to be expected.

Naturally the state has had to do something, but all its efforts have been uneasy. It may for instance give away books couched in popular scientific language on how to raise children. The books, however, merely reproduce the hollow education of personality that is the current style. "Through training in regularity of feeding, sleeping, and elimination," says one such guide, a United States Government Children's Bureau publication, "the tiny baby will receive its first lesson in character building." Well put, but is this the ideal man that the community wants, one that is regular in feeding, sleeping, elimination, and in everything else; or are there other ideals of character that should be preferred? Again, in the face of a sickness that steadily spreads, the state, doubting its competence in the area and unwilling to legislate a mountain of law, turns the moral guidance of a mental hygiene program over to private practitioners in psychotherapy.

There is much renovation to be done in modern religion before it can recover its rightful place. As it teeters on brinks it is not a religion of the whole spirit. It has become a victim of biblical legalism and pharisaical moralism. Like everyone else today, it believes that when one talks of morals one favors "stricter morals." But the founder of Christianity invited men to a feast.

That morality is static is a notion just as false as that it is restricting.[11] Morality is more flexible than the king's law or the people's voting. Even in the stablest of communities morality changes. When the community expands or shrinks a changed natural law governs it. Morality, too, changes to match these new principles. The community grows; the religion that does not grow with it is outgrown. Modern churches, unable to forgive, were trapped in old incrustations. They could not realize how much the community had changed because they were cut off from communication. Their members were afraid to tell them of their moral dilemma.

Before religion can heal again it must find a place for all of modern life within its worship of God, for not alone the deep fervor of the *Kyrie eleison* but the wild joyful shout of the *Gloria.* It must realize that a poet, like the Egyptian Abu Hurairoh of centuries past, when he sings:

> *Let me be impious, O God, let me be unlucky*
> *Only let one of my hands all my life*
> *Rest on the loved one's thigh*
> *And the other hold the cup of wine,*

is a pious man. Piety is more than genuflection. Religion must stand for all art. To Bishop Bossuet's demand, "Who would dare say that he is at the theater for the love of God or to please God?" it must answer straight out, *"We* do." Religion must stand for all ecstasy. It must reconcile the Bacchanals to the Orphics, for both were trying to attain unity with God, the first by intoxication, the other by abstinence. In a religion of the whole spirit, unlike things must meet and mate.

The church still knows how to bear suffering. This is good. Man's life is not a lark. He needs the church's help here but he needs it for the joy and beauty in his life too. Not these things of spring are the church's enemy, but pride, which by this token is also the community's enemy.

A religion, then, must stand for art and suffering and exultation, must prompt all the magnificent creations of the spirit, and lead the way to the poet's eternal festival of gods and men.

Coda

Now there are climates, regions, and conditions of men. And when one stands in one's own community and looks at the morality in others, one is prone to say that morality is a chance or arbitrary thing. It differs from land to land. Rather does morality represent the community's efforts to reach a natural law on the just relations of men. As both the Greeks and Romans saw, the law and customs of one land can be right for itself and wrong for another. But when lands come together through the changes of the world, and through peace or through war make a larger community, a new morality comes to being which is likewise an attempt to reach the natural law. Someday there will be a community of the world, and its morality, too, will strive for the perfect commonwealth that mirrors natural law.

Until this perfection is at hand crime and neurosis in the community are signs that it is off the beam of natural law. There are in the world fundamental principles of goodness or justice. Man, the half-perceiving, half-creating being, tries to learn these principles. All his science is bent toward their discovery. Those who are thought to know the natural law best are invested with the authority of the community.

Built into man is this institution—community. The natural love of the good in every man is its product. Moral rules change but the moral call is unchangeable and insists always on the *realissimum*—Men were born to be together. If God's finger had made its furrows in rock when He gave His law, He would have used those letters or the older ones: God is your father and all ye are brethren. You can, if you will, call this institution divine. In community the objective and subjective aspects of religion coalesce.

There were some who were fond of pointing out that everyone's religion is like a family with God as the father. They liked to cite this as proof that everyone projected his own family onto the screen of the sky and saw there the family writ large. They seldom paused to think that there is no way for men, including themselves, to escape this idea. They never conceived the possibility that the projection could be a divine projection writ small onto man's institutions. Community is stamped on man's soul.

It is not that man in his early years was put into a family mold and pressed out of shape. It is not a mere analogy that compares the family to the state and the church. Instead it is that man in his later years, too, has a relationship to a community that parallels the family. The small theater prepares for the larger stage and that larger one for the eternal festival. Man, if he would live with other men, must have his law and morality and his authorities to help teach him what is the best of his knowledge of himself and of God. Such is the tissue of the universe.

This book seems to have begun with gods and made its way to God. But the ancient Greeks used to say that God is in the beginning and end and middle of everything. Man is not his own. He belongs to someone else. Through authority he reaches out beyond the outlines of his bodily self into the life of a larger self that moves toward a divine likeness.

To the extent that the loves and dreams of men are shared, to that extent the community lives. The dreams are the ideals sought by law and morality. In so far as a man shares those dreams he is part of the community. If he does not partake of them he not only *feels* himself alienated—it is not a mere impression he has—he actually is outside the community. He must be restored not solely to relieve the torment in his own soul but also because every such person is literally a loss of part of the community. If the community parts with him, part of itself is amputated. After many such excisions the organism is cut into a mess of wiggling sections.

The political and religious authorities of the community are the ones best able to say, "Of these dreams of yours, of these loves and passions you have, this one is fair and this one foul. This is the truth and therefore this is the way." Only those can say this who are brought up to see more clearly than other men the valley of vision. They are the ones put in front.

And what of the political scientist? He knows his station. Politics is the frontier of man's knowledge. Hence the definition of the work of the political scientist is a sliding one. Sometimes his task is the means of brute subsistence, sometimes the expression of ideals in art, at other times defense and war and peace, sometimes psychotherapy, sometimes the formation of character, sometimes all these together, at all times the goals the community regards as most important and as most difficult to achieve. At all times to see that truth is one, and all things to each other turn.

But the political scientist has a just reward. When he dies he goes aloft to rule a star. He has Plato's word for it. Until then he works, knowing that there is no more necessary work than his.

It was not pleasant to have to point out that today there is no healing. But better to know than to let what is an endless trickle of blood become a spurting wound. Better to know the distinguishing marks of a true psychotherapy than to clash by dark. Mental disorder and psychotherapy now can be seen for what they are, problems of morality and law. This in itself gives hope. No more is psychotherapy a mystery of an untouchable science. The political community now has not only a concern but a direct and rightful power. It cannot recognize a psychotherapy that is all in pieces.

In and beyond this there is much to do.

Notes

1. The reluctance of social scientists to make totals of these figures is understandable. In the form in which the statistics exist today there is no way of estimating the overlap of the various categories. But the following figures taken from "Statistics Pertinent to Psychiatry in the United States," *Hospital Committee of the Group for the Advancement of Psychiatry,* Report No. 7 (March 1949), might indicate roughly their dimensions in the United States.

Psychiatric cases	8,500,000
Divorces, female	822,563
male	624,398
Crimes, including juvenile delinquency	1,700,000
Alcoholism	750,000
Narcotic addiction	100,000
Suicides	16,152

The figure cited above for psychiatric cases is a conservative one. E.g., J. Wilder, "Facts and Figures on Psychotherapy," *Journal of Clinical Psychology,* VII (1945), estimates from military neuropsychiatric rejections in World War II that the figure should be 21,000,000. M. Fishbein, "Mental Hygiene," *Hygeia,* XXVII (1949), estimates that half the United States population has psychoneuroses and a third ought to be treated. H. J. Eyesenk, reporting an English study of over 3000 workers in *Dimensions of Personality* (1947), estimates that approximately one out of every three of them is neurotic, with ten per cent of the entire group suffering from a neurosis that is definitely disabling. See also B. Malzberg, *Social and Biological Aspects of Mental Disease* (1940), a thoughtful study of the statistics of the State of New York, which concludes that the objection that the marked increase in mental disorder is only apparent cannot be maintained. "The population of mental hospitals is constantly increasing, incurring ever greater financial burdens upon the State. If present trends continue, mental disease will soon become our foremost health problem." From a military standpoint it should be mentioned that twelve per cent of all males examined at the induction stations of the United States during World War II were rejected as neuropsychiatric cases. The figure amounted to thirty-eight per cent of all rejections.

2. Sebastian de Grazia, *The Political Community* (1948).

3. Of recent books representing various aspects of this view, which can be said to have had its first full expression in J. S. Mill's *Representative Government* (1861), see F. Biddle, *The World's Best Hope* (1949).

4. Albert Einstein and Sigmund Freud, *Why War?* (Paris, 1933), pp. 11–13.

5. Respectively, G. A. Lundberg, *Can Science Save Us?* (1947), p. 104, and A. H. Leighton, *Human Relations in a Changing World,* (1949), p. 40. See also B. Wooton, *Testament for Social Science* (1950); S. Chase, *The Proper Study of Mankind* (1948); and C. Kluckhohn, *Mirror for Man* (1949).

6. "Once a new idea has seized the imagination of the race nothing can stay its advance. I believe that a new social power of this kind is now emerging: an idea. The time for it is ripe, and it may be that neither war nor economic chaos will prevent this century completing its task: the establishment of a true science of man. . . . I believe its day has come." L. L. Whyte in "Towards a Science of Man," *The Listener* (London), Jan. 15, 1948. And Kluckhohn (op. cit., p. 288) declares in like vein: "The new stage of development of the social sciences, still largely unrealized by the general public, may prove to have consequences as revolutionary as those of atomic energy."

CHAPTER ONE, PAGES 17–18

1. Sigmund Freud, "Fragment of an Analysis of a Case of Hysteria," *Collected Papers* (5 vols., 1925 50), III, 11–146.
2. A tendency to see in communication the distinguishing medium of the psychotherapeutic situation can be seen in F. Shaffer, "The Problem of Psychotherapy," *American Psychologist,* II (1947); E. J. Shoben, Jr., "Psychotherapy as a Problem in Learning," *Psychological Bulletin,* XLVI (1949). J. E. Finesinger, "Psychiatric Interviewing: I," *American Journal of Psychiatry,* CV (1944); and H. S. Sullivan, "Theory of Anxiety and the Nature of Psychotherapy," *Psychiatry,* XII (1949). For the limited view of communication generally held in psychotherapy, see Chapters Five and Six above.

CHAPTER TWO, PAGES 19–28

1. The group of studies referred to includes the following: R. P. Knight, "Evaluation of the Results of Psychoanalytic Therapy," *American Journal of Psychiatry,* XCVIII (1941–42); C. A. Landis, "A Statistical Evaluation of Psychotherapeutic Methods," in L. E. Hinsie, *Concepts and Problems of Psychotherapy* (1937); K. E. Appel, "Psychiatric Therapy," in J. McV. Hunt, *Personality and the Behavior Disorders* (2 vols., 1944), II; J. Wilder, "Facts and Figures on Psychotherapy"; L. Kessel and H. T. Hyman, "Value of Psychoanalysis as a Therapeutic Procedure," *Journal of the American Medical Association,* CI (1933); J. Bierer, "Psychotherapy in Mental Hospital Practice," *Journal of Mental Science,* LXXXVI (1940); E. H. Truex, Jr., "Psychogenic Deafness," *Connecticut Medical Journal,* X (1946); S. B. Hadden, "Group Psychotherapy," *American Journal of Psychiatry,* C (1944); L. W. Gerhart, "The 'Question-Box' Method of Group Psychotherapy," *Mental Hygiene,* XXXI (1947); and J. N. Rosen, "The Treatment of Schizophrenic Psychosis by Direct Analytic Therapy," *Psychiatric Quarterly,* XXI (1947).

The more comprehensive of these studies are Knight, Landis, and Appel. The others are more or less typical of the small

numerical study of psychotherapy found in the technical jour-
nals. Many statistical studies of hospital remissions can be consulted but they usually have little to say about the therapeutic
measures used. There exist also many statistical studies of shock
therapy which have in general the same limitations as the above
group. See, e.g., L. Jessner and V. G. Ryan, *Shock Treatment
in Psychiatry* (1941). For a discussion of the relation of shock
and physical therapies to communicative psychotherapy, see
Chapter Nine. Also available are many small numerical studies
of individual psychotherapists or sanitaria. Amalgamation or
even citation of all of them is not worth while in light of their
imprecision and incomparability.

2. Appel, "Psychiatric Therapy," p. 1155; for his reservations
about the statistics, see p. 1151. Knight, "Evaluation of Results," and Landis, "Statistical Evaluation," mention other
qualifications. Freud himself was well aware of the limitations
of existing psychoanalytic statistics. See his *Introductory* and
also *New Introductory Lectures on Psychoanalysis,* 1929 and
1933 respectively.

3. Bierer, "Mental Hospital Practice," pp. 945–46.

4. Shaffer, "Problem of Psychotherapy," p. 461.

5. For this case, see J. Gillin, "Magical Fright," *Psychiatry,* XI
(1948).

6. For the Hawaiian case, see M. F. Long, *The Secret Science
Behind Miracles* (1948). The statement following, made by
a group of Yale University social scientists in *The Bulletin of
Associates in the Science of Society,* was reported by R. Froman
in *This Week* (April 3, 1949), p. 23. See also Renzo Sereno,
"Obeah, Magic and Social Structure in the Lesser Antilles,"
Psychiatry, XI (1948); and M. Bartels, *Die Medizin der
Naturvölker* (Leipzig, 1893), p. 50: "The shaman has been
known to effect cures where the efforts of the white physician
have been expended in vain."

7. Appel, "Psychiatric Therapy," p. 1155.

8. Landis, "Statistical Evaluation," p. 169. See also Shoben, "Psychotherapy," pp. 368–69. Janet's remark appears in a communication quoted by Landis, ibid., p. 161.

9. Choosing the method of similarities does not preclude an
explanation or theory of the causes of differences. For the

significance of variations in psychotherapy, see below, Chapters Four, Six, Eight, and Nine.

CHAPTER THREE, PAGES 29–41

1. This is one of the fragments of Aelian to be found transcribed in E. J. and L. Edelstein, *Asclepius* (2 vols., 1945). See Testimony 399, and also, e.g., Testimonies 318, 346, 394, and 581. For some general works on the psychotherapy of other civilizations, see G. G. Dawson, *Healing: Pagan and Christian* (1935); G. Zilboorg, *A History of Medical Psychology* (1941); R. H. Major, *Faiths That Healed* (1940); M. Hamilton, *Incubation* (1906); W. A. Jayne, *The Healing Gods of Ancient Civilization* (1925); L. F. Calmeil, *De la folie* (2 vols., Paris, 1845); K. Chimin Wong and Wu Lien-teh, *History of Chinese Medicine* (Shanghai, 1936); T. C. Allbutt, *Greek Medicine in Rome* (1921) including the essay on "Byzantine Medicine"; C. Singer, "Medicine," *The Legacy of Greece*, ed. R. W. Livingstone (1921); W. R. Dawson, "Medicine," *The Legacy of Egypt*, ed. S. R. K. Glanville (1942); P. Bassoe, "Spain as the Cradle of Psychiatry," *American Journal of Psychiatry*, CI (1945); and E. G. Browne, *Arabian Medicine* (1921).
2. Among the biblical allusions to healing are the following passages: Exodus 4:11; 15:26; 23:25; II Chronicles 6:28; Deuteronomy 7:15; 28:60; Job 5:18; Psalms 15:38; 41:3; 51:9; 64:7; 69:26; 21:15; 103:3; 147:3; Jeremiah 30:14; I Kings 8:37; Acts 4:10; 8:6; 9:33; 14:8; Mark 2:1; 9:2; Matthew 8:1; 9:2; 17:1; Luke 9:28; James 5:13; John 5:1. For a study of the ideas of mental disorder in ancient Hebrew writings, see B. Morris, *Scriptural Psychiatry* (1946).
3. This case, along with numerous others, is described in J. Sprenger and H. Kraemer (Institoris), *Malleus Maleficarum* (1928), pp. 169–70. The work originally was printed sometime between 1487 and 1489.

The generalization quoted would include the views of the physicians as well as the theologians of the period. G. Zilboorg, in *The Medical Man and the Witch* (1935), rightly points to gross differences in the views of priest and physician concerning the dangerousness and handling of the mentally disordered but overlooks the fact that both priest and physician (even the most enlightened example Zilboorg could find, namely Johannes Weyer) saw alike on the issue of etiology, on moral causation. Zilboorg also takes confusing positions by discussing at one time as mentally disordered the witches, at another time the priests, at still other times the entire population. Such a tendency among modern writers has been criticized in some detail by E. H. Ackerknecht, "Psychopathology, Primitive Medicine, and Primitive Culture," *Bulletin of the History of Medicine,* XIV (1943), and by F. Schneersohn, "Zur Gründlegung einer Völker und Massenpsychopathologie," *Ethos,* I (1925–26).

4. A. I. Hallowell, "Sin, Sex and Sickness among the Salteaux," *British Journal of Medical Psychology,* XVIII (1939). For surveys of the primitive conception of mental disorder, see W. H. R. Rivers, *Medicine, Magic and Religion* (1924); Ackerknecht, "Psychopathology, Primitive Medicine"; J. L. Maddox, *Medicine Man* (1923); Bartels, *Die Medizin;* W. G. Sumner and A. G. Keller, *Science of Society* (3 vols., 1927), II, 1342, 1388, 1420; and F. E. Clements, *Primitive Concepts of Disease,* Vol. 32, No. 2, University of California Publications in American Archaeology and Ethnology (1932). Clements' work would have been much more valuable had he distinguished between concepts of mental and physical disease and had not the categories he chose overlapped completely the central one of taboo violation. Even in his restricted sense, however, the breech-of-a-taboo disease concept is found in every major culture area of the world except for a small number; and for almost each one of the exceptions evidence for the existence of the concept can be found in the bibliographical materials of this chapter. Rivers' division of disease concepts into human (witch, sorcerer, etc.) and supernatural agencies similarly overlooks the cause common to both, namely improper thought or conduct. For an example of the detailed connections of bewitchment to thought and conduct among primitives, see E. E. Evans-Pritchard, *Witchcraft, Oracles and Magic among the Azande* (1937). For some localized studies of the moral transgression idea of mental disorder, see the work of Sereno, "Obeah"; E. and P. Beaglehole, *Some Modern Maoris* (1946);

Robert and Margaret Park Redfield, *Disease and Its Treatment in Dzitas, Yucatan,* Vol. VII, No. 32, Contributions to American Anthropology and History (1940); F. C. Nicolas, "Aborigines of the Province of Santa Maria, Colombia," *American Anthropologist* III (1901); and W. La Barre, "Primitive Psychotherapy in Native American Cultures: Peyotism and Confession," *Journal of Abnormal and Social Psychology,* XLII (1947).

5. Hippocrates, "Ancient Medicine," *The Genuine Works of Hippocrates* (2 vols., 1849), p. 164. Indeed it is difficult to find therapeutic nihilists anywhere. Not even Christian Science seems to fit the term; see H. W. Steiger, *Christian Science and Philosophy* (1948).

6. For this expectation of the Greek physician, see Edelstein, *Asclepius;* for that of the modern physician, see the cases of referrals in any of the books on psychosomatic medicine cited in Chapter Eight, n. 21. For primitive discrimination among illnesses, see, e.g., Hallowell, "Sin, Sex and Sickness," p. 191; Beaglehole, *Some Modern Maoris;* Clements, *Primitive Disease;* and Sumner and Keller, *Science of Society,* II, 1384. For examples of the size and effectiveness of primitive pharmacies, see Maddox; *Medicine Man,* pp. 227 82. Evans-Pritchard's *Witchcraft* should be referred to for an example not only of the range of the primitive materia medica but of the complexity of primitive thought on therapeutic topics generally.

7. K. Horney, *The Neurotic Personality of Our Time* (1937), p. 23; see also her *New Ways in Psychoanalysis* (1939), pp. 193–206. Freud's statement occurs on p. 111 of *The Problem of Anxiety* (1936). See also his *General Introduction* (1921) and *New Introductory Lectures.* See further H. S. Sullivan, "Theory of Anxiety"; A. Freud, *The Ego and the Mechanisms of Defense* (1937); and Shoben, "Psychotherapy," which specifically notes the presence of anxiety as a common element in clinical cases.

8. Horney, *New Ways,* p. 232. See also n. 13, below.

9. S. Freud, *New Introductory Lectures,* pp. 148–51. One can also see Freud's interest in guilt in *Totem and Taboo* (1918). See, too, H. Nunberg, "Sense of Guilt and the Need for Punishment," *International Journal of Psychoanalysis,* VII (1926),

and "The Feeling of Guilt," *Psychoanalytic Quarterly*, III
(1934); and J. C. Flugel, *Man, Morals and Society* (1945).

10. W. Stekel, "The Harvest," *Journal of Criminal Psychopathology*, VII (1945–46).

11. Of the cases that follow in brief statement of moral conflict,
the first four are taken from F. Alexander and T. M. French,
Psychoanalytic Therapy (1946), the next seven from C. Berg,
Casebook of a Medical Psychologist (1948), and the last three
from W. Snyder, *Casebook of Non-directive Counseling*
(1947).

The clarification that comes to a case once the moral conflict
can be delineated leads to the hope that someday neuroses
might be classified in this fashion. Such a classification might
be attempted today and could serve as a guide to existing
moral confusion were it not for the fact that there is no collection of all or even a sample of all cases handled by psychotherapists. The cases they now publish are at best theoretical
contributions and at worst merely sensational. The bulk of
cases, monotonous in their ordinariness, never see the light of
day.

12. The first sentence is a quotation from H. S. Sullivan, *Conceptions of Modern Psychiatry* (1947), p. 102.

13. R. Burton, *The Anatomy of Melancholy* (3 vols., 1923).
Rank's statement appears in "Beyond Psychoanalysis," *Psychoanalytic Review*, XVI (1929). For Jung's views, see his
Modern Man in Search of a Soul (1934); for Adler, see *Practice and Theory of Individual Psychology* (1929). For the
moral concept in French psychotherapy, see J. J. Dejerine and
E. Gauckler, *Psychoneuroses and Their Treatment by Psychotherapy* (1913). For an early Spanish work, see C. A.
Puertas, *Gobierno moral y médico para conservas la salud y
buenas costumbres* (Pamplona, 1694).

The distinction made by F. Alexander in *Fundamentals of
Psychoanalysis* (1948) between guilt and inferiority feelings as
leading to different kinds of action, even if a valid distinction,
would not affect their indentity as presented here. Feelings both
of guilt and of weakness, in his sense, depend on a judgment of
conscience. "Weakness" as used by Alexander connotes moral
self-condemnation.

Even the physiological or behaviorist theory of neurosis involves a hidden acceptance of the moral theory. Thus I. P.
Pavlov in *Conditioned Reflexes and Psychiatry* (1941), wrote,
in describing the theory, that "with the collision of . . . excitatory and . . . inhibitory processes, there appears either a
predominance of the stimulating process, disturbing the inhibi-
tion . . . or in other cases a predominance of the inhibitory
process . . . disturbing the excitatory process." For excitatory
read "emotional"; for inhibitory, read "moral" or "conscience."

14. Military medical examinations in the United States during
World War II, e.g., usually were given collectively, while
psychiatric interviews were held in private. For the confessional, see J. Tixeront, *History of the Seal of Confession*
(1927), and Chapter Eight above. The secrecy of psychotherapeutic communication, however, is not one of the universals of
psychotherapy; in many places the therapy is given in the
presence of kinsmen or other persons. See, e.g., Gillin, "Magic
Fright," Hallowell, "Sin, Sex and Sickness"; and n. 3, pp. 264–
65, below.

For the important question of communications privileged at
law see J. Wigmore, *A Treatise on the Anglo-American System
of Evidence in Trials at Common Law* (3rd ed., 1940), Vol.
VIII, Chaps. 82, 86, 87. In a recent murder trial in Iowa a
university counselor, not having medical, legal, or clerical
status, was forced to submit the details of his interviews with
the accused, although as is customary (and untruthful) the
secrecy of the interviews had been implied. See E. J. Shoben,
Jr., "Psychologists and Legality; A Case Report," *American
Psychologist* (1950). Psychiatrists and psychoanalysts, nearly all
of whom possess the Doctor of Medicine degree, do not have
this restriction and can truthfully guarantee secrecy. However,
it is the accident of their status as doctors and not their work
as psychotherapists that gives them this privilege. See Chapters
Eight to Ten above.

CHAPTER FOUR, PAGES 42–65

1. The quotations in this sentence are respectively from Maddox,
Medicine Man, p. 114; Bartels, *Die Medizin,* p. 50; Sumner

and Keller, *Science of Society,* II, 1395; and Evans-Pritchard, *Witchcraft,* p. 251. See also S. M. Shirokogoroff, *The Psycho-mental Complex of the Tungus* (1935); W. Z. Park, *Shaman-ism in Western North America* (1938); R. F. Fortune, *Sorcer-ers of Dobu* (1932); W. Lloyd Warner, *A Black Civilization* (1937); Kluckhohn, *Navaho Witchcraft* (1944); and B. Mali-nowski, *Coral Gardens and Their Magic* (2 vols., 1935). For variations in the status of doctors, see J. Hermann Baas, *Out-lines of the History of Medicine and the Medical Profession* (1889).

For data on women as healers, see R. Briffault, *The Mothers* (3 vols., 1927), I, 485–91; Maddox, *Medicine Man,* pp. 72–90; and M. A. Czaplicka, *Aboriginal Siberia* (1914).

2. C. Rogers, *Counseling and Psychotherapy* (1942), p. 53.

3. W. U. Snyder, "A Comparison of One Unsuccessful with Four Successful Non-directively Counseled Cases," *Journal of Con-sulting Psychology,* XI (1947). See also B. J. Covner, "Non-directive Interviewing Techniques in Vocational Counseling," *Journal of Consulting Psychology,* XI (1947), which learned that "most clients" had the same expectation.

4. National Opinion Research Center, *National Opinion on Oc-cupations* (Chicago, 1947; mimeographed). Thanks are due Dr. Clyde W. Hart, director of the Center, for the use of this study.

5. S. Freud, *The Problem of Lay-Analyses* (1927). In the last few years there has been a stir among some psychoanalytic groups to train candidates who are not Doctors of Medicine. On thera-peutic training see Chapter Seven above.

6. S. Freud, *Introductory Lectures* (1936), p. 374. For some ex-amples: in industrial counseling, the case of "Bill" in S. G. Law, *Therapy Through Interview* (1948); in a criminal case, R. M. Lindner, *Rebel Without a Cause* (1944); in social service work, H. J. Mills, "Prognostic Value of the First Inter-view," *Smith College Studies in Social Work,* VIII (1937).

7. See, e.g., L. R. Steiner, *Where Do People Take Their Troubles?* (1945); and H. L. Mencken, *The American Language: Sup-plement I* (1945), pp. 525–64.

8. R. Landau, *God Is My Adventure,* (1936), pp. 149–59. For

healing in modern American cults, see, e.g., C. S. Braden, *These Also Believe* (1949).

9. F. G. Crookshank, "The Psychological Interest in General Practice," *British Medical Journal,* No. 3717 (1932).

10. *The Case of Mrs. Ett* (Chicago: Counseling Center of the University of Chicago, 1947; mimeographed), pp. 40, 94, 142, 157. Thanks are due Dr. Carl Rogers, executive secretary of the Center, for the use of this case.

11. Berg, *Casebook,* pp. 210–13.

12. Alexander and French, *Psychoanalytic Therapy,* p. 296.

13. See, e.g., T. M. French and R. Ormsby, *Psychoanalytic Orientation in Case Work* (1944).

14. C. Rogers, *Counseling,* p. 109. For hypnosis allegedly without authority see L. R. Wolberg, *Medical Hypnosis* (2 vols., 1948), I, 436–39, and II, 364–65.

15. Alexander and French, *Psychoanalytic Therapy,* p. 17; on p. 73 the phrase "figures of importance" is used in the definition. See also O. Fenichel, *Psychoanalytic Theory of the Neurosis* (1945), pp. 559–64.

Freud's statement is to be found in *Lay-Analyses,* p. 176. His clearest statements of the concept of transference are in the case of Dora in *Collected Papers,* III, 11 146, and in *Introductory Lectures,* pp. 360–88.

A handful of psychiatrists and psychologists now see the existence of authority in the psychotherapeutic situation, but it is more clearly recognized by the anthropologist R. Linton in *The Science of Man in the World Crisis* (1945), p. 447; and better yet by the sociologist T. Parsons in *Essays in Sociological Theory* (1949), 288–95.

Originally the psychoanalysts held, and many of them still have not clarified their thoughts on the subject, that the transference included the re-enactment of relationships the patient had in childhood with anyone—brothers, sisters, peers, and so on. Their theory of the transference with its explanation of the patient's love and compliance is inconsistent, however, unless it includes the assumption that with any of these figures the patient must have had a filial relationship, as a child might have with an older sister if his mother were dead or working away from home much of the time.

16. Berg, *Casebook,* p. 206.

17. Alexander and French, *Psychoanalytic Therapy,* pp. 259–60.

18. E. Glover in *Technique of Psychoanalysis* (1940) and S. Ferenczi in *Further Contributions to the Theory and Technique of Psychoanalysis* (1926). Eyesenck's study, *Dimensions of Personality,* also shows the prominence of suggestibility in the neuroses but apparently assumes it to be a cause rather than an effect.

19. *The Case of Mrs. Ett,* p. 179.

20. Alexander and French, *Psychoanalytic Therapy,* p. 36.

21. W. E. Hocking, *Science and the Idea of God* (1944), p. 40.

CHAPTER FIVE, PAGES 66–102

1. Nicholas, "Aborigines," pp. 639–40. For the life-and-death powers of the shaman, see especially Bartels, *Die Medizin.*

2. A. Salter, *Conditioned Reflex Therapy* (1949), p. 134; also pp. 69, 111, 169, 181, 273. See, too, e.g., A. Herzberg, *Active Psychotherapy* (1945).

3. The statements are taken respectively from C. Rogers, *Counseling,* p. 88; N. Cantor, *Employee Counseling* (1945), p. 98; Fenichel, *Theory of Neurosis,* p. 5; and Freud, *Collected Works,* II, 398.

4. A. Green, "Social Values and Psychotherapy," *Journal of Personality,* XIV (1946). See also J. Wortis, "Freudianism and the Psychoanalytic Tradition," *American Journal of Psychiatry,* CI (1945); and K. Davis, "Mental Hygiene and the Class Structure," *Psychiatry,* I (1938).

5. Cantor, *Employee Counseling,* pp. 108–9.

6. This quotation and the preceding one are from *The Case of Mrs. Ett,* pp. 30, 13.

7. Ibid., pp. 57, 63.

8. P. Federn, "Employment of Neurotics," *Journal of Clinical Psychology,* VII (1945–46). For "A Note on the Architecture of the Psychiatric Ward," see B. Merrill in *American Journal of Psychiatry,* CV (1948–49).

9. B. Bettelheim and E. Sylvester, "Milieu Therapy," *Psychoanalytic Review,* XXXVI (1949). See also Bettelheim's *Love Is Not Enough* (1950).

10. The first example is from C. Rogers, *Counseling,* p. 285; the second from Earl F. Zinn, *A Psychoanalytic Study of a Schizophrenic* (5 vols.; New Haven, Conn.: Institute of Human Relations, Yale University, no date; typewritten). Thanks are due Dr. Mark A. May, director of the Institute, for the use of this case.

11. *Case of Mrs. Ett,* pp. 16, 59. Sometimes such therapists make a point of saying that what they do is not to repeat what the patient says but to respond to his feeling. This, however, by increasing the ambiguity merely enlarges the problem. Suppose that a patient says to his therapist with heat, "I think you're dead wrong!" What does the therapist try to do, reproduce the heat? And how does he do that without some words or gestures on which to attach the heat? Suppose, then, that he "responds to the feeling" by saying, "You think I am completely mistaken!" and grant him the ability to generate the exact amount of heat with which the patient spoke. Is this the patient's feeling, or even his meaning, or did he wish to say to his therapist, "I hope you are wrong and I wish you were dead"?

Such circuitous efforts to avoid making judgment are not only impractical but lacking in merit.

12. Berg, *Casebook,* p. 99. For another case in which silence of a different kind played an important role see Law, *Therapy Through Interview,* the case of "Bill."

13. C. Rogers, *Counseling,* p. 329, and see note, p. 330.

14. The first example is from the *Case of Mrs. Ett,* p. 102. (Details of the article the patient saved for the therapist have been deleted to help preserve anonymity.) The second example is from Zinn, *Psychoanalytic Study,* II, 632. For another instance of the use of language differing from the first case, see S. Freud's "Rat-man case," *Collected Papers,* III, 304. See also the policy on obscene words expressed by S. Ferenczi in *Contributions to Psychoanalysis* (1916).

15. The first interview is from E. E. Evans-Pritchard, *The Nuer* (1940), pp. 12–13 (see also the author's remarks, p. 15, on the Nuer as an equal); the second is from the *Case of Mrs. Ett,* p. 98.

For some of the subtler responses of psychotherapeutic patients see, e.g., E. W. Lazell, "Group Psychic Treatment of

Dementia Praecox by Lectures in Mental Re-education," *U. S. Veteran's Bureau Medical Bulletin*, VI (1930); T. A. Watters, "The Ego and the Eye," *North Carolina Medical Journal*, IX (1948); K. R. Eissler, "Limitations to the Psychotherapy of Schizophrenia," *Psychiatry*, IV (1943); J. Layard, "Primitive Kinship as Mirrored in the Psychological Structure of Modern Man," *British Journal of Medical Psychology*, XX (1944–46); T. Benedek and A. Rubenstein, *Sexual Cycle in Women*, Vol. III, *Psychosomatic Medical Monographs* (1942).

16. C. Rogers, *Counseling*, pp. 309–10, 312, 316.

17. The case excerpt is from Snyder, *Casebook*, p. 147; the patient's report is from C. Rogers, "Some Observations on the Organization of Personality," *American Psychologist*, II (1947). For the terminology of the non-directive or client-centered school see the works of C. Rogers and W. U. Snyder. For two others considered sometimes as belonging to this school, sometimes as comprising another school, called "relationship therapy," see F. H. Allen, *Psychotherapy with Children* (1942), and J. J. Taft, *Dynamics of Therapy in a Controlled Relationship* (1933). The terminology of these therapists can be illuminatingly compared to that used by a psychoanalyst; see, e.g., C. Berg, *Deep Analysis* (1947). On pp. 84, 154–55, 174, e.g., the patient's repetition of the therapist's jargon should be compared with that in Rogers, ibid.

S. Deri in *An Introduction to the Szondi Test* (1949) remarks appropriately: "I have noticed, although I have made no systematic study, that different schools of psychotherapy tend to effect different 'K' constellations in the patient, depending on their explicitly or tacitly implied value-judgments in regard to social behavior."

18. All published modern verbatim cases were consulted for this study, and possibly also the majority of unpublished recorded cases whether typewritten, mimeographed, or phonographically, wire, or tape recorded. The number of truly verbatim cases is much smaller than is usually realized, an understandable fact in view of the cost and labor involved in recording one. Fully verbatim psychoanalytic cases are extremely rare, analysts generally being reluctant to record their interviews. The largest collection of verbatim cases is that at the Counsel-

ing Center at the University of Chicago, almost exclusively handled, however, in the non-directive fashion that dominates the Center.

19. The case is from Berg, *Casebook,* pp. 78–80.

CHAPTER SIX, PAGES 103–131

1. If the presence of authority in therapy is not only a universal but also a causal factor, it should be true that when authority is not present therapists discover that their efforts are ineffectual. In the case of persons involuntarily brought to the therapist this has been shown to be the result. In addition to the works cited in n. 6, Chapter Four, see B. Karpman, *Case Studies in the Psychopathology of Crime* (2 vols., 1944). The inutility of the friend has been noted by Freud, *Collected Papers,* pp. 313–14. It is sometimes said that a stranger can act as a therapist. Sociologists especially have noted that persons find it easier to talk about intimate matters with strangers to a community There are two possible reasons for this: first, the stranger may have some status or authority in his own right; second, he has been exposed to at least two different environments, his old community and the new, and as a result is conversant with at least two varying moralities. Accordingly he is less likely to be morally shocked at immoral disclosures, is in other words more tolerant. But unless he has some authority his tolerance will not provide more than the temporary relief one gets from any person with coincident morality. This temporary relief explains the phenomenon of "listeners," persons in big cities who advertise that they will listen to anyone at a certain price per fractions of an hour without ever responding. Their authority, augmented only by the advertising they do, is no greater than that of any other person; their moral tolerance—since they merely sit and listen and respond little more than a stick of wood—is greater perforce.

Other evidence for the causal validity of the theory of authority exists (1) in cases where the therapist's authority, first present and accordingly effective, is for some reason broken; and (2) in cases where conflicts in authority exist. For the latter instance, see, e.g., A. Stanton and M. Schwartz, "Observations on Dissociation as Social Participation," *Psychiatry*, XII (1949), which depicts the harmful results in mental hospitals when diverse therapists give diverse counsel to the same patient. The same problem exists in "multiple" psychotherapy. See, e.g., J. Warkentin, et al., "A Comparison of Individual and Multiple Psychotherapy," *Psychiatry*, XIV (1951). On a national scale the results of the conflicting directives of political rulers was analyzed in *The Political Community*. Of the former instance, authority present and then broken, see, e.g., the case of B. Bandler reported in C. P. Oberndorf et al., "Symposium on the Evaluation of Therapeutic Results," *International Journal of Psychoanalysis*, XXIX (1948). For another relevant case, see above, Chapter Seven, pp. 135–36; see also n. 5, pp. 258–60, below.

2. G. B. Chisholm, "The Reestablishment of Peacetime Society; The Responsibility of Psychiatry," *Psychiatry*, IX (1946).

3. The word "passion" was used in this study because it can mean today an intense desire or feeling for an end or goal without connoting that the desire or feeling is either innate or acquired, or moral or immoral; and because it has a long history in political philosophy, appearing in such diverse writings as those of Locke, Hobbes, Thomas, R. G. Collingwood, Fourier, and before these, in the works of Aristotle, Epictetus, and Seneca. See also Chapter Ten above.

4. A recent expression of the "state of good nature" theory put in the form of a commandment: "Thou shalt honour the need of every human organism to persist in its own being and to reach its normal completion or actualisation" (Wooton, *Testament for Social Science*, p. 181). For educational works stemming from this theory for which Rousseau's *Émile* was a trail blazer, see, e.g., Bertrand Russell, *On Education* (1926); M. J. Radke, *Relation of Parental Authority to Children's Behavior Attitudes* (1947); R. Lippitt, "An Experimental Study of the Effect of Democratic and Authoritarian Group Atmospheres," *Studies in Topological and Vector Psychology* (1940); and K. Lewin et al., "Authority and Frustration," *Studies in Topological and Vector Psychology*, III (1944). R. Demos describes the state of affairs in "On the Decline of Authority," *International Journal of Ethics*, XXXVI (1926). The view

so thoroughly permeates the field of educational study that it is perhaps more important to cite the works of educators whose views are diverse. See E. T. Campagnac, *Education in Its Relation to the Common Purposes of Humanity* (1925); A. Meiklejohn, *Education Between Two Worlds* (1942); B. Brickman, "Relation Between Indoctrination and the Teaching of Democracy," *Social Studies,* XXXV (1944); Max Horkheimer, ed., *Studien über Autorität und Familie* (Paris, 1936); K. D. Benne, *A Conception of Authority* (1943); J. S. Plant, *The Envelope* (1950); J. H. Nelis, *Die Autorität als pädagogisches Problem* (Kallmung, 1933); W. H. Kilpatrick, *Education for a Changing Civilization* (1926). For a recognition of the error in the psychoanalytical contribution to educational theory see E. Kris, "On Psychoanalysis and Education," *American Journal of Orthopsychiatry,* XVIII (1948).

5. Sereno, "Obeah," p. 24; the description of the Indians is from J. F. Lafitau, *Moeurs des sauvages Amériquains* (2 vols.; Paris, 1724), II, 274, 280, 284–86.

A difficult theoretical question arises here. Prolonged torture has been known to drive men insane. How does such insanity fit the general theory of neurosis here presented? The question can be resolved theoretically in two ways. One can say that it is possible though not perfectly understood that prolonged intense pain physiologically damages the organism. (This would mean that the resultant insanity belongs to the category of organic damage.) One can also maintain that, depending on early training such as that of the Indians, the organism can sustain pain until the person becomes mercifully unconscious or dies. This second view would hold that the essential condition is the education of the child for a world in which torture is a recognized part; that where this education has not been had, torture is so extraordinary and unexpected that the protracted pain will signify the collapse of the person's world, its abandonment by God to the fiends, or alternately, as in the dilemma of Job, that the person is guilty of some transgression and thus visited by punishment. See n. 3, pp. 269–70. In this second case the moral element is present.

There is no way of deciding which of these views is correct, direct evidence is happily non-existent, and in fact for the purpose at hand there is no need to decide one way or the other. The essential fact here is solely that torture considered unbearable has been borne by the members of some communities and this tolerance of pain is attributable to their rearing.

6. The first quotation is from B. J. F. Laubscher, *Sex, Custom and Psychopathology* (1937), p. 29; the second is from M. Covarrubias, *Island of Bali* (1937), p. 351.

7. Wolberg, *Medical Hypnosis*, I, 90, 116. For an example of hypnotic phenomena, see L. F. Cooper, "Time Distortion in Hypnosis," *The Bulletin, Georgetown University Medical Center*, I (1948). See also below, n. 5, pp. 258–60.

8. R. Underhill, "Autobiography of a Papago Woman," *Memoirs of the American Anthropological Association No. 46* (1936), p. 5. See also R. C. Cabot, *Psychotherapy and Its Relation to Religion* (1908), pp. 38–39, for the use of a similar method in psychotherapy. For the related but not identical (because of the relative absence of authority) subject of sleep-learning, see the article by J. D. Ratcliff, "Learn While You Sleep," *Look Magazine*, March 14, 1950, which summarizes conveniently the unpublished work of C. R. Elliott and M. Sherover.

9. W. L. Warner, *Black Civilization*, p. 288.

10. For a work describing such cases, see, e.g., J. Paul de River, *The Sexual Criminal* (1949).

For modern political studies that discuss authority seriously and with discrimination, see W. W. Willoughby, *The Ethical Basis of Political Authority* (1930); Yves Simon, *Nature and Functions of Authority* (1940); C. E. Merriam, *Political Power* (1934); R. M. McIver, *Society: Its Structure and Changes* (1931); and H. D. Lasswell and A. Kaplan, *Power and Society* (1950). In contrast to these works are those that make a political use of the term that imitates the psychological and educational use already observed. See, e.g., H. V. Dicks, *The Psychological Foundations of the Wehrmacht* (a report made for British military use, 1944); B. Schaffner, *Fatherland* (1948); H. Becker, "The Regimented Man," *Social Forces*, XXVIII (1949); and T. W. Adorno et al., *The Authoritarian Personality* (1950).

In political science it is to be regretted that the meaning of authority and its central position in the discipline has been forgotten. The Latin word *auctoritas* comes from *auctor* which in turn comes from *augere*, meaning "to increase" or "to produce" (a sense now absorbed in the English "author"), and from *augescere*, signifying "to further." These meanings, "to produce" and "to further," are of the utmost importance for political science in its conceptions of authority, rules, and rulers. (On *rulers*, see *The Political Community;* see also Sebastian de Grazia, "The Principle of Authority in Its Relation to Freedom," *Educational Forum*, Jan. 1951, and "Authority and Rationality," *Philosophy*, XXVI [1952], articles of which extensive use was made in this chapter.)

The confusion in most political studies, even the good ones, results either from an inability (due to disinclination or to insufficient analysis) to put authority in anything but a tangential theoretical position or from a Thrasymachian confusion of authority with its trappings or with power or force. Thus in Lasswell and Kaplan, *Power and Society*, pp. 133–37, authority is defined as formal power, thereby confounding it with its always varying trappings in the manner of King Lear's phrase, "There thou mightst behold the great image of authority: a dog's obeyed in office." Again in such propositions as "Authority alone is power of low weight . . ." or "Weight of authority varies with the prestige of the authorities," there exists a misunderstanding of the fact that political authority is extended to those who are thought to have the most important mortal power that the community values. It is therefore impossible to state as a general proposition that this is a power of low weight. Either the power is unimportant or those said to have it are found really not to have it or to exercise it not for the common good—in all three cases political authority then ceases to exist. The same can be said for proposals, the most recent of which seems to be that of J. Maritain in "The World and the Wise," *Common Cause*, III (1950) to establish a council of the wise "endowed with unquestionable *moral authority*." Political authority cannot be extended the wise unless the community believes the things these wise men are wise in are the attainment, preservation, and furtherance of the things it cherishes most of all. When people believe that the handling and disposition of military forces are vitally important, the political and moral authority of generals will be greater than that of mandarins.

11. On the healing of kings and rulers specifically, see M. Bloch, *Les Rois thaumaturges* (Paris, 1924); J. G. Frazer, *The Golden Bough* (2 vols.; London, 1890); and for modern times, K. Martin, *Magic of Monarchy* (1937). See also Shakespeare's *Macbeth*, Act IV, Scene iii, lines 139–58. The stars of film or theater or sports also have a healing power with those for whom they are idols. E.g., see the case of the fourteen-year-old crippled girl reported in "The Town Crier," Chicago *Daily News*, March 28, 1949; similar items are a common occurrence in the day's news. Royal processions, visits to hospitals of kings and dictators and presidents, frequently produce healing phenomena.

12. M. G. Ernst, "A Psychotherapeutic Approach in Schizophrenia," *Journal of Mental Science*, LXXXVI (1940). For the ancient ceremony of the laying on of hands, see J. Coppens, *L'Imposition des mains et les rites connexes* (Paris, 1925).

CHAPTER SEVEN, PAGES 132–162

1. B. Bandler in Oberndorf et al., "Symposium," pp. 26–27. See also, e.g., R. Kapeller, "The Post-Analytic Migratory Symptom," *Journal of Criminal Psychopathology*, VII (1945–46). For a typical imputation of this theory to other schools, see A. Noyes, *Modern Clinical Psychiatry* (1948).

2. Stekel, "Harvest," p. 127. This case also clearly illustrates the effect on psychotherapy of conflicting authority; see n. 1, pp. 251–52.

3. W. Reich, *Sexual Revolution* (1945), pp. 14–15. For a modern discussion of the theory of appetites, see H. A. Murray, "Facts Which Support the Concept of Need or Drive," *Journal of Psychiatry*, III (1937). The hope is sometimes indulged by various writers that, once more is known about the biological ingredients of the appetites, the problem of a scientific psychotherapy will be solved by the use of drugs, injections, or operations. Even were such a hope realized, the problem would remain stationary. The question asked about the girl in the case above—what about her sexuality as such?—would remain still

to be answered. Why should one use such drugs? The use of lobotomy today, e.g., poses similar problems. See the discussion of shock therapy above, Chapter Nine.

4. For this theory, see, e.g., P. Bergman, "Germinal Cell of Freud's Psychoanalytic Psychology and Therapy," *Psychiatry,* XII (1949), and for the most recent psychoanalytic version, H. S. Sullivan, *Conceptions,* pp. 102, 117, 141. For an example of the idea that everybody should be psychoanalyzed, see S. Freud, *New Introductory Lectures,* pp. 204–5. Freud never could shed his interest in building a system of psychology out of what began as therapy—psychoanalysis. One sees him often like a detective in hot pursuit of a clue, a name, or a number, until he has traced to his satisfaction all the converging psychological elements. The result is not the health of the patient but a brilliant mosaic, a monument to Freud's belief in psychological determinism. Freud himself was well aware of a distinction between therapy and a theory of learning and psychology. See ibid, pp. 207, 214–15, and Vol. III of his *Collected Papers.* K. Abraham once said in "Notes on Coué's Method of Self-Mastery, *International Journal of Psychoanalysis,* VII (1926), "Let us quote his [Coué's] own words: 'It is better not to know from where an ill comes and yet to drive it away, than to know and not to be able to get rid of it.' The psychoanalytic method is at the opposite pole to this." However, the conflict between therapy and either psychological theory or an emphasis on diagnosis is one that can be exaggerated. Each aspect helps the other; one of the purposes of a psychological theory, but not the only one, is to help understand the process of therapy and thus indirectly to help heal. The important thing is to recognize that often while collecting psychological data about the patient one is not helping to heal him.

For various works exemplifying the normative use of words like "oral," "anal," "infantile," "immature," and "regressive" see J. Ruesch, "The Infantile Personality," *Psychosomatic Medicine,* X (1948); H. A. Overstreet, *The Structure and Meaning of Psychoanalysis* (1930); E. A. Strecker and K. E. Appel, *Discovering Ourselves* (1931); and C. Saul, *Emotional Maturity* (1947). Naturally the effort to discover a non-ethical psychological definition of maturity fails even in such serious attempts as those of G. W. Allport in both *Personality* (1937) and *The Individual and His Religion* (1950).

5. For an example of this gradual letting out of the true story, see Berg, *Casebook,* pp. 192–95. For recognition of the fact that psychological knowledge of oneself, or insight or the recovery of memories, is insufficient for therapy, see, e.g., C. P. Oberndorf, "Factors in Psychoanalytic Therapy," *American Journal of Psychiatry,* XCIX (1941–42); Dejerine and Gauckler, *Psychoneuroses;* and S. Ferenczi and O. Rank, *Development of Psychoanalyses* (1925), p. 22, which speaks of the kind of patient "who, after a lengthy analysis, has the whole analytic knowledge of his analyst in his little finger, and can even surpass him in analyzing his own symptoms without having been in the least helped in regard to his suffering."

The essential points in the discussion above are (1) that therapists operating with the theory find it no longer corresponds to their clinical experience; (2) that the moral conflict concerns present adult, not past childhood, standards; (3) that the patient's gradual entrusting of the memory of certain experiences to the therapist, rather than a sudden revelation from the unconscious, can be explained as his gradual coming to believe in the "no moral judgment" doctrine of his therapist; (4) that a full assembly of *temps perdu* is humanly impossible; and (5) that the psychoanalytic practice of free association selects certain types of memories.

The last point deprives the theory of facts, for it applies not only to the psychoanalytic situation as such but also to what is now the deepest cache of evidence—hypnosis. Free association, reverie, the recounting of dreams, and their interpretation can all be shown to be not free but influenced by the authoritative presence of the therapist. The most that remains of support for the theory is what is supplied by hypnosis in such articles as M. H. Erickson and L. B. Hill, "Unconscious Mental Activity in Hypnosis," *Psychoanalytic Quarterly,* XIII (1941), where the subject under hypnosis is directed to perform certain actions and not to reveal his motives ("motives" in this case meaning the source of his instructions). Here, however, the very same considerations that applied in the analytic interview apply in even greater force. The subject wants to do what the hypnotist tells him. As in the therapeutic relationship, he not only listens to the therapist's words but divines his meaning from the subtleties of his acts and the situation. When the subject is later asked, "Why did you do this?" and if as a reason he gives some answer other than "You told me to," he is merely taking his cues. This is evidence not for an unconscious but for an extraordinary fidelity to the therapist's wishes. The instructions can be brought to recall by anyone who can fulfill the role of hypnotist for the subject. Indeed it is amusing to watch how much rival hypnotists can learn about one another's instructions when they can have, as sometimes happens, the same subject. Under such conditions of divergent loyalties, the so-called unconscious becomes obvious and most apparent to him who wins the subject's greatest loyalty.

Apart from the lack of evidence, to ask whether the unconscious exists is to ask paradoxically whether memory exists. If memory exists, experiences can be recalled and relived (for memory involves a partial re-experiencing) but until recall they are unconscious. Thus if there were no memory there could be no unconscious. To object that the unconscious is that part of recorded experience that influences action serves no purpose. All a man's past affects his action, some experiences more than others. And all of it is unconscious until the moment of recall. Nor is it correct to say that unless he knows the full history of an act a man in acting it acts from unconscious motives. In ordinary usage a man's acts are considered consciously motivated if he can give an acceptable motive for them. If one asks a man why he often eats an orange after lunch, he may say he likes the aftertaste of something sweet and refreshing. This, as an expression of the resultum of past experience, is generally accepted as an answer. If one wants to go into the history of this taste for oranges, one may find that the experiences associated with it are extremely difficult to recall because the act never was a matter of great passion. These unimportant experiences, like subliminal figures in the periphery of vision, are those that in the sense of difficulty of recall are more unconscious than the passionate experiences. Though they influence behavior they may never be recalled except through accident, e.g., of another experience nearly parallel. How to get at these memories makes up another field of psychology.

In fact there is a utility, an economy, in not being aware of the history of one's acts that at times becomes vitally important. For a soldier to stop to recall why he acts to protect his comrade —before pulling him down out of a line of fire—could be fatal.

Usually one is not interested in the history of an act unless one wants to do something about it—preserve it or change it or remove it. But (1) knowing the history of an act does not change it, though applying new moral standards to it can and often does; and (2) there are many other ways of changing the acts of men without resorting to a detailed recall or reliving of past experience.

In any case the theory of the unconscious is clinically useless and legally harmful (see Chapter Ten). It should be replaced by a theory of the conditions under which past experiences can be recalled and related. Women say things to women that they keep "unconscious" when talking to men. A man may find a friend to whom he can speak about some parts of his past that to others of his friends remain "unconscious." As one gets older one's ideas about the moral tribulations of one's youth may so change that experiences that hurt greatly to remember while young become mellow recollections, recountable to almost anyone. Not the mysterious and contradictory doctrine of the unconscious should guide study but the problem of to whom and under what circumstances can parts of the past be recalled and recounted.

It should be noted that not all conceptions of the unconscious have been discussed but only the main features of the psychoanalytic doctrine, the most influential in modern therapeutic and legal practice. For a thoughtful consideration of sixteen different conceptions, see J. G. Miller, *Unconsciousness* (1942).

6. L. S. Kubie, *Practical Aspects of Psychoanalysis* (1936), pp. 201–2. For the theory, see, e.g., Shoben, "Psychotherapy."

7. For a modern representative, see H. S. Sullivan, *Conceptions*, p. 141.

8. The quotations are respectively from Horney, "What Is a Neurosis?" *American Journal of Sociology*, XLV (1939–40);

Freud, *Anxiety*, p. 148; and C. A. Séquin, "The Concept of Disease," *Psychosomatic Medicine*, VIII (1946).

9. The long quotation is from A. Gregg, "A Critique of Psychiatry," *American Journal of Psychiatry*, CI (1944); the short one is from M. Moore, "The Private Practice of General Psychiatry," *American Journal of Psychiatry*, XCVIII (1941). For various aspects of the training required of and recommended for psychotherapists, see S. Rado, "Graduate Residency Training in Psychoanalytic Medicine," *American Journal of Psychiatry*, CV (1948–49); D. D. Blocksma and E. H. Porter, Jr., "A Short-Term Training Program in Client-Centered Counseling," *Journal of Consulting Psychology*, XI (1947); F. Fromm-Reichmann, *Principles of Intensive Psychotherapy* (1950); J. G. Miller, "The Mutual Dependence of Professional Training in Psychology and Psychiatry," *American Journal of Psychiatry*, CV (1948–49); L. M. Herrick, "The Employee Counselor in the Federal Service," *Pi Lambda Theta Journal*, XXI (1943); and G. S. Speer, "Certification of Counselors and Psychological Services by Professional Organizations," *Occupations* (February 1949).

One psychotherapist who sometimes used the word "teach" was Adolf Meyer; see, e.g., "The Role of Mental Factors in Psychiatry," *American Journal of Insanity*, LV (1908). The disadvantage of the word is that one is almost obliged to say what it is that one teaches. Other phrases which identify their makers as members of this group are the "corrective emotional experience" of F. Alexander, the "learning" of T. M. French, the "adjustment" of K. Menninger (*The Human Mind* [1945]), the "extensionalization" of A. Korzybski (*Science and Sanity* [1933]); and the "inadequate to the situation," the "excessively complex," the "illusory persons," and the "ineffectiveness of behavior" of H. S. Sullivan.

10. For various attempts to introduce some clarity into the confused question of health, disease, and cure, see O. H. Mowrer, "What Is Normal Behavior," in L. A. Pennington and I. A. Berg, eds., *Introduction to Clinical Psychology* (1948); R. P. Knight, "Evaluation"; K. Goldstein, "Idea of Disease and Therapy," *Review of Religion*, XIII (March 1949); P. E. Meehl and H. McClosky, "Ethical and Political Aspects of Ap-

plied Psychology," *Journal of Abnormal and Social Psychology,* XLII (1947); M. Mead, "Concept of Culture and the Psychosomatic Approach," *Psychiatry,* X (1947); T. Burrow, *Neurosis of Man* (1949); R. W. White, *The Abnormal Personality* (1948); H. F. Darling, "Definition of Psychopathic Personality," *Journal of Nervous and Mental Disease,* CI (1945); F. J. Hacker, "The Concept of Normality and Its Practical Significance," *American Journal of Orthopsychiatry,* XV (1945); J. P. Foley, "The Criterion of Abnormality," *Journal of Abnormal and Social Psychology,* XXX (1935); and L. J. Saul, "The Nature of Psychogenic Cure," *American Journal of Psychiatry,* CI (1944). As long as the problem remains in its present confused state one can expect that every year or so a new and startling method of psychotherapy will be discovered. Since no one knows what cure is, no one can check the wild growth of a lunatic fringe. This should not be taken, of course, as a discouragement to the trying or combining of new methods (see, e.g., F. J. Mott, "Drama and the Evocation of Unconscious Images," *Journal of Clinical Psychology,* VII (1945–46), but rather as an expression of the impossibility of distinguishing the center from the fringe.

11. For various examples of conflicting moral guidance representative of those presented and in addition to the cases presented in previous chapters, see Oberndorf, et al., "Symposium," p. 10; J. F. Cuber, "Functions of the Marriage Counseler," *Marriage and Family Living,* VII (1945); Berg, *Casebook,* p. 53; L. Hutton, *The Single Woman and Her Emotional Problems* (1935); N. G. Harris, ed., *Modern Trends,* p. 62; Watters, "Ego and Eye," p. 13; W. M. Marston, *Emotions of Normal People* (1928); S. W. Ginsberg, "Psychiatry and the Social Order," *Mental Hygiene,* XXXII (1948); K. Davis, "Mental Hygiene"; Federn, "Employment," p. 813; O. Rank, *Will Therapy* (1932), p. 282; F. Alexander, "The Influence of Psychologic Factors in Gastro-Intestinal Disturbances: I," *Psychoanalytic Quarterly,* III (1934).

12. J. M. Mackintosh, *The War and Mental Health* (1944). See also R. Ekstein, "Ideological Warfare in the Psychological Sciences," *Psychoanalytic Review,* XXXVI (1949).

13. For this quotation on homosexuality and the one immediately

above, see respectively De River, *The Sexual Criminal,* and
H. Greenspan and J. D. Campbell, "The Homosexual as a
Personality Type," *American Journal of Psychiatry,* CI (1945).
14. The phrase on the physician's love is Ferenczi's, reported in
I. D. Suttie, *Origins of Love and Hate* (1945), p. 212. The
three sentences before the phrase belong to K. Menninger,
"Mission of Psychiatry," *University of Chicago Magazine*
(March 1951). The phrase on acting sadistically is Salter's in
Conditioned Reflex Therapy, p. 122.

Some persons may believe that a central tendency or two
exists in modern psychotherapy, and that this may indicate that
psychotherapy thus is helping the community move toward a
new morality. Whoever is of this opinion cannot be aware of
the varieties of therapies that exist and of the differences among
them. Some may think, e.g., that the attitude toward sex is
commonly "more liberal" in modern healing. But the secular
healers clash not only with the religious on this point (see above,
Chapters Eight and Nine) and with mental hygiene literature
(see, e.g., K. Davis, "Mental Hygiene") but also among themselves (see, e.g., Chapter Five). Perhaps almost all of them
agree on a horror of suicide. Yet, for Freud's view see Oberndorf, et al., "Symposium," p. 10; and for one whose technique
is impaired by his views, the case in Snyder, *Casebook,* pp. 103–
4.

15. For "The Content of Mental Hygiene Literature," see R.
Tyson in *Journal of Clinical Psychiatry,* V (1949); and K.
Davis, "Mental Hygiene." For some examples of newspaper
counseling, see Beatrice Fairfax, *Personal Reply* (1943); and
John J. Anthony, *Mr. Anthony Solves Your Personal Problems*
(1945). For the radio, see W. U. Snyder, "Personal Advice
Over the Radio," *American Psychologist,* IV (1949); and
Federal Communications Commission, *Public Service Responsibility of Broadcast Licensees* (1946). On the related question of
bibliotherapy, see, e.g., J. M. Schneck, "Bibliotherapy in Neuro-
psychiatry," in W. R. Dunton, Jr., and S. Licht, eds., *Occupational Therapy* (1950); and S. Lazarsfeld, "Use of Fiction in
Psychotherapy," *American Journal of Psychotherapy,* III
(1949).

16. The long quotation is from J. R. Rees, *Shaping of Psychiatry*

by War (1945), p. 31; the short one from Wilder, "Facts and Figures," p. 338. See also The Council of State Governments, *The Mental Health Programs of the Forty-Eight States: A Report to the Governor's Conference* (1950), p. 45; Bureau of Labor Statistics, "Employment Outlook for Psychologists," *Occupational Outlook Summary,* (U. S. Department of Labor, 1949; mimeographed) ; and above, n. 1, p. 237.

17. On the problem of rehabilitation which even under the best circumstances is a difficult and delicate task, see T. F. Main, "Rehabilitation and the Individual," in N. G. Harris, ed., *Modern Trends,* pp. 386–411; N. J. Demerath, "Social Solidarity and the Mental Hospital," *Social Forces,* XXI (1942–43); and G. S. Stevenson, "Crisis in the Psychiatric Functions of the State," *Public Welfare* (March 1946). For an example of how rehabilitation is provided for in primitive tribes, see the work of W. L. Warner, who shows an exceptional grasp of the problem in *Black Civilization,* and "The Social Configuration of Magical Behavior," in *Essays in Honor of A. L. Kroeber,* ed. R. H. Lowie (1936).

CHAPTER EIGHT, PAGES 163–187

1. Radin, *Crashing Thunder,* pp. 175, 188–90, 193–94. For peyotism, see also La Barre, "Primitive Psychotherapy." In general for aboriginal confession, see R. Pettazzoni, *La Confession des Péchés* (2 vols.; Paris, 1931).

2. See, e.g., E. W. Hopkins, *The Religions of India* (1895); H. C. Lea, *History of Auricular Confession* (1896); J. H. Hopkins, *History of the Confessional* (1850); R. Pettazzoni, "Confession of Sins in the Classics," *Harvard Theological Review,* XXX (1937); and J. T. McNeill, "Historical Types of Method in the Cure of Souls," *Crozer Quarterly,* XI (1934). For a recent work on the intimate phases of religious development, see R. A. Knox, *Enthusiasm* (1950).

3. See, e.g., Lea, *Auricular Confessional;* J. H. Hopkins, *Confessional;* W. Bright, *Some Aspects of Primitive Church Life* (1898); C. M. Roberts, *History of Confession to A.D. 1215* (1901); O. D. Watkins, *History of Penance* (1920); and J. T. McNeill and H. M. Gamer, *Medieval Handbooks of Penance*

(1938). For the Christian idea of confession as therapy, see J. T. McNeill, "Medicine for Sin as Prescribed in the Penitentials," *Church History,* I (1932). For some cases of public confession among primitives, see Hallowell, "Sin, Sex and Sickness"; Gillin, "Magical Fright"; Pettazzoni, *La Confession;* and La Barre, "Primitive Psychotherapy."

4. H. E. Lucock and P. Hutchinson, *Story of Methodism* (1926), pp. 168–69.

5. W. James, *Varieties of Religious Experience* (1902), p. 463.

6. For examples of psychotherapeutic and psychological criticisms of the confessional, see Shoben, "Psychotherapy"; J. R. Oliver, *Psychiatry and Mental Health* (1932); and especially G. W. Allport, *The Individual and Religion.*

7. This last quotation is from the "Penitential Ascribed to the Venerable Bede"; the previous three are from the "Penitential of Theodore" and the "Corrector of Burchard of Worms"; all to be found in McNeill and Gamer, *Medieval Handbooks,* pp. 184–86, 223, 324–25, 340.

8. See L. Geddes and H. Thurston, *Catholic Church and Confession* (1928); C. E. Schieler, *Theory and Practice of the Confessional* (1905); I. F. Hapgood, *Service Book of the Holy Orthodox-Catholic Apostolic (Greco-Russian) Church* (1906); S. Zankor, *Eastern Orthodox Church* (1929); E. E. Yelverton, *The Swedish Rite* (1921).

9. See, e.g., H. C. Lea, *Auricular Confession;* J. H. Hopkins, *Confessional;* C. Chiniguy, *Fifty Years in the Church of Rome* (1886); and W. Hogan, *Auricular Confession* (1859). For discussions of confession from a religious and therapeutic view, see, e.g., R. May, *Art of Counseling* (1939); J. S. Bonnell, *Pastoral Psychiatry* (1938); F. J. Sheen, *Peace of Soul* (1949); W. F. Halliday, *Psychology and Religious Experience* (1929); and F. Kunkel, *In Search of Maturity* (1943).

10. John Cosin quoted in H. Bettenson, ed., *Documents of the Christian Church* (1947), pp. 419–20, 425–26. The point of absolution in the Anglican Church should not be confused with the previous point of obligatoriness of confession. Anglicans are much more united on the former than on the latter.

   For the modern Roman Catholic confessional, see Geddes and Thurston, *Catholic Church;* Schieler, *Theory and Practice;*

and Sheen, *Peace of Soul.* For an idea of the lack of the sense of obligatoriness in the Catholic attitude toward confession, see, e.g., C. Houselander, *Guilt* (1951).

11. James, *Religious Experience,* pp. 462–63; and P. Janet, *Les Obsessions et la psychasténie* (2 vols.; Paris, 1903), II, 707.

12. Jung, *Modern Man,* p. 41.

13. See Sebastian de Grazia, "Toleration and Forgiveness" (Bicentennial Address, King's Chapel, Boston), *Vital Speeches,* December 15, 1949.

14. Figures on the extent to which the Catholic (or the Anglican) confessional is used seem to be unobtainable. There is some evidence, however, in the published secular cases, where one sees cropping up instances of failure of Catholic pastoral care. See, e.g., Cantor, *Employee Counseling,* pp. 110–11; and C. Towle, *Social Case Records from Psychiatric Clinics* (1941) pp. 197–252. Furthermore, while in a country like Italy without competing religions the problem of psychoneurosis is comparatively simple, in other countries like England (though the rate for Catholics everywhere is still relatively low, as Jung points out) the number of Catholics diagnosed as neurotic is increasing. See, e.g., E. J. Slater, "Neurosis and Religious Affiliation," *Journal of Mental Science,* XCIII (1947). In ascribing reasons for these developments two facts should not be overlooked: (1) the diminished authority of the Catholic clergy in Protestant countries, and (2) the assumption by that clergy of the prevailing Protestant attitude toward sin with its neglect of forgiveness.

15. For the more abstract Protestant concern with forgiveness, see, e.g., A. E. Taylor, *Faith of a Moralist* (1930); H. R. Mackintosh, *Christian Experience of Forgiveness* (1927); E. B. Redlich, *Forgiveness of Sins* (1937); W. E. Barnes, *The Forgiveness of Jesus Christ* (1936); J. M. Schulhof, *The Law of Forgiveness* (1901); V. Taylor, *Forgiveness and Reconciliation* (1941); Daniel Day Williams, *God's Grace and Man's Hope* (1949); P. Lehmann, *Forgiveness* (1940); also see n. 8, p. 273, below.

16. This statement is by Jung, *Modern Man,* p. 290; the previous one is by J. Leuba, "The Neurotic Family and the Family Neurosis," *Revue française de psychoanalyse,* Vol. IX, No. 3

(abstracted in *Psychological Abstracts*, XXVI [1939]), p. 579; Hocking's statement appears in *Science*, p. 43.

17. For some anthropological materials bearing on this point, see B. M. G. Sundkler, *Bantu Prophets in South Africa* (London, 1948); Evans-Pritchard, *Witchcraft;* and Sereno, "Obeah." See also n. 10, pp. 261–62, above.

While it is possible to say without question that the number of persons, secular and religious, devoted to psychotherapy has increased greatly in proportion to population during this century (n. 16, pp. 263–64, above), it is extremely difficult to get precise figures on other times. For some figures on the proportion of priests empowered to hear confession in relation to the total population in a few medieval communities, see A. C. Flick, *Decline of the Medieval Church* (2 vols., 1930) II, 314; Lea, *History*, p. 205; and J. C. Russell, "Clerical Population of Medieval England," *Traditio*, II (1944).

18. Freud, *Collected Papers*, III, 296. For the different state of affairs today, see, e.g., the mental hospital cases reported by Demerath, "Social Solidarity." One patient said that some of her friends "seemed to think I was engaged in an orgy of sex talk with the doctor." Another said, "I thought it was necessary to make love to someone to get out here [the hospital]. That's why I came, wasn't it? I came to find freedom in love and I thought I would have love here."

For short psychoanalytic treatment today, see Alexander and French, *Psychoanalytic Therapy*. Two other reasons should be mentioned for the decline in length of treatment. First, as pointed out in Chapter Seven, n. 4, Freud, who set the pattern of analysis, seemed to be more interested in developing a general psychology than a psychotherapy. Accordingly he spent much time tracing ideas of numbers, proverbs, phrases, and so on, working out in the process interesting studies in associational psychology. Psychotherapists are just beginning to abandon this process. Secondly, the authority of secular therapists has grown tremendously since the days of the early twentieth century. As Ferenczi and Rank point out (*Development of Psychoanalysis*) p. 22, "What Freud was already able to foretell in 'The Future Chances of Psychoanalytic Therapy' (in his Congress speech, 1910), that our therapeutic results will be much better when we shall have obtained the authority commonly attributed to other specialists, has since then come to pass to some extent." Of course, as Chapter Four recorded, the authority of the healer is greater than that of most specialists.

19. Jung, *Modern Man,* pp. 263–64.

20. The passage is quoted and translated by Wilhelm Pauck in "The Nature of Protestantism," *Church History,* VI (1937). His book, *The Heritage of the Reformation* (1950), should also be consulted for the departure in general of modern Protestantism from the teachings of the Reformers.

21. See such works as C. P. Blacker, *Neurosis and the Mental Health Services* (1946); F. Dunbar, *Synopsis of Psychosomatic Diagnosis and Treatment* (1948); J. L. Halliday, *Psychosocial Medicine* (1948); R. E. Faris and H. W. Dunham, *Mental Disorders in Urban Areas* (1939); and E. Weiss and O. S. English, *Psychosomatic Medicine* (1943) which contains such inclusive statements as (p. 41), "All medicine is psychosomatic medicine."

22. "Over 2000 Protestant clergymen have taken clinical training [etc.]. . . . The writer knows of no medical school that has made a special point of insuring that some member of its psychiatric faculty has drunk comparably at the wellsprings of theology and religion" (L. H. Woodward, "Concluding Statement on the Relationship of Religion and Psychotherapy," *Journal of Psychiatric Social Work,* XVIII [1948]). For various other grievances against the *odium temporale* of psychotherapists, see, e.g., W. Kluge, "Problem of Cooperation Between the Psychotherapist and the Spiritual Advisor," *Journal of Psychiatric Social Work,* XVIII (1948); I. Kristol, "God and the Psychoanalysts," *Commentary,* VIII (1949); R. J. Fairbanks, "Cooperation between Clergy and Psychiatrists," *Journal of Pastoral Care,* I (1947); Sheen, *Peace of Soul;* T. V. Moore, "Pathogenesis and Treatment of Homosexual Disorders," *Journal of Personality,* XIV (1946); and "Pastors and Morals" (editorial), *Journal of Pastoral Care,* II (1948).

CHAPTER NINE, PAGES 188–214

1. See, e.g., K. A. Menninger, "Polysurgery and Polysurgic Addiction," *Psychoanalytic Quarterly,* III (1934). The phenomenon is so common that therapists speak of patients "provoking" operations. See, e.g., Oberndorf et al., "Symposium," p. 25.

2. H. Palmer, "Recent Technique of Physical Treatment and Its Results," in N. G. Harris, ed., *Modern Trends,* pp. 254–55. The lengthy quotation is from R. Good, "Some Observations on the Psychological Aspects of Cardiazol Therapy," *Journal of Mental Science,* LXXXVI (1940).

3. J. Atkins, in "Psychology of Shock Therapies and of Leucotomy," *Journal of Clinical Psychology,* VII (1945–46), says, "There are certain circumstances, however, in the therapies with which we are here concerned, that made one suspect deeper and darker motives, at least in some instances." D. W. Abse in "Psychology of Convulsion Therapy," *Journal of Mental Science,* LXXXVI (1940), remarks, "This aspect of the treatment [contraction and stretching of muscle groups and visceral disturbances] inevitably reminds us of the hot and cold douches to which patients were exposed, and even (historically) to the thrashings to which they were once so brutally subjected." W. Mayer-Gross, in a paper reviewed by the *Journal of Clinical Psychology,* VII (1945–46), holds, "The following psychological factors deserve attention when treating depressive and neurotic patients with electrical convulsion therapy: The patient's dread and apprehension; 'flight into the soma'; self-punishing tendencies; the suggestive atmosphere of healing by electricity; memory disturbances, including retrograde amnesia; post-convulsive motor automatisms; repression of the state before treatment and failing insight; lack of explanation for the curative effect; mild euphoria immediately after treatment and superficial shallow politeness lasting several weeks; resistance against psychoanalytic procedure if applied by the same doctor who handled the 'magic' of the switch." Other articles speak of associated deaths and spinal lesions. The Group for the Advancement of Psychiatry warned in 1947 against certain abuses of electro-shock therapy but was mainly

concerned with indiscriminate, immediate, and exclusive use. No state mental hospital in the United States disapproves of its use. See *The Mental Health Programs of the Forty-Eight States,* Table 28, pp. 304–11.

Since shock or convulsion therapy may obtain its effects as physical punishment, a theoretical word on the subject is in order. The administration of physical punishment by authoritative figures is encountered almost universally in early education (if not the fact, at least the idea). Such treatment in later life, when paralleled in severity, has an effect in changing the conduct of patients in almost all strata. For some it may signify that a desired course of action must be abandoned because those who have such overwhelming sanctioned force must be right in their displeasure; such patients will try to find the right path in their therapists. For others it may seem to be just payment for whatever wrongdoing they believe they have done or even, when the punishment leaves a cataclysmic impression, may seem that they have made a complete atonement or expiation and that they are thereafter purified or reborn. Yet for others it may mean humiliation, degradation, resistance, and a conviction that those who administer the treatment are on the side of the forces of evil. Much depends on what the significance of authoritatively applied physical pain is to the particular patient. See n. 5, pp. 253–54, above. This view resembles that of the psychoanalysts who also, in general, consider the effects of shock therapy to be due primarily to its punitive aspect. For a summary article see E. Stainbrook, "Shock Therapy," *Psychological Bulletin* XLIII (1946).

4. Atkins, "Psychology," p. 732. He continues: "The [melancholiac] patient may readily agree to [treatment] in a phase of acute mental agony, but he would also as readily agree to being killed outright. . . . [His] feelings during his insane phase cannot be regarded as a valid criterion for action. One must take a longer view."

5. This use of the term "schizophrenia" is justified also by the prevalence of the diagnosis despite the inability of clinicians to define the disorder. C. S. Sherrington's quotation is from *Man on His Nature* (1940), p. 357. Another favorite expression— "the problems of the neurotic are *emotional*"—also falls short

of accuracy. Rage, love, fear are emotions or effects. Yet their experience or expression is not what brings the person to the psychotherapist, but the conflict of emotions with moral standards—rage inexpressible, love illicit, and fear despised.

6. The psychologist quoted is H. A. Murray, "What Should Psychologists Do About Psychoanalysis," *Journal of Abnormal and Social Psychology,* XXXV (1940). Dejerine and Gauckler's statement in *Psychoneuroses,* p. v, is also apropos: "The psychotherapist is nothing more than a confessor or director of the lay conscience." As the substitution of the pastor by the therapist becomes gradually more complete, the similarity of their roles becomes more evident. See, e.g., Part III of Fromm-Reichmann, *Principles,* which deals with events traditionally calling for the pastor's presence—death of close relatives, pregnancy and childbirth, engagement, marriage, divorce, requests for advice, severe illness and accidents.

"As soon as the problem of authority really lifts its head," wrote P. T. Forsyth, "all others fall to the rear." Certainly the disastrous effects on religious healing of the weakening of Protestant authority cannot be denied. The Decree of Papal Infallibility of 1870 had its effect, but indirectly, in a way the Pope never dreamed of. In their reaction Protestant theologians cut the ground from under them. To combat the Roman Church's claim to authority by apostolic descent, they renewed and re-emphasized the importance of conscience and individual moral judgment but in so doing tried to separate the two from authority. This they accomplished by confronting the internal judgment of conscience and morality with the so-called external judgment of established authority. A distinguished line of Protestant writers from 1870 on set the pace for an idea that entered easily into the "state of good nature" ideology and endures today in educational, psychological, and political thought. The idea, which appears fresh in recent books such as E. Fromm, *Escape from Freedom* (1941) and *Man for Himself* (1947) and D. Reisman, *Lonely Crowd* (1950), with their internal submission versus spontaneity and inner- versus outer-directed man, began in 1872 with the magnum opus of James Martineau, *Seal of Authority in Religion.* The train of works passes then through A. Sabatier,

Religions of Authority and the Religion of the Spirit (1904);
J. Oman, *Vision and Authority* (1902); T. B. Strong, *Authority in the Church* (1903); J. M. Sterret, *Freedom of Authority* (1905); and culminating in 1912 in Forsyth's *Principle of Authority*. (In the educational field, Kilpatrick, *Education*, had a similar interest.) The point where all these works necessarily fail is at Forsyth's question: Agreed that the seat of authority is the conscience but what is the nature of conscience? Neither Oman nor Forsyth (nor J. N. Figgis, *Fellowship of the Mystery* [1914]), whose works come closest to the correct answer, had the evidence that is today available and of which Chapter Six made use. The answer is that the call of conscience, too, is a product of the continuous creative stream of authority with which man welds a community of himself and his fellows. (See Chapter Ten and Coda above.) The distinction between the commands of conscience and those of external authority is solely a point in time. All authority was once external. Nothing to which the name "man" can be given has ever been found living outside a community of men. This external authority, to be embedded in conscience, was once internal to other particular men. And that conscience, that internal authority, is never exclusively internal but remains reachable and grants all the force of its early nature to the new authorities who evoke its love and trust. Forsyth grasped something of this when he counseled Protestants "to a daily, practical, unashamed recognition" of authority (p. 362).

For the history of the idea of conscience, see G. S. Brett, *A History of Psychology* (2 vols., 1921). No modern psychology claims explicitly that ideals are inborn. That there is a faculty of conscience, however, few would deny. See H. B. Acton, "Autonomous Ethics," *Hibbert Journal*, XLVIII (1949).

7. S. Ferenczi, *Further Contributions*, p. 445; and see pp. 97–99, Chapter Five above. For another example of legal language, see the New York Penal Code's attempt (Art. 106, Sec. 1141) to ban comprehensively all obscene literature. For studies of the agreements and disagreements of the U. S. Supreme Court, see the pertinent writings of C. Herman Pritchett, e.g., "The Divided Supreme Court," *Michigan Law Review* XLIV (1945). Close examination of those times and places in which

constitutional or scriptural authority exists in the form of wide-spread faith in the literal words of written documents reveals the concomitant presence of a small body of aristocratic, specialized literary interpreters. Without the consensus of an aristocratic group and with interpretation extended to everyone who can read, the written word loses its definiteness with surprising rapidity. The point, though, is that even when the authority exists it depends on human exegesis. To avoid absolutely a reliance on men one must devise, for difficult cases of right or wrong, a system such as the Azande poison-oracle. The written or printed word will never do.

8. F. Fromm-Reichmann, "Transference Problems in Schizophrenics," in S. S. Tomkins, ed., *Contemporary Psychopathology* (1944), pp. 377, 379–80. Contrast this case of forgiveness, that at the close of Chapter Six above, and that of "Thomas Corrigan," in Towle, *Case Records,* with a case of toleration, e.g., "Case 6. David McGruder," in H. L. Witmer, ed., *Psychiatric Interviews with Children* (1946).

Some religious writers are able to mention the word "forgiveness" even in the teeth of psychiatric discussion. See especially A. T. Boisen, "The Problem of Sin and Salvation," *Journal of Religion,* XXII (1942); and also, e.g., J. S. Bonnell, *Pastoral Psychiatry;* R. B. Nichols, "Anxiety," *Journal of Pastoral Care,* II (1948); D. C. Shaw, "Some General Considerations on the Religious Care of the Mentally Ill," *Journal of Clinical Pastoral Work,* I (1947); O. R. Rice, "Christianity and Psychotherapy," *Journal of Psychiatric Social Work,* XVIII (1948). There is religious healing today but, outside of the churches using private confession, it is almost all to be found in the devotion and direct ministry to the sick of the modern small sects (see n. 8, pp. 246–47, above).

CHAPTER TEN, PAGES 215–233

1. See, e.g., B. Beck, *Short-Term Therapy in an Authoritative Setting* (1946); and E. A. Haggard, "Psychological Causes and Results of Stress," in *Human Factors in Undersea Warfare* (National Research Council, 1949). The same conclusion applies to all psychotherapy or counseling done on the part-man

basis. For the industrial counselor the mark of therapy is a worker who works well and causes no friction; whether he beats his wife at home does not enter the counselor's province unless work is not efficiently done. For the marriage counselor the aim is to "preserve the marriage" (see, e.g., J. Lottier, "Marriage Counseling: Goals and Techniques," *Marriage and Family Living*, IX (1947), 60. If a marriage threatening to disintegrate is preserved, the therapist chalks up a score on the side of successful therapy.

For the relation of the ideal of the individual to the "state of good nature" theory, see Chapter Six; for the relation of both to economic theory, see the articles of Walter A. Weisskopf, "Psychological Aspects of Socio-Economic Thought," *Journal of Political Economy* (August 1949), and "Individualism and Economic Theory," *American Journal of Economics and Sociology* (April 1950); and recall the classic statement of Adam Smith: "Every individual is continually exerting himself to find the most advantageous employment for whatever capital he can command."

2. For some current examples of psychotherapeutic writings that consciously go over into the fields of politics or theology, see R. E. Money-Kryle, "Some Aspects of Political Ethics from the Psycho-analytical Point of View," *International Journal of Psychoanalysis*, XXV (1944); *Proceedings of the International Congress on Mental Health, London, 1948* (1949); F. Alexander, "The Bomb and the Human Psyche," *United Nations World* (November 1949); and J. H. Masserman, "Psychological Medicine and World Affairs," in N. G. Harris, *Modern Trends*. For criticisms of such efforts, see, e.g., Hocking, *Science;* H. Finer, "Psychiatry and World Peace," *Common Cause* (February 1950); K. Davis, "Mental Hygiene"; and A. Green, "Sociological Analysis of Horney and Fromm," *American Journal of Sociology*, LI (1946).

It might occur to some that, since therapy must consider communal or group standards and ideals, perhaps the point favors the form of treatment known as group therapy. The way in which group therapy is conceived and practiced, however, has small relevance. It involves the bringing together by therapists of neurotic patients and having them converse, listen to lectures, act plays, or do other things in common. Assembling together a group of persons acknowledgedly neurotic gives each one the face-to-face awareness that he is not alone in his illness, and under the leadership of the therapist (whose authoritative position has not changed) often forms a bond among them, thus creating a small community. But this is a special microcosm of selected persons living under hothouse conditions. By no stretch of the imagination is it the great community to which they must be restored. In fact the special environment of group therapy (though it often, as in individual or special school therapy, lessens the patient's guilt) wrongly informs him about life outside the therapeutic group. For group therapy, see, e.g., S. R. Slavson, *Introduction to Group Therapy* (1943); N. Blackman, "Ward Therapy," *Psychiatric Quarterly*, XVI (1943); J. L. Moreno, *Psychodrama* (1946); U. S. War Department, *Group Psychotherapy*, Technical Bulletin No. 103 (1944); E. N. Snowden, "Mass Psychotherapy," *Lancet*, No. 239 (1940), and for some of its authoritative aspects, F. Redl, "Resistance in Therapy Groups," *Human Relations*, I (1947–48); and F. Powdermaker and J. D. Frank, "Group Psychotherapy with Neurotics," *American Journal of Psychiatry*, CV (1948–49).

3. Ethical problems connected with psychotherapy are being discussed today but among them the central problem of health is neglected. Present legal discussion concentrates too much on the certification of patients for mental hospitals (see *Mental Health Programs*, pp. 46–49); present psychological discussion (and the American Psychological Association must be praised for its recent efforts toward clarification) concentrates too much on the certification of psychotherapeutic practitioners (see, e.g., Dael Wolfe, "Legal Control of Psychological Practice," *American Psychologist*, V [1950]).

Expectedly in a profession that deals with moral disclosures and guidance, many points of contact with the law exist. Expectedly also, in secular psychotherapy with its principle of toleration, many conflicts with the law exist. That is, not only do the directives given by therapists clash both among and with themselves and with many religious standards but they clash also with the law of the community. To take an example, the laws on abortion are an instance of the law of the commonwealth, of the state's relation to the physician, of a clear moral injunction. How does the psychotherapist treat the subject of abortion? of adultery? or fornication? all of which are illegal in many states. Just what is the state of legal control over the psychotherapist, what are its channels? Is he supposed to report all legal transgressions like other citizens? Are California psychotherapists, e.g., ever accessories to the violation of Sec. 288 A of the State's Penal Code? (See H. Benjamin, "A Case of Fatal Air Embolism, *"Journal of Criminal Psychopathology,* VII [1945–46].) What does the psychotherapist do about dead-letter laws? What tells him a law is dead letter? How often does his theory of practice violate the legal conception of the reasonable and prudent man? How often does he promise secrecy when he legally cannot? (See n. 14, p. 245, above.) (The problems of professions in respect to the common good are instructively treated in T. H. Marshall, "Recent History of Professionalism," *Canadian Journal of Economics and Political Science* [August 1939], and A. M. Carr-Saunders and P. A. Wilson, *Professions* [1933].)

4. Some students, especially those associated with anthropology, have begun to show an interest in the ideal of man in various societies but have used the idea for classificatory rather than reconstructive purposes. See R. Linton, *Study of Man* (1936), who states, p. 436, "All societies have concepts of the ideal man"; A. Kardiner et al., *Psychological Frontiers of Society* (1945); and H. A. Murray and C. Kluckhohn, eds., *Personality in Nature, Society and Culture* (1949). For some philosophical considerations, see S. Johnson, "Old Norse and Ancient Greek Ideals," *International Journal of Ethics,* XLIX (1938); W. Mueller, *Charakter und Moral* (Munich, 1939); and H. C. Brown, "Ethical Evaluation of a Social Order," *International Journal of Ethics,* XLV (1935).

5. J. Dollard, "Mental Hygiene and a 'Scientific Culture,'" *International Journal of Ethics,* XLV (1935). (In other respects, however, the article shows keen understanding of the communal significance of mental hygiene.) Similar ideas are expressed in Lasswell, *Psychopathology and Politics* (1930).

6. H. A. Murray, "Psychologists," p. 163. On the same point, see K. Davis, "Mental Hygiene."

A work typically affected by the "civilized restriction of needs" theory is Murray and Kluckhohn, *Personality*. An extreme example, particularly concerning the compulsiveness of sexual behavior and its "outlets," is A. C. Kinsey et al., *Sexual Behavior in the Human Male* (1948). For some of the prejudicial results that this view assigns religious activity, see L. M. Terman, "Kinsey's 'Sexual Behavior in the Human Male,'" *Psychological Bulletin*, XLV (1948).

Yoga, with its emphasis on the control of the flesh, and to a lesser extent Stoicism, with its belief in the harmful character of unrestricted desires, may be considered to be at the other pole of this theory.

7. For the insuperable difficulties in the way of setting up an experiment on *The Biology of Human Starvation*, see A. Keys et al. (2 vols., 1950).

8. See, e.g., F. Pollock, *A First Book of Jurisprudence* (London, 1896). In this chapter law is spoken of principally in its intention or purpose. As Stammler put it, "All positive law endeavors to be just law." On the general relation of *Law and Morals*, see Roscoe Pound (1924). For works related to the view here presented, see James Lorimer, *Institutes of Law* (1880); R. Stammler, *Wirtschaft und Recht* (Leipzig, 1896); and for the idea of minimum ethics, G. Jellinek, *Die sozialethische Bedeutung von Recht, Unrecht und Strafe* (Berlin, 1878). For the importance of morality in international law, see, e.g., J. B. Whitton, ed., *The Second Chance* (1944); and Hans Morgenthau, *La Réalité des normes* (Paris, 1934).

9. Statement made at the third annual institute of crime and delinquency by R. Lindner, Chicago *Daily News* (March 30, 1950). On the doctrine of the "irresistible impulse" see Davis v. U.S., 160 U.S. 469, 16 Sup. Ct. 353. For a recent work describing the effects of the doctrine in sending one criminal for medical treatment in Stepney and another to jail in Whitechapel for the same offense, see C. Binney, *Crime and Abnormality* (1949). For the idea of the mental hospital as the place where one can be "crazy comfortably," see H. S. Sullivan, *Conceptions*, and Demerath, "Social Solidarity." It is an error

for criminal psychologists to think of the law's penalties and punishments as solely retributive. Even the *lex talionis* was also reformative and deterrent in intent, as the slightest observation of a man in a violent vengeful rage with his "I'll teach you . . ." attitude supports. These considerations can be seen in greater detail in the writings of Plato, Hobbes, Bosanquet, and Beccaria's *Crimes and Punishments*.

Concerning the question of the state's forgiveness, there is a dilemma similar to that in religion and psychotherapy. The judge under the influence of the ideas of analytic jurisprudence usually conceives himself as the knower and applier of a black and white written law. The problem is treated in Pound's *Law and Morals* but is brought clearly into significance by J. D. Frank in his *Law and the Modern Mind* (1930). Instead in his interpretation and decisions on facts, relevance, etc., the judge actually makes new law, new moral judgments. The dilemma appears over the question of whether students of law should acknowledge publicly that black and white law (as with black and white holy books) is a fiction. If so, it is thought, the authority of the law and the judge crumbles. To a certain extent this is true but it is true for the false authority they now assume. To perpetuate the fiction is immoral, but the basis of authority can be clarified. The judge (and the priest and the healer) can have a real authority. The judge's political authority is a moral authority that assigns wide powers of discretion and forgiveness to compensate for the limitations of man's foresight and the written word of the law.

10. The child in any community inevitably acquires religious and political ideas and because of their natural resemblances links them together. The later separation of political and religious education breaks the harmonious relationship. For some recent pertinent works on the educational separation of church and state, see A. P. Stokes, *Church and State in the United States* (1950); W. Moberly, *Crisis in the University* (London, 1949); L. A. Lardner, "How Far Does the Constitution Separate Church and State?" *American Political Science Review*, XLV (1951); and Eric Voegelin, *Die Politischen Religionen* (Stockholm, 1939). It should be remarked that there are many forms of separation of church and state besides the present

mutually exclusive dualism, which resembles the solution of Pope Gelasius I. For the Western history of church and state relations, see C. H. McIlwain, *Growth of Political Thought in the West* (1932); and A. J. Carlyle and R. W. Carlyle, *A History of Mediaeval Political Theory in the West* (6 vols., 1903–36).

11. For the flexibility of morality among primitives, who are often thought to be bound to rigid custom, see B. Malinowski, *Crime and Custom in Savage Society* (1926); for some considered remarks on the modern history of morals, see M. Oakeshott, "Tower of Babel," *Cambridge Journal,* II (1948); for an example of the changing of educational morals in an aristocracy, see J. H. Hexter, "Education of the Aristocracy in the Renaissance," *Journal of Modern History,* XXII (1950).

Index

Absolution. *See* Forgiveness

Anthropology, and ideal of man, 276; and morality, 107; and role of authority, 115; *see also* Social sciences

Anxiety, caused by guilt in neurosis, 34–35; of patient, 46, 243; in psychoses, 144; theory of cure by removal of, 143–44; *see also* Guilt; Moral disorder; Passions

Appetites, experiments on, 277; and needs theory of cure, 134–36, 277; and stoicism, 277; and yoga, 277; *see also* Passions

Authority, absence of, in prognosis, 48–49, 54, 62, 251; of apostolic succession, 199–200; and application of pain, 253, 270; as causal factor in psychotherapy, 251; and childhood conformity, 61–62; and confession, 187; conflicting, result of, 251, 256; confused use of term in political science, 254–55; and conscience, 112; and culture, 112–13; definition of, 42, 48, 59; differing trappings of, 49–50, 53; of documents, 199–200, 272–73; early healing by, 118; in education, 76; and excommunication, 128; fallibility of, 224; and forgiveness, 187; of friend, 54; and gods, 53–54, 235; in hypnosis, 119–22, 254; increased in transference, 59; influence of, on guilt, 104; influence of, on perception, 115–21; internal vs. external, 126, 271; of judge, 278; lan-

guage of, 213; of law, 111–12, 199–200, 278; loss of, results of, 251; and love, 109–10; of medicine man, 43; in milieu therapy, 76; mistaken ideas of, 60, 112–13; and negative transference, 61; odor of word, 60, 84, 199; parents as first, 54–55, 57; persistence of, in psychotherapy, 62; of physicians, 43; and political community, 127–28, 236, 254–55; of priests, 42; in Protestantism, 271; psychological study of, 112; psychotherapists' position of, 42–65, 103; in psychotherapy, denial of existence of, 60, 188–214, 217, 267–68; and Puritanism, 126; religious, 127, 178, 236, 271; of secular healer, 145–48; in sleep learning, 254; and teaching, 112, 122–23, 126; for unforgiveness, 200–3; *see also* Political community, Religious community

Beliefs and religious community, 175–76

Body-mind dichotomy, in Buddhism, 29; and "mental" disorder, 197–98; and neurosis, 197–98; and organic theories of psychotherapy, 197–98; in primitive therapy, 32; and psychosomatic medicine, 184–87, 268

Case history excerpts, 30–31, 35–36, 50–53, 55–58, 61–64, 67–69, 71–73, 75–77, 79, 83, 85–87, 89–90,

ualism, 200; reformers' teachings on confession in, 177, 180–81; *see also* Catholicism; Psychotherapy; Religion; Toleration

Protestants, departure from reforms of, 268; and psychotherapists, 50, 180–87

Psychiatrist, training of, 148–49; *see also* Psychotherapist

Psychiatry, moral disorder theory in, 39, 244; and secrecy, 245

Psychoanalysis, authority in, 61, 112; and childhood, 107; as a creed, 92; as general prescription, 138; cure in, by talking, 17; implications of studies in, 126; influence of, on other therapies, 96–97; jargon of, 250, 257–58; and morality, 68, 94, 107, 184; as psychological system, 257, 267; as a psychotherapy, 257; and science, 95, 198; and secrecy, 245; and shock therapy, 198, 270; short treatment in, 184; transference in, 55–64, 247

Psychoanalysis, theories of, educational, 115, 252–53, 257; therapeutic, 132–61; unconscious, 258

Psychoanalyst, authority of, 146, 161, 198; training of, 147–49; *see also* Authority

Psychology, conflict of, with law, 229; and criminal, 229; psychoanalytic contributions to, 257, 267; psychotherapeutic training in, 148–49; and role of authority, 112, 115; *see also* Psychotherapy

Psychopath, lack of authoritative situation with, 48–49; and the law, 229

Psychosis, anxiety in, 144, 196–97; definition of, 206; description of, 144–45; and guilt, 206; as index of political scientist, 225; vs. neurosis, 145; and separation from community, 206; suffering in, 196–97; system of beliefs in, 144–45; and guilt, 206; as index illness; Moral disorder

Psychosomatic medicine, and polysurgery, 189; rise of, 184–85; and symptoms, 185–87; *see also* Body-mind dichotomy

Psychotherapist, the, authoritative position of, 42–65, 103, 145–46, 267–68; Catholic and Protestant consultants of, compared, 50; changing of, 212; characteristics of, 44–45; confession of one to another, 209; conflict of, with religion, 152; and dead-letter law, 276; dedication of, 208; differences among, 19–22, 27, 42, 48, 152–55, 211–12; direction of patient by, 66–102; as expert on reality, 146–50; fees of, 208; and legal concept of reasonable man, 176; legal right to secrecy of, 40, 245, 276; limitation of stranger as, 251; "listeners" as, 251; and love, 208; mass communication by, 158–59; medical man as, 213–14; and morality, 66–102, 104; need for, 159, 183; numbers of, 267; occupational risk of, 220; political writings by, 274; as priest, 198–99; as representative of community, 212; status of, 42, 46–47, 267–68; training of, 44, 145, 213–14, 246; women as, 246

Psychotherapy, ancient, 19; authority for, 187–214, 217; authority in, 60, 251–52, 257; and bibliotherapy, 263; Christian, 20, 241; common factors in, 150, 205, 240–41; communication in, 27–28, 69–70, 238, 263; confession in, 163–87, 209; conflicts of, with law, 223; conflicts of, with religion, 268; as creeds, 92–93; and the criminal, 277–78; definition of, 19; differences in, 42, 104; and doctors of medicine, 184; exorcism in, 66, 102; and female attire, 58; and friendship, 54, 104, 251; goals of, 216–17; by gods, 128–29; good, criteria for, 205–6; and healing materials of childhood, 118; ideals in, 206–7, 217, 273–74; jargon of, 96, 250, 257–58; by kings, 128–29, 256; and law, 236; learning vs., 257; modern, 20; moral disorder perpetuated by, 157–58; and morality, 67–69, 160–62, 184, 209, 236, 262–63; multiple, 251–52; parental, 118; and passions, 270–

71; and political community, 206–7, 236; and polysurgery, 269; by popular idols, 256; by priests, 129; primitive, 19, 25–26, 32, 133; as a profession, 275–76; psychoanalysis as, 257; and psychopaths, 229; and psychosomatic medicine, 184–85; and quacks, 24, 53, 205, 262; and reality, 261; rehabilitation in, 213, 264; religious, 50–53, 163–87, 246–47, 273; and religious community, 229; religious nature of, 214–15, 220, 271; results of physical view of, 189–90; by rulers, 256; schools of, 18, 21–27, 262; and science, 95, 205, 207–8, 236; scientific, and use of injections, drugs, and operations, 256–57; secrecy in, 245; secular, 184, 203–4, 273; selection of patients in, 147; shock, 269; short, 184; speed in, 206, 217; statistics of, 20–21, 23, 239–40; and talking, 95–96; and teaching, 261; termination of, 212; theories of, 103, 132–62, 190–91, 258; and therapeutic nihilism, 243; as toleration therapy, 104; by touch, 128–29, 256; transference in, 55–64, 247; universal elements of, 29–41, 66–103, 270–71; universal and local standards in, 210

Punishment, in childhood, 113; contrasted with psychotherapy, 277–78; functions of, 277–78; and good works, 210–11; neurotic need for, 35; physical, 114; and polysurgery, 189, 210–11; and psychosomatic medicine, 210–11; separation as, 111, 114; and shock therapy, 269–70; and "state of good nature," 113; see also Authority; Pain

Quacks, in psychotherapy, 24, 53, 205, 262

Radio, and non-verbal communication, 74; use of, by psychotherapist, 158–59, 263
Reality, psychotherapist as expert

on, 146–50; in theories of cure, 146–50, 261

Religion, apostolic succession in, 199–200; authority in, 178, 198–200; authority in, for healing, 129–30, 188–214; book in, 199–200, 272–73; in childhood, 109–10, 278; and doctrine of individual conscience, 198–99; and exemplary character, 214; and family, 235; and good works, 210–11; humility in, 233; and ideals, 109–10; and love, 109–10; modern, 187, 233; and morality, 220, 228; objective vs. subjective, 235; and psychosomatic medicine, 184–85; and psychotherapy, 92, 152, 187, 214–15, 268; separated from political beliefs and education, 230–31; see also Catholicism; Confession; Protestantism

Religious community, confession as healing instrument of, 163–87; and forgiveness, 183, 229; ideal of man in, 215–33; importance of, 231; membership in, 175–76; modern, lack of communication in, 233; moral disorder in, 209–10; as natural order of man, 235; and psychopaths, 229; psychotherapist as representative of, 212; psychotherapy in the, 206–8, 218, 229; restoration to, 225; separation from, 111; subjective and objective coalescence in, 235; see also Authority; Morality

Rulers, authority of, 44, 112, 255; conflicting directives of, 252; healing by, 128–29, 256; and healing touch, 128–29; see also Authority; Political community

Salvation, in democracy, 9, 238; by psychotherapy, 92, 138, 160–61, 208, 232; by religion, 10, 232–33; by social sciences, 10–12, 162, 225–27, 238
Science, and mental hygiene, 208; moral neutrality in, 160; and non-verbal communication, 73–74; as part of psychotherapeutic creed, 92; and psychoanalysis,